PACIFIC OCEAN

OCEA

BOLIVIA

AREQUIPA
LAKE TITICACA
TACNA
LA PAZ
ARICA
ANTOFAGASTA
GRAN CHACO
Cattle
Rubber
Coffee
ASUNCION
PARAGUAY
VALPARAISO
MENDOZA
SANTIAGO
SANTOS
RIO DE JANEIRO
SALVADOR
PORTO ALEGRE
URUGUAY
CONCEPCION
BUENOS AIRES
MONTEVIDEO
BAHIA BLANCA
ARGENTINA
CHILE
BUENOS AIRES LAKE
FALKLAND IS.
CAPE HORN

Route of the

D0582018

LNS

SOUTH
BY
THUNDERBIRD

By the same Author

THE STORY OF BERMUDA

THE PAGEANT OF CUBA

SOUTH BY THUNDERBIRD

STREET SCENE IN RIO DE JANEIRO SHOWING INLAID PAVEMENTS

SOUTH BY THUNDERBIRD

HUDSON STRODE

HAMISH HAMILTON
90 GREAT RUSSELL STREET
W.C.1

FIRST PUBLISHED 1937

PRINTED IN GREAT BRITAIN BY
THE STANHOPE PRESS LTD.
ROCHESTER : : KENT

For
Admiral Sir Vernon Haggard
and
Peter Davies
with admiration of their qualities

"Comprehension must be the soil on which shall grow all the fruits of friendship."

Woodrow Wilson

"The present century is the century of South America."

Theodore Roosevelt

CONTENTS

ILLUSTRATIONS

PREFACE

"*To the South! To the South!*"

Peter Martyr

PREFACE

In 1537 the prodigious excitement in Europe over conquests and settlings of various parts of South America was still at flood tide. But only yesterday the great Southern continent remained virtually undiscovered to most North Americans and Britishers, even in their libraries.

"Comprehension," said Woodrow Wilson, speaking of the relations of the United States with Latin America, "must be the soil on which shall grow all the fruits of friendship." The statesman knew that too many of his countrymen are ever ready to call barbarous anything that departs widely from their own taste or experience. When Señor Pezet was Minister of Peru to the United States, he commented courteously on the average American's lack of interest in the other fellow's point of view. "We South Americans have a funny quality in us," he explained. "We like to be rubbed the right way. We are quick in giving. We are willing to meet more than half way, but then we crave a smile, a kind word, something nice. We want culture, we want politeness. We want just the middle course—the same as you do when you are driving a bargain with other Americans. You know how to approach them. You know how they are going to receive you. Well, try the same thing with us. . . . But don't thrust things down our throats, because they are made by you, as you use them, you wear them, and you like them."

Some students from South America are indignant to discover the Anglo-Saxon public's ignorance of even the geography of their continent. Thousands of otherwise intelligent English and North Americans confess quite blandly that they have only a vague conception of South America and its people. Many admit they have never distinguished Uruguay from Paraguay. Naturally all the republics regard themselves as separate entities, and the opinion of these individual countries can no more be summarized than the opinion of the United States, Canada, Mexico, San Salvador, and the Dominican Republic in the Northern continent.

Although I had travelled considerably, all the lands that lay south of Texas and Florida, except Cuba, were as unknown to me as the smell and taste of exotic fruits I had read of, but never savoured. During two years of research, 1932-33, in preparing to write an informal history of Cuba, I had come upon alluring cross references to South America that spurred my interest and determined me to see the other half of the hemisphere at the first interval of leisure. I wanted to clear away the mists of my own ignorance, and I was frankly excited about the Southern continent's imagination-stirring potentialities.

Starting on a voyage of discovery, I wondered what would come out of it, what shape it would take in my mind. Particularly, I wondered about contacts with my fellow-man in the various countries. I was perhaps more interested in human relationships than in gems of Spanish-Colonial architecture, ancient civilizations, the contours of the Cordilleras, or even modern progress. I was embarking with senses receptive, interests catholic. I was not going in the attitude of a sentimental pilgrim or for the purpose of riding any special hobby. I was not an archæologist, a salesman, an engineer, a diplomat, an ornithologist, or a propagandist. I was setting out as an eager observer, not as a passionate participant. I was just as interested in the social legislation of Uruguay, the slaughter-houses of Argentina, the cotton-planting campaign of Brazil, as I was in the position of women in modern Lima, the race track at Santiago, and the superb scenery of Rio de Janeiro.

I was going to get a bird's-eye view of the whole show. I knew that, for all its alien glamour, South America had a great many attributes of the United States, and I was quite prepared to believe that the South Americans order certain matters far better than North Americans do. I knew, too, that Englishmen had almost always maintained a happy way with South Americans, the way of friendly attitude, of co-operative effort, of fair dealing. I knew that the "word of an Englishman" was still—with one exception—a proverbial expression for honesty. I knew that the United States was beginning to cultivate valuable international relationships with the Southern republics, which the English had been enjoying for more than half a century. I knew that the magnetic needle of North American interests, which had always pointed east and west, was definitely turning south, and I was assured that president Franklin Roosevelt's Policy of the Good Neighbour and Cordell Hull's reciprocity trade treaties were making an unwonted and inspired conquest of friendship.

In my time I had read some three score volumes of Latin American history and impressions, and hundreds of magazine articles and pamphlets, and I had found something of interest in every one, and yet I was not in the least sure what the various people were really like—of how a Chilean differed in temper, say, from an Argentinian. So I have aimed in this book to present a clearer comprehension of South Americans by revealing intimate contacts with the people themselves. I have tried to convey this feeling of the "daily life" of individual countries by taking the reader with me wandering down dark and narrow side streets, as well as motoring along resplendent boulevards; by reproducing people's actual conversation in their homes, at their parties, their offices and amusement places. Conversations in the book are as nearly as possible verbatim talk, which I wrote down within twenty-four hours of their happening. With the exception of six or seven instances, I have used the real names of the people I met and talked with.

From copious notes and reams of statistics I have selected such scenes and facts as seemed most illuminating—to help the reader to distinguish the individual flavour of one country from another. Of course, I realize that from any specialist's point of view there are striking deficiencies. Despite my inherent sympathy with the underdog, I shall stand accused by Marxians of not going deeper into obvious social abuses, but that was not in the scope of this volume. (For those interested primarily in the Marxian attitude, there is Waldo Frank's brilliant *America Hispana*, which I recommend with profound admiration.) On the other hand, the aristocracy of Bogotá has every reason to consider my impression of their interesting city distorted, because I confess I could not avail myself of an opportunity to meet their distinguished intelligentsia. It was not in the purpose of this book to delve into the complexities of Inca culture and collectivism, or to summarize the history of conquistadors and the general revolt from Spain in the first quarter of the nineteenth century, or to list the countless subsequent political revolutions and the frequent setting up and throwing down of dictators. I have touched on history only as certain moments along the flight recalled vivid decisions, achievements, and failures.

For those who are not already familiar with the literature on South America and who wish to read further and profit by diverse opinions, attachments, and criticisms, I recommend that they begin with Humboldt, Darwin, Prescott, Hudson, and Graham; then read Bryce and Tomlinson; and afterwards read all that Waldo Frank has to say on the subject, and Philip Guedalla, Morand, Siegfried, Keyserling, Kasimir Eschmid, William McFee, Clarence H. Haring, Blair Niles, Peter Fleming, Harry A. Franck, and the ever-provocative Carleton Beals. Certainly included as required reading should be Conrad's novel *Nostromo* and the magazine and newspaper articles of that most clear-sighted and unprejudiced of Latin American commentators, Hubert Herring. For a guidebook there is none better in facts and figures than *The South American Handbook.*

I am also grateful to the following for the pictures listed below:
Frontispiece by Margaret Bourke White, from Pictures, Inc.
Photographs 2 and 3 by Foto Sport, Guatemala City.

Photographs 9, 16, 17, 19, 26 and 27, courtesy of Pan American Airways.

Photographs 10 and 11 by Runcie, Lima, Peru.

To avoid the constant recurrence of the personal pronoun, which I have suffered from in other travel books, I have arbitrarily adopted the convention of writing in the third person. I have created a character to whom I give virtually no personal description—so that the reader may more easily put himself in the place of the traveller. But everything that happened to me happened to the man I have called Norbourne. I have no special reason for selecting the name; it belonged to a man I met fifteen years ago on a fishing trip in the Gulf of Mexico, and when I resolved to write in the third person his was the first name that came into my mind. Besides avoiding the personal pronoun, I have eschewed wherever possible foreign phrases, and I have refrained from recording "quaint expressions in broken English."

Since Brazil alone is larger than the United States by another Texas and I had only three months in which to "explore," it was necessary that I should fly. In "doing" the continent in three months I had the precedence of James Bryce, who wrote his admirable work on South America after only three months of travel by slow ocean steamer in 1911. By flying I could travel paradoxically with more leisure than he, and have more time in the various towns for intimate contacts with the people. For instance, Mr. Bryce had seven hours in Lima; I had six days. Considering the violent topography of the South American continent, with its contrasting jungles and deserts and mountains, its lack of roads, its uncertain railways, I believe it is impossible to over-emphasize the value of travel by aeroplane. For those who have never flown, I have indulged in many descriptions of the actualities of commercial flying as they impressed me along the way.

When the Indians of the Bahamas beheld the white-masted caravels of Columbus in 1492, they thought they were birds from heaven. When the Indians of to-day stood amazed to see and hear great aerial ships roaring over their waters and jungles and mountains, they called them "thunderbirds." Hence my title, *South by Thunderbird.*

Although my flight began at Miami, shuttled by way of Cuba over Mexico, then continued through Central America, down the west coast of South America, over the Andes, up the east coast and through the islands of the Caribbean back to Miami again, I thought it more valuable to attempt to give a more comprehensive picture of the South American continent than to include Mexico and the republics and colonies of the Caribbean. So I have begun my book at the take-off from Panama and ended with my last glimpse of the Green Continent.

HUDSON STRODE

February 3, 1937

PRELUDE

PRELUDE

In the centre of the great lobby of the Pan American Air Terminal at Miami, in a circular pit sunk several feet below the marble floor, a replica of the world revolved. Above on a sky-blue ceiling, painted in silver, the twelve signs of the Zodiac hovered at their aerial stations. With its cities and seas and silences, the restless globe whirled, but not "through unsounded time." For it had been caught and fixed. Here the world, brought within a conceivable intimate space and robbed of its vast immensities, seemed symbolical of the magic of aviation, which has eliminated Time and Distance, those chief obstacles to international commerce and comprehension. The intimate effect was further emphasized by a loud speaker system which courteously broadcast the departure and arrival of planes. And on an electrically illuminated bulletin board, indicating foreign stations along the various routes, schedules were recorded—the hour one would arrive at destinations 6,000 miles away.

Norbourne joined the passengers already gathered at the proper gate. A bell sounded. The pilot, the co-pilot, the radio operator, the flight mechanic, and the steward walked in informal procession and boarded the plane. The four giant engines were droning out a powerful synchrony. In each of them was the driving power of seven hundred horses. When the second bell sounded, the gate was thrown open and the passengers filed down under the striped marquee. They went up the short gangplank over the side on to the rubber-covered walk. Down the stairs of the companionway they descended into the yacht-like atmosphere of the passenger compartments, where the carpets were soft, the cushions silken, the ceiling lined with inlaid walnut-balsa-wood panels. Hidden underneath the panels, pads of rubberized horse-hair lay protectively to damp the vibration and deaden the sound. In compartments between the hatch and the tail lay the mail bags, luggage, express parcels.

The field manager waved a chequered black and white flag. The pilot thrust the throttle forward. The flying chariot was off in a flash across the foam-flecked bay. Then as if a driver had tightened his reins, signalling responsive thoroughbreds that knew their paces, the twenty-eight hundred silver horses leapt into the air and climbed an aerial hill to a height of two thousand feet. Pointing their noses south, they raced down a stretch of invisible track toward the golden capital of that heavy-blossomed, heavy-fruited island of Cuba.

The phantom shadow of the seaplane skimmed the sea's mirror-smooth surface lightly. The coral atolls and the fishing smacks looked small as river gnats. Norbourne was caught in a spell of magic, held in the ivory tower of this flying observatory where time and distance were telescoped. He had breakfasted in Miami at the airport's veranda dining room. At ten-thirty he was drinking iced pineapple juice in Havana. And, having changed from the luxurious Clipper to one of the smaller Sikorsky amphibians, he flew westward over Cuba's long mosaic of sugar cane and tobacco plantations. At noon he ate a boxed luncheon while whizzing through the air above the incredibly blue Yucatan Straits, somewhere between the western tip of Cuba and the Isle of Cozumel, where Cortez began his spectacular conquest. When an ugly range of oyster-coloured clouds loomed up ahead of them, the pilot neatly swerved forty miles to the right and dodged a nasty squall.

Just as they circled a green lagoon edged with desultory white cranes, Captain Schultz, the pilot, handed Norbourne a radiogram from Miami. It said that his flight reservations had been finally confirmed by all South American stations and that he could have six days in Lima instead of three, if he preferred. He was to radio his choice. The office at Mexico City would make the alteration in his ticket. He wrote "Yes" on a pad, signed his name, and a radiogram was dispatched. To the radio operator the matter was commonplace. Norbourne was naïvely thrilled.

The amphibian touched the water and taxied to a little pier, left mail, took petrol. The passengers had black coffee and plates of sliced pineapple. At four o'clock they flew over the wondrous Maya temples at Chichen Itza in the jungle. By four-thirty they had arrived on the landing field of Merida, and the first day's flight was done.

For a fortnight Norbourne beheld the marvels of Mexico and the delights of five republics of Central America. He took the experience carefree, without notebook, as an appetizer to the continental feast. The prelude to South America ended in the wasp-waist geography of Panama.

I

THE TEMPLE OF THE WARRIORS IN THE JUNGLES OF YUCATAN

2

VOLCANO ON LAKE ATITLAN, GUATEMALA

3

RUINS OF ANCIENT CATHEDRAL, ANTIGUA, GUATEMALA

4
ANTIGUA, GUATEMALA

I

COLOMBIA

"There cannot be a more breath-taking experience for any reader than to discover a whole continent whose history is new to him. . . . For here is a vast region of the world, of which our knowledge, apart from a vague notion that it once belonged to Spain, is an almost total blank. . . . It is singularly refreshing to breathe the new air of a scene where every landmark is quite unfamiliar."

Philip Guedalla

COLOMBIA

Strange Cargo

Norbourne was called by telephone at 4.45. He switched on the bedside light and looked at the French windows. They were black as jet. The rain had not ceased. Downstairs the night clerk told him in the constrained tones of early morning that three inches of water had fallen in the night. After a fortifying breakfast, he was driven through a thick, colourless soup to the aerodrome in Cristobal, Colon's twin city. The formalities of weighing men and luggage were finished. The airport manager, the pilot, the radio men, the Negro attendants, the passengers looked up at the dark sky resentfully. The rain drizzled on. It was as dismal, unlovely a morning as Norbourne had ever known. There would be no glory of a sunrise out of the Pacific.

At 6.40 the pilot, Captain Mathis, made his decision: "Let's go." In the company bus they sloshed across the watery field to the Duck. UMCA was still using the little Sikorsky S-38s for the flight between Cristobal and Medellín. The only other passenger was a North Carolinian going to sell electric trains to the Colombians. If this fog and clouded visibility continued all the morning, Norbourne wondered how they would see to get down again. Well, he had confidence in the skill of the pilot, Captain Mathis, who was to be married next month, and who said the sun would be shining in Turbo. Also he knew, of course, that hazardous flights are not begun on guesswork or the hunches of pilots, but on careful studies by trained meteorologists and data based on radio reports of actual conditions ahead. With these sustaining thoughts he ascended the step-ladder and entered the maw of the Duck from the roof. He paused, bewildered, as a penetrating screeching assailed his ears.

The shrieks came from green cardboard boxes piled up on six of the eight seats. From out the half-inch perforations stuck beaks of agitated baby chicks stretching their tender jaws wide in terrified protest. They had been hatched only three days ago in Avon Park, Florida, and were consigned to a Mr. Pascual Jaranillo in Medellín, Colombia. On foreign shores they would grow up and multiply and interbreed and improve the scraggly stock of native poultry.

Norbourne and the North Carolinian made themselves comfortable amid the deafening chorus of cheeps. The aeroplane rose into greyer gloom and flew blindly through thick blankets of fog. The scream of the three-day-olds drowned the noise of Wasp engines, penetrated the cotton which the pilot, the radio man, and the two passengers had stuffed in their ears.

Norbourne peered at the printing on the boxes. "Important. Open this box in presence of your postmaster or carrier. Count the live chicks—not the dead ones. We guarantee 100 per cent *live* chicks of number ordered on arrival." If they continued to scream so, he thought, surely they would all be dead from exhaustion by the time they reached Medellín. Whatever it was they yelled for—mothers they had never cuddled under or food they had never known (chicks require no nourishment the first three days of their existence)—it was no weak or whimpering noise they emitted. It was a throat-straining, authoritative, implacable complaint. Incredible, thought Norbourne, that such energy, such fantastic vitality, could be enclosed in a thing the size of an egg.

The gentleman from North Carolina and he endeavoured to exchange some conversation. They took the cotton out of their ears and shouted futilely. The clamour of the chicks lay between like the Great Wall of China. The cabin began to smell as if they were stabled with elephants. With a portentous shrug, the North Carolinian opened his travelling case and passed over a flask of

Canadian Club. Norbourne took a grateful swig from the bottle and settled back in resignation.

Below there was no more to be seen than if he had been in a rocket on his way to the moon. But he knew what lay at the bottom of those layers of fog and drizzle: fœtid jungles, sluggish small streams, occasional naked brown savages in little clearings with their houses of grass, their banana trees, their canoes, their alligator neighbours. No white man had ever yet traversed that region. In routing the international highway that would extend from New York to Buenos Aires, that strip lying between the Canal and the highlands of Colombia was the section that was giving more pause to the engineers than the Cordilleras of the Andes.

After an hour of enveloping fog, bits of blue sky began shooting through the thick vapour like luminous will-o'-the-wisps. Through occasional rifts in the clouds beneath them, glimpses of forests thick as those of eastern Yucatan were to be seen. Then the green sea of tree tops turned to the green of the real sea.

Mathis handed a message back to Norbourne along with the pilot's map. "If you inspect this map closely," the note read, "you will find we fly *east from* the Atlantic *to* the Pacific, and continuing in one straight line, again we arrive on the Atlantic side! We cross the continent twice in one straight flight." Norbourne scrutinized the map. The hemisphere writhed like a snake in its wasp-like middle region called Panama and twisted itself twice about the aeroplane's straight line of direction. They had passed from one ocean to the other and again to the first within the space of less than two hours. The phenomenon was a fitting overture to the lessons and wonders he was to discover on this ancient continent which he knew only by hearsay and desultory reading.

Again clouds obscured the view of earth and sky. In the dim light Norbourne glanced through some pamphlets and let his mind run through what he knew of this strange land of bananas, petroleum and platinum, and the finest coffee and emeralds in the world. In area Colombia ranks fourth among the South

American republics, following Brazil, Argentina, and Peru. Slightly larger than the combined areas of England, France, and Germany, its population is estimated at barely nine million. Four-fifths of the land is virtually unknown and uninhabited. The only country of the subcontinent that borders on both the Pacific Ocean and that part of the Atlantic called the Caribbean Sea, its coast line extends for 641 miles on the former, 448 miles on the latter. West Coast-bound ships call at historic Cartagena and the busy seaport of Barranquilla on the Caribbean and stop for a few hours at black Buenaventura on the Pacific. But rarely does anyone except a diplomat, a travelling salesman or an oil man venture beyond the coastal fringes. Even writers who crossed the Atlantic for the avowed purpose of interpreting South America—James Bryce, Paul Morand, André Siegfried, Count Keyserling, Kasimir Eschmid—failed to fit the high interior of Colombia into their schedules.

The country's rugged topography, due to the three ranges of the Andes running in parallels north and south, has retarded the construction of roads and railways. The consequent lack of facilities for transportation has baulked the development and exploitation of opulent natural resources and made Colombia one of the least visited of countries. A nearer neighbour to the United States by many thousand miles than Argentina or Chile, Colombia is considerably more of a stranger. Like himself, Norbourne knew that the average North American had only a foggy conception of the country and its culture, even though everybody had recently read about the Virgin's emerald crown, containing 453 jewels and appraised at $4,500,000, which the Pope had given permission to a Colombian Archbishop to sell to a Chicago gem syndicate and to use the proceeds for a charity school.

A Royal Way

At 9.45 the Duck alighted in Colombian territory in a yellow bay near the village of Turbo. Just as the pilot had predicted, there was neither rain nor fog. The sky was like unclouded marble. The Duck docked at a rude float, and the passengers got out to have their passports examined. Norbourne looked about him with the strange emotion he always felt at a first view of a foreign land. But this was like the heart of Africa. Black dugouts manned by half-naked blacks slithered in and out of green portières of bayous as they went about their primitive business with ageless casualness. There was not a breath of wind stirring. The silence was intense, thick as the enclosing jungle vegetation. The hushed land and the still water; the unquestioning officials stamping the passports; the cautious, barefooted, dark attendants refuelling the amphibian—all seemed bound together in some compact of quietness. It was as if nature and man were unconsciously paying a last tribute to the death of one epoch and homage to the birth of another. A rose-coloured ibis flew up out of the green drapery with great, ostentatious wing-flappings. "Flying is not really so miraculous," it might have been saying; "we felt just as awed a million years ago when man first walked among us."

"You know," said Captain Mathis, while the plane was being refuelled, "Colombians who have never yet seen an automobile, a train, or a wheeled vehicle of any sort have grown quite accustomed to the aeroplane. The Indians call them 'thunderbirds.' They tell a story about an old Indian chief, who was much excited when he first saw one of the Pan American scouting transports fly over his country. In due course, by some primitive means of smoke signals and runners, news was brought that the great bird was resting in such-and-such a place. Thereupon the wily savage sent two of his most trustworthy warriors to the place where the bird was nesting. He instructed them to sneak up under it and try to get one or two of the eggs. He hoped to hatch them and use the birds in his wars against his enemies."

When the attendants had finished refuelling, Mathis gave emphatic orders for a rearrangement of the cargo. The screaming chicks were stored fore and aft. "Never again will any chicks be put where we can smell 'em," the pilot said apologetically. "You are about the last passengers who'll ever be able to boast you have sat among crates of chicks in the pioneering days of international aviation. We're getting larger planes for this run—where baggage will be always in baggage compartments." Crates of Borsolina hats from Italy and bundles of samples from Hamburg now took up the empty passenger space. Here was speaking evidence of the bid European countries were making for the great stake of South American trade. The goods had come by European steamer to Cristobal and thence were transferred to air express route. Eighty per cent of the goods carried by UMCA was of European or Asiatic origin.

"Obviously the kingpin in the trade situation between the two continents," said the North Carolinian, reading the express tags, "is going to be the air lines linking them together. Of course, the vast bulk of air traffic from the States enters Colombia at Barranquilla. Did you know that Colombia is now only twenty-four hours from New York?"

"It isn't possible," said Norbourne.

"Absolutely. By the new schedule, a business man can leave New York by air at 5.30 p.m. He arrives in Miami early in the morning, connects with the Barranquilla Clipper at 8.0, stops at Jamaica for lunch, and arrives in Barranquilla in time for five o'clock tea."

The plane rose out of the jungle water and headed towards the mountains. The sound of the chicks' unmitigated screaming was only a faint echo now. The lulling monotonous drone of the engines was conducive to sleep. Norbourne looked down at the matted terrain stretching beneath. A wild, poisonous region without roads or trails—a sickening place to travel through, a deadly place in which to be lost. When in 1915 Knox Martin flew over the mountains to Bogotá in a small Curtiss plane, the people thought him raving mad, little dreaming that what the young American did as a death-defying stunt was a harbinger of tremendous significance. Here, today, in a commercial transport,

Norbourne was scorning nature's hostilities as casually as the ibis. He opened his box of luncheon prepared by the Hotel Washington at Cristobal in another continent and began to eat fried breast of chicken.

Up from Mule Back

By one o'clock they were in sight of Medellín, the town named after the birthplace of Cortez in Estremadura. In six hours they had made a trip that ordinarily took three to six weeks by boat, depending on the season and the state of the Magdalena river bed. The second city of the republic, one of the world's greatest coffee markets, lies in a gracious valley at an altitude of five thousand feet. With its thermometer registering close to 72°, season in, season out, Medellín has the boon of as perfect a climate as any place in the subcontinent.

The sun was shining joyously. Rows of Lombardy poplars, big-bellied white cows at pasture, and a sparkling river rushing by houses with flowering patios gave the place a charm that should go with prosperity, but so rarely does. This industrial town of forty factories was like a garden city.

On the landing field the uniformed SCADTA airport manager, a Viennese named Carlo Hermann, approached the plane as if he were host of a country estate greeting his week-end guests. Captain Mathis introduced Norbourne to him. He invited Norbourne to have a cup of Colombian coffee at the little open-air café. The Austrian was lithe and lean, with auburn hair and moustache, and a ready, warming smile. The dark hazel eyes behind the horn-rimmed glasses were frank, thoughtful, sensitive, alert. In three minutes Norbourne felt at complete ease with him.

"Doubtless you know this is the first permanently operating air company in this hemisphere, and the oldest in the world," Hermann replied obligingly, when Norbourne asked him about the beginning of Sociedad Colombo-Alemana de Transportée Aereos, popularized to SCADTA. "A countryman of mine, Dr.

Peter Paul von Bauer, a war ace, organized it in December 1919. German capital backed the venture."

"Germany's quick gesture to get back old markets after the war," Norbourne commented, draining the last drop of coffee, which was as superior in taste as in reputation.

"Precisely. And commercially it proved a success—besides diplomatically. So, after a few years, the Germans began further aeronautical activities in Bolivia and Argentina. In 1927 they secured the first licence in Brazil under the flying name of Condor. Within six years after the establishment of SCADTA here, von Bauer looked across the Canal with purposeful interest. He flew over the uncharted jungles of Central America, thence across the Gulf of Yucatan to Havana and on to Key West. He hoped to establish his own international airline. But Washington denied his request for landing bases in the Canal Zone and Florida. Who can blame Washington? The U.S. entered the field just in the nick of time. Germany had all but plucked the plum." He smiled without a trade of resentment. "The establishment of the U.S.'s international airways through South and Central America is to my mind the most significant event since the Monroe Doctrine."

He stopped suddenly, and called out sharply to one of the attendants: "Hi! Watch what that little devil is doing!"

Norbourne turned. A monkey in a crate was reaching his paws between the slats, jerking off express tags on the bundles and boxes piled close to him, and chewing them up.

Hermann excused himself and rushed to see the damage.

There is something completely cosmopolitan about the Viennese that is peculiarly refreshing, Norbourne said to himself, as Captain Mathis came up to say good-bye and to introduce him to the pilots who were to take him to Bogotá. The German captain was named Schuler. He was a soft-spoken, rosy-cheeked Prussian, four years under thirty. He introduced Norbourne to the Managing Director of UMCA, Gonzalo Mejía, a stout, Moorish-looking Colombian with a hearty deep laugh.

"Not stopping in Medellín!" he exclaimed in *basso profondo*.

"Give up a day in Bogotá, spend Sunday with us here, and I'll show you some fine *casa de campo*. How can you tell what we are like merely by looking down on our roof tops?"

After the little Duck, SCADTA's tri-motored Ford seemed spacious as an ocean liner. From the air, the neat *fincas* lying about the sun-soaked landscape looked very self-respecting and well-ordered, their red tiled roofs half hidden in a luxury of green vegetation. All the valleys were under cultivation. Beyond, through fleecy clouds, purple patches of higher mountains shone above gold and russet hills.

The boy steward looked with clinical eye at the faces of the various passengers. As he made his swift diagnoses, he drew down the brown silk blinds at the windows and adjusted the seats to semi-reclining positions for those he thought would welcome a siesta.

The plane vaulted a mountain ridge and descended on Palanquero, a town on the Magdalena River. The passengers got out for a walk and cooling drinks. It was hot and low here. Norbourne and a senator from Barranquilla, who had got on at Medellín, walked together down to the river's edge along a short newly-made street planted with almond saplings. A corps of labourers were squatting on the lawn, deftly chopping out sticker grass from the turf with machetes. On the river, black men in loin cloths were poling dug-outs.

"I understand," said the Senator from Barranquilla, "in the rest of the world it is still thought to be something of an adventure to travel by air. Here only the poor or those to whom time is of no value patronize the boats. According to the state of the river the trip used to take two to four weeks from my home to Bogotá. It still does—for those who do not fly. A few years ago when you travelled in Colombia you took your mule or horse with you. You bought a ticket for the animal as well as yourself. The beast travelled in a flat boat lashed to the steamer, and then in the mule car on the same train with you. You had to take your own bed linen and drinking water too."

"It was hardly worth being a senator," suggested Norbourne.

"Quite," he agreed; "it was most uncomfortable." They had reached the river bank. A flock of blue herons rose from the marshy land across the river and glittered metallically in the heat. "The Magdalena is capricious as a bird, eternally changing its channel. It is now high and swift, now flowing through mud flats where you are apt to get stuck for a fortnight. These old river boats we still use are like the stern wheelers you once had on your Mississippi. We call them 'wet grass' boats. They have such a shallow draught—only three to four feet—that we say they can be navigated on wet grass."

"I should think they might turn over."

"Oh, it is not uncommon at all. One turned over with me once in the middle of the night."

"Really? How?"

"No one has ever known. Perhaps two of the crew stood at the port rail together at the same time. Some say an alligator nosed it over. Five people were drowned. I lost all my luggage and was stranded on a sand bar in my nightshirt." He smiled reminiscently. "I beat myself black and blue, slapping at mosquitoes. But I came near dying of malaria just the same."

They turned and walked back. The motors in the plane had been set humming. "How different now! Breakfast with my family this morning; dinner in Bogotá tonight!" The expression on his face was benign. "No country in the world has been so benefited by aviation as Colombia. It was a startling innovation. We jumped direct from mule back to flying machine."

As they were about to enter the plane some men coming up recognized the senator. They rushed up and put their chests against his chest one by one with dignified cordiality and he patted their shoulders six pats in return—three on the left, three on the right.

The plane climbed higher and higher into the clouds to gain a great margin of altitude over the mountains. "We go really up now," said the steward. "It is safer to take lots of altitude. Sometimes those innocent-looking clouds have hard centres." He winked to be sure the passengers would catch the joke.

Norbourne looked ahead at the higher Andes barring the way. For centuries those adamantine mountains had stood in formidable opposition to man's activities. They halted his steps, broke his bones, froze his flesh, filled him with despair, sometimes killed him. It took the Conquistador Quesada nine painful months to make the journey from the coast to the plateau of Bogotá. Of his thousand men eight hundred died from fevers and privations on the march. Today Norbourne was covering a greater distance in a handful of daylight hours. The Andes had been humbled by scientific ingenuity. By a superhuman trick man had devised a royal way of scaling their cold forbidding heights with an alacrity like that of a pole vault and a security like that of sitting by one's own fireside. Surely, Norbourne said to himself, despite what the unimpressed ibis may have thought, no achievement of mortal man is more miraculous than his conquest of the air.

A Different People

At the feet of the peaks of Guadalupe and Monserrate, which reminded Quesada of the grim crags of Moorish Granada, Bogotá stands on a plateau 8,500 feet above the sea, 5° above the equator. In the bus ride from the landing field, Norbourne felt as if he had entered an entirely different country. The cool air smacked him in the face sharply. The sky was grey. The mountains, the flocks of sheep, the shepherds, the workmen's houses, out at heel, with débris scattered about, made him think of an unkempt Switzerland. The people on the road were moving fast. They were not Indian or Spanish, but peons evolved from both races. Their features and physique had been moulded by climate and the topography peculiar to the region. The women were neither pretty nor ugly. They had pleasant, flattish, slightly masculine faces. Their bodies were thick, enduring. There was no allure in the young girls, only an earthy animality. They all looked alike, with broad high cheekbones, straight black hair. Their large dark eyes were without illusion, but uncomplaining, and not averse from smiling. There was no colour in their costumes, no crimson petticoats, no bright shawls. Instead of Latin flowers in their hair, over-sized men's felt hats with the crowns uncreased were pulled down to the eyebrows to keep the wind from blowing them off. All the women, young and old, wore men's hats. And on their feet they all wore rope-soled canvas sandals. Their stout ankles were grimy with mountain dust.

"The people on the roadside are very different from the Indians of Guatemala and Mexico," Norbourne commented to the Senator from Barranquilla.

"Yes, we are not an Indian country. Our population is only two per cent full-blooded Indian, and those live mostly in the hinterland. Five per cent are pure-blooded Negro—in the banana lowlands. Blacks don't thrive in high altitudes. One-third of us are pure white, almost exclusively Spanish. Over half are of mixed blood, white and Indian, white and Negro, and Negro and Indian in varying combinations—*mestizos*, *mulattoes*, and *zambos*."

"The peasant girls here look extraordinarily sturdy."

"Since babyhood they've been trained to do the heavy farm work of boys and men. The peons in this region choose wives not for feminine charm, but strength of arms and the potential ability to bear stout sons. It's the mountain in them—and the strain of Indian."

Sketch in Charcoal

Remote Bogotá is a closed-in, narrow-streeted city of grey stone, austerely colonial Spanish in type. Its population numbers approximately 300,000. Thoroughfares were jammed with pedestrians up to the middle of the tram tracks. The steady drone of a thousand conversations was punctuated by incessant honkings from Chevrolets and Fords and clangings of exasperated tram-drivers' bells. Citizens hanging to the sides of trams brushed against citizens on sidewalks who pressed their fellow men against the walls of shops. The crowd was sombrely dressed: the better classes in black formal attire with spats and sticks, the poorer with their heads thrust through squares of dingy black woollen cloth called a *ruana*, the Colombian variant of the *poncho*. Black or dark grey were the only colours to be seen. When there were neckties, they too were black or grey. The few women to be seen were dressed in grey or black. Around the edges of formal plazas, bootblacks, at work or soliciting, knelt in the gutters with their boxes on the curb, while men stood above them like black storks on one leg, as the shoe of the other foot was shined. Black-skirted, sallow priests were ubiquitous—lingering in arcades, in shadows of doorways, buzzing about church doors, getting in and out of trams and taxis.

"The right picture of Bogotá," Norbourne remarked to Schuler, "should be done in charcoal."

"Do you know what the less religious Bogotános call those priests?" Captain Schuler said, as the bus swung around a corner. "*Gallinazos*. Buzzards."

"Is the church powerful here?"

"Is it!" Schuler made a slight movement with his eyes upward. "Listen to that." From the open belfry of a church came a fiendish clamour of bells beaten violently with metal rods: a terrific din to make angels writhe and demons rejoice. Norbourne had heard a noise equal to it only in Santiago de Cuba, where in the cathedral loft an old man belabours the bells at unreasonable hours throughout the day and night as if he were fighting bees.

By the time the bus had struggled through the crowded streets and stopped at the entrance of the Hotel Granada twilight had fallen. The shadow of Monserrate lay upon the city. Yellow lamps began to glow here and there in the evening greyness.

A blast of chill mountain air whipped about the passengers as they got out. Norbourne looked gratefully towards the warm refuge within. But he was fooled. It was almost as cold indoors as out. This modern hotel, which possessed every other known comfort, did not possess a heating system. In his room the rich mulberry red of the wall paper, the hangings, the carpets, the bedspread made a futile effort to warm the atmosphere. Norbourne punched the button for the bell boy. He would have his suit pressed while he cheered himself in a hot bath. He took off his trousers. A maid appeared. She was a strapping, apple-cheeked wench with playful eyes and fine teeth. She stood pleasantly waiting his command. In his confusion he had suddenly forgotten the word "to press." He handed her his trousers and made motions. She accepted the trousers, smiled broadly, and waited for him to be more explicit. Norbourne shivered slightly with cold. "*Frio!*" he said cheerfully. The maid nodded and laughed, holding his trousers between her finger tips. He took one trouser leg from her and imitated passing an iron over it and shivered again. She grinned and pulled, as if they were about to begin a playful tug-of-war. He shivered again and dropped his end. Wait, she said, and gave him a knowing smile. She left him standing there and ran off down the hall with his trousers. In a minute she was back with the grin of a successful conspirator. She beckoned him. She had something to show him. He hesitated. She was insistent. He slipped his arms into his dressing gown and went down the hall after her, hoping he wouldn't be seen with his bare shanks showing like that. Round the corner of the corridor the door of another red room was open. The girl urged him in. She walked to a projection that jutted out into the room and placed her broad palm against it. She smiled triumphantly. Bewildered, Norbourne walked over and put his palm flat against the wall. It was deliciously warm. The chimney for the hotel's hot water system was concealed behind that projection. There was only one room on each floor that was so warmed. The maid raised a questioning eyebrow, and without waiting for a sign telephoned the manager that the gentleman was changing his room. Norbourne regarded the grinning girl as a frostbitten Alpine climber might regard a succouring St. Bernard. He reached at his pocket to give her a tip and caught up his shirt tail. At that moment the Senator from Barranquilla passed on the way to his suite. Both were too confused to be completely nonchalant. The girl broke into an unrestrained giggle and ran out to get his luggage.

Hero

Schuler had telephoned Captain Helmuth Grautoff to meet Norbourne and himself for whiskey and soda before dinner. He said Hermann had suggested the idea to him. At one end of the lounge a fire of sticks blazed in an enormous fireplace, but the space about it was so thick with people reading periodicals or drinking cocktails, that Schuler and Norbourne sat down on a leather chair at the other end of the room to catch what cheer they could from the reflection of the blaze on the white marble mantel.

A smiling dark giant of about thirty came quietly through the swinging glass doors from the lobby. Norbourne was introduced to the great bulk of Helmuth Grautoff. Was this overgrown boy with the round, ingenuous, wondering eyes that pioneer who had made the first non-stop test flight of the German mail plane from Africa to Brazil? Norbourne ordered drinks.

"No-o, no-o," Grautoff was saying slowly and ruminatingly, wrapping his huge left fist gently about his glass, "no adventure, no romance. It's really very simple, just seventeen hours of flying over the ocean. Berlin, Stuttgart, Marseilles, Seville, Las Palmas, Bathurst—then over the ocean to Brazil. There's nothing more. That's all there is to it." He tilted his glass into his small mouth. "No-o, no-o, it's very easy to keep awake. I never get sleepy. I always took off from Bathurst at midnight and got thirteen hours of light out of the seventeen. I flew low, generally only about five metres above the water. It was faster that way and avoided the winds. Then, you see, if anything went wrong, it was such a short little drop to the water." He smiled. "No danger at all, really."

He clinked his wedding-ring finger against the glass and peered into the future. "I want to fly now direct from here to Manáos on the Amazon. There might be some danger in that. It's savage country. No one has ever been through it or over it. But we'll have a transport line one of these days from here to there, as Pan American already has an air service there from Pará. Manáos is run down now, but in 1900 it was a city rolling in money—centre of the world's rubber trade. It had the finest opera house in South America and the best French whores in the world, the old-timers say. It still has the opera house."

Glancing at the tiny watch on his powerful wrist, he stood up, towering and bulky—sixteen stone of modest, fearless vitality. "Sorry I can't dine with you. But my wife is expecting me. I married a French girl and they do not like to be left alone. Now if I had married a Spanish woman—I could have stayed with you with pleasure." He held out a huge, affable hand.

Norbourne regarded the heroic back that went out of the door uncommented on by the hotel guests. "No, no; no adventure, no romance—it's very simple—you just take off and fly over the ocean——." He had flown over the Atlantic twice a week on routine mail schedule with as little seeming concern as a skipper piloting a night boat between New York and Boston.

"Yes," said young Schuler, as they went in to dinner, "he could have stayed if his wife were Spanish. The Spanish American girl makes no demands on her husband."

Urbane Ducking

After dinner they got their overcoats and went for a walk. The drab streets were as deserted and silent as if an air raid warning had made the inhabitants scurry under cover. But it was the chill of night that had sent them to bed or to huddle about the tables of the undecorated coffee shops, drinking infinite cups of steaming coffee.

"Unlike other South American capitals, Bogotá has no vestige of night life," Schuler said.

"But I've heard American managers of oil companies boast of the fantastic stakes they play for at bridge here."

"Oh, yes—at the country clubs. There's wealth here, of course."

Norbourne stopped short, as amazed as if he had confronted Norway's midnight sun in the tropics. The plaza was blazing with colour. The four great fountains were illuminated like Versailles. Green, yellow, scarlet waters spurted high into the night air like liquid fireworks and dropped in a cascade of jewels. The waters changed to amethyst and aquamarine as the controls of an electric switch were juggled.

"Tomorrow is their Independence Day," Schuler explained. "In 1810 a Spanish soldier and a Colombian had an altercation. The Spaniard got a chamber pot smashed on his head. That was the beginning of the independence."

They walked up close to one of the fountains. A group of people muffled to the nose stood in awed quiet before the miracle of colour. "Here, in these basins," said Schuler, "the bootblacks douse the unfortunate matador who has not been valiant or sensational enough for them in the bull ring.—You know they have one of the finest arenas in the world here.—They bear him ignominiously spread-eagled like a hog going to slaughter and duck him again and again in these fountains until he is almost drowned."

"Don't the police interfere?"

"Never. They stand by and cheer while the poor devil splutters." They turned away from the coloured waters and went down a dim side street. "It is claimed that the mortality of men in the Bogotá *corridas* is two hundred per cent higher than in those of Spain or Mexico."

"Lack of skill or fear of bootblacks?"

"Both. They can't afford the cream of the Spanish toreadors, and besides the bulls are more ferocious and more clever. They are black Andalusian stock crossed with the fierce native longhorn of the *llanos*. But I think the bootblacks spur them into taking crazy chances. One bullfighter committed suicide from chagrin last year after a ducking."

Bless the Go-Getter

Back at the Granada, Norbourne stopped in the lounge to glance at the papers. Sunk in the deep leather of a semicircle of armchairs a group of men, three Colombians and three Americans, sat about the embers talking business—the need for roads and railways and the advantages to be gleaned from Cordell Hull's bilateral reciprocity treaty. Norbourne got into conversation with them.

Up to the time of the World War few new ideas had penetrated beyond the coast of Colombia. Since the stirring days of the conquest and the piratical raids on treasure-filled Cartagena in the sixteenth and seventeenth centuries, Colombia had been content with a somnolent existence. The Spanish ruling class of Bogotá lived in aristocratic seclusion, drawing their money from coffee, bananas, salt, and metals. They travelled little. They were content with their mountain views, their blue-blood lineage, their own poetic compositions. Business as the United States knows business was a factor unknown and undisturbing to the even tenor of their slow traditional days. The transportation problem made towns across the mountains from each other as remote as New York and Berlin.

During the World War Colombia woke up to the fact that she was making very little out of her bounteous natural resources and began to bestir herself. By selling their raw materials, Colombians were able to buy European luxuries and American conveniences. They began to modernize their business and their daily life, as Germans seeking new frontiers introduced new trading methods. Isolated districts began to get in touch with the great outside world.

Through the United Fruit Company, Colombia long ago knew the value of her bananas, which rank today third among her exports. But her oilfields were idly neglected. However, petroleum has now jumped to second place among her commodities. From

1926 to 1929 the production of petroleum increased from six million to twenty million barrels annually. With a double pipeline running 365 miles from an American concession in the Department of Santander to the Bay of Cartagena 50,000 barrels can be pumped daily from the interior to the coast for foreign export. This liquid gold that pours out of the soil is worth far more than all the loot of the conquistadors.

Today Colombia is the second coffee-producing country in the world, and coffee heads her list of exports. In the depression years Colombia's revenues from coffee averaged about $50,000,000 annually. Ninety per cent of the production from her 450,000,000 coffee trees goes to the United States. And because their coffee industry depends almost exclusively on that market, the Colombians, while not forgiving the United States the loss of the Panama Canal Zone, throttle their resentment. The United States also takes the bulk of Colombia's petroleum and virtually her entire crop of bananas.

"Because of its present inaccessibility," one of the American oil men said to Norbourne, "the mineral wealth—gold, silver, copper, salt, platinum, emeralds—has only been slightly exploited. And even now, except for coffee production, primtive methods of agriculture are still largely practised. Industries are just commencing. Colombia is only at the threshold of her expansion.

"Her trade is something all the big nations are competing for. Though far and away her best customer—in 1934 we bought ten times as much from Colombia as France did, and forty times as much as England—the United States has been given a comparatively small share of the nation's business. However, by the new reciprocity trade treaty between the two countries signed in 1935, Colombia is giving us an increasingly greater share of her trade and becoming more and more cordial through mutual economic benefits.

"There's one significant thing you may not notice down here and I hope you don't mind my calling it to your attention," the oil man went on, as the group broke up. "Out of the new necessities and new opportunities, a new type of native industrialist and business man is being evolved. Nothing much has ever been written about business men because their careers are supposed to be pretty prosaic. Yet without them, nations would remain with civilization stopped in its tracks. When you people visit these Latin American nations, you are apt to find only the peons picturesque and the aristocrats worth remembering. But you should remember that what makes your visit more comfortable and convenient is due to the native industrialists who had the will to do things despite the huge handicaps of tradition—and transportation."

Norbourne thanked him for his lesson, and went up to sleep soundly in the most comfortable bed he had found south of the Ritz in Mexico City.

Bolos

The *fiesta* bands began playing early on Colombia's Independence Day. When Norbourne went out, he was pursued by a host of *bolos*. His shoes did not need a shine. But there was a look in the eyes of the least aggressive of the bootblacks that beguiled him to sit on a cold marble bench under the statue of a hero and offer patronage. The ragged lad, the size of a thirteen-year-old, knelt on a minute square of frayed blue carpet and began rubbing the inside of a sucked orange around the edges of the shoe sole. His uncreased man-size felt hat rested on his ears. On his feet he wore frayed canvas sandals. His ankles were an unhealthy blue from the chill. A wisp of silky moustache on his unwashed upper lip prompted Norbourne to ask his age. "Twenty-one," the boy said, looking up with joyless, unambitious eyes.

A competitor *bolo* joined them. He squatted on his blacking box up-ended, and regarded both the foreigner and the job in process with cool appraisal. He was handsome in a picaresque way like a ragamuffin from a Murillo canvas. His blue-black hair curled like hyacinths from under the rakish slant of a battered felt hat. His eyes were impudent, untrustworthy; his mouth, chiselled in sardonic lines. Doubtless he was one of those who relished the spectacle of a proud toreador spattering in the pool. Norbourne offered them Philip Morris cigarettes. They accepted them like men of the world. The second *bolo* struck a match and held it to Norbourne's cigarette with a mature gesture.

"How much do a pair of those sandals cost?" Norbourne asked, rising, his rump numb from the cold marble. The answer was the equivalent of thirty cents. "Go and buy yourself a new pair," he said, handing the boy the money. He looked at it hesitatingly, then accepted the unaccustomed kindness with a shrug.

More *bolos* barred Norbourne's way down the street. He pointed out that his shoes had just been shined. They were not impressed. They wanted to do it over again. Before the cathedral, in the midst of fiesta hubbub, bootblacks plied their trade with assiduity. Nineteen *bolos* squatted in a gutter before morning-coated gentlemen standing on one leg and conversing with their neighbours in dignified, rhetorical Castilian. The church bells of Bogotá are not more vehement in clamouring for the cleansing of souls than the *bolos* are for the salvation of shoes.

The main plaza was thick with stirring humanity. The water of the fountains had become the colour of water again, but the red, yellow, and blue flags of Colombia were being borne in parade. *Mestizo* soldiers were marching in bright blue uniforms with black and gilt Germanic helmets on their heads. Many of the soldiers were out of line. At a halt they did not stand straight, but leaned forward as if a band were tied about their foreheads and a weight of stones rested on their backs — a posture inherited from burden-bearing Indian ancestors. Thick on the heels of the soldiers came nuns and Red Cross nurses and bands of little orphanage girls in sober grey serge uniforms, their eyes almost popping from their faces with the unwonted attention.

In and out of the great cathedral door, like flies buzzing about the mouth of a molasses jug, went women in black shawls and men's felt hats, with lack-lustre pigtails tucked inside their dress backs. With a bow to feminine graces, a few wore their masculine headgear grotesquely above rusty lace mantillas. Within the illuminated church women laid their babies on the cold stone pavement and knelt beside them. In their transports of adoration some of them bent forward and licked the dusty floor. When the foreign diplomatic corps in all its formal elegance entered to join the President of the Republic at High Mass, two women had to be prodded out of their ecstasy to save their infants from being trampled on.

So this confusion and jostling and noise, this gawking and gaping was the fiesta that people looked forward to weeks in advance. Norbourne was relieved to drive out into the country that afternoon to see Bogotá's famous rendezvous for suicides.

Theatre Manners

A young Colombian who had been educated in Philadelphia went with Norbourne. He was the first in his aristocratic family ever to work, a local manager for an American film company. He was tall and pale, with distinguished features, sad eyes, and a gentle manner of speaking.

On the country roadside rugged peons were on the brisk move. They were covered with dust but they smiled unresentfully at the passing cars. Though there was not a pure-blooded Indian among them, they belonged to the landscape in their way, as much as the Indians of Yucatan and Guatemala did to theirs. They looked hewn from the yellow-brown rock.

"What is the explanation of all these poor people?" Norbourne asked.

"It has always been the way with Spain—two great classes: the few extremely rich, the many very poor. Only gradually is there developing that middle class, of which your country, for instance, is mostly made up. What is known as England's upper and lower middle class is just beginning to come about in Colombia—extraordinarily clever peons who prosper and younger sons of old families who lost their money two generations ago are beginning to form a middle class. They are the industrialists and the retailers. This country's progress has not been made by Americans or Germans or English. It has been made by native sons. But English, Germans, and Americans have furnished us with ideas and systems and capital, and the United States has lent us her engineers."

"The peons' taste for felt hats and canvas sandals is unanimous apparently," said Norbourne.

"Yes, and it is so with their pleasures," said the young man. "In the picture houses they are a thousand bodies with one mind. Nowhere do managers have to cater so to the taste of an audience. The patrons don't get up and go out if displeased—they stay and demand something better. The management always has to have extra films to substitute. If a picture is slow, they begin the *pateo*, that is, to stamp their feet—a most disturbing sound to the manager. He continues the reel to see if it can regain their favour. Unless it picks up quickly the stamping becomes menacing. Then the patrons get out their match boxes. They stick the ends of the matches under their fingernails, light the tips and hold up their hands as if challenged by highwaymen. Soon the darkened theatre is blazing with hundreds of these little five-branched candelabra. If the management has not changed the picture by the time the matches have burnt down to the fingernails, the audience begins to split the chair bottoms into kindling wood."

"How can you tell what will displease them?"

"We can't. But we've learned they hate slow motion above everything else. Some years ago they got bored with Eddie Cantor in *Whoopee*. The manager had been so sure that the picture would be popular he had no reserve on hand. They nearly wrecked the theatre. For years he was afraid to give them more Cantor. Then he risked *The Kid from Spain*. The bull fight scenes won them. Now Cantor in anything is a huge success."

Rendezvous for Suicides

Thirteen miles from the capital the Bogotá River swirls about a rocky ledge projecting over the edge of an abyss, contracts to a width of twenty-five yards and drops precipitously four hundred and forty feet. As it plunges down with a thundering detonation, the water bursts into iridescent spray and reflects the caprices of the sky and the sylvan luxuriance rioting rankly about the rocky fall. Norbourne and his companion stood on the drenched terrace of the Hotel Salto, which juts from an opposite precipice like a flying buttress. Norbourne looked down into the depths of the gorge. A legion of ghostly blue vapours rose like shrouded spirits making an ascension. Instinctively he stepped back from the rail.

"In Bogotá we say, 'If anything goes wrong I'll take a bath in the Tequendama.'" The young Colombian spoke in a gentle shout at Norbourne's ear. "Only last Sunday two soldiers bathed here. After luncheon in the hotel they stood on the rock over there and held each other by the arm and leaped. The police could find no motive."

"No letter in their pockets?"

"No trace of anyone who went over the falls has ever been found down there. It's a bottomless hole."

"Perhaps it's the lost entrance to Hades," Norbourne said. He regarded the subtle magnificence of the scene. It was a hundred times more stirring than obvious Niagara. Both fascinating and repelling, it was a natural setting for some unwritten Wagnerian opera. "But this place is for gods and heroes to commit suicide in," he said, "not puny man."

"Well, plenty of puny men make use of it. The Tequendama is said to be the best *suicidadero* in Colombia, because if you do it here your family is spared the humiliation of your body's being stowed away in the cemetery for suicides."

They passed through the small unheated reception room of the hotel where some *mestizos* were dancing the *pasillo*, a fast native two-step. Two couples of sturdy girls were dancing violently; their four boy-friends sat about in straight chairs drinking cold beer. In the gloom of the small bar beyond, two glum black-bearded peons with their heads stuck through fuzzy black *ruanas* were also drinking cold beer. As Norbourne drank his sad-eyed companion's health, he was thinking: Bogotá would not be the place for an acute attack of the blues.

Emeralds

As they passed the University on their return, Norbourne asked why the epithet "Athens of the New World" was always attached to Bogotá in the guide books. Its bleak exterior suggested a barracks and nothing Hellenic.

His companion smiled ironically. "In vice-regal days Bogotá was so remote from the world the citizens who were literate wrote verses to beguile the time. Cypresses were planted in the plazas so that they could stroll under them and declaim their own compositions. Today in a country where eighty per cent of the people are illiterate, there's little to justify the catch phrase. But even yet we speak the purest Spanish of South America and our poets are still considered the best outside Spain."

As they neared Norbourne's hotel the young man said, "I'm sorry the Zipaquirá salt mines are closed during the holidays. They are really extraordinary, with their gigantic galleries and arcades gleaming like diamonds in the electric illumination. When visitors are properly bowled over by the white magic, we say, 'But this is nothing—you should see the emerald mines of Muzo!' "

"What are they like?" Norbourne asked, falling into the trap.

"Like the salt mines, only green."

Norbourne laughed. "Too bad that isn't true. Tell me about your emeralds. I know Colombia is the greatest emerald country in the world and the only one producing them just now."

"The emerald mining country is prodigiously inaccessible. I've been there once. Mules furnish the only transportation. The Muzo mines are located seventy-five miles north of Bogotá in the bowl of an extinct crater. They were worked by the Spaniards as early as the middle of the sixteenth century. The Muzo mines have produced tens of millions of dollars' worth of the gems. Indian labourers break a trail of green quartz out the surface of the crater with pickaxe and crowbars. The quartz is collected and washed by a forceful stream of water. Great care has to be taken in the washing, for the stones are fragile when in the matrix and do not harden until after exposure to air.

"I haven't seen the Chivor mines. They are eighty miles northeast of Bogotá. For a century they were closed and lost to civilization and only rediscovered buried under jungle thirty years ago. Other lost mines are still being sought. Why don't you come down and help us find them? The government would give you a percentage. A percentage would net a nice fortune. The emeralds are there. A flawless Colombian emerald sometimes brings three times the price of a diamond the same size. All anybody needs is pluck and capital."

"That's all anybody needs anywhere," Norbourne answered.

"Sometimes you don't have to have much of either."

"No?"

"No. I have some cousins in Cartagena who merely bought an old house that had stood there since the days before Morgan's raid."

"Don't tell me they discovered an emerald mine in the cellar."

"Something like it. In doing some repairs to enlarge the drawing room about fifteen years ago they tore down a thick wall, and, believe it or not, found a jar of emeralds hidden in the stones. Very quietly one of the women of the family took the next steamer for Paris. The people in Cartagena believe a relative in Europe left my cousins their fortune."

Norbourne had regretted missing Cartagena on many counts. "The Queen of the Caribbean" with its fabulous tales of wealth and pirate sackings had stirred his imagination since childhood, but he had had to leave out Colombia's most historic spot simply for lack of time. But now he decided he would not miss Medellín. He felt, however, that he was missing much in cutting a party of the literati of Bogotá to which he was invited the next afternoon. Yet he felt too that no matter how long he stayed in aristocratic Bogotá or how many charming people he met, it would always remain to him pictorially a sombre sketch in charcoal.

That evening he sent a radiogram to Hermann asking him to reserve a room at the Europa and one to Don Gonzalo saying he would be honoured to visit the country estates of his relatives. The next morning he flew to Medellín. Grautoff was his pilot.

Gardens and Parasites

From his hotel window in Medellín Norbourne looked down through glossy foliage of great trees at the ravine cutting through the centre of the city. The little silver river bounding over the ravine's rocky bed made a pleasant rural music that took the edge off modern traffic noises. He thought now it was particularly the abundance of trees that had beguiled him to return to Medellín—it possessed far more than most Spanish American towns. Trees tempered the severity of Spanish façades in the business district. Immense shade trees bordered the streets of the better residential districts. And in the suburbs grey-green willows, called *sauces*, shot straight and sharp as geysers along the ferny banks of nameless tributary mountain rills. In a climate where all seasons merged together in a perpetual spring, like the end of an English May, trees of the tropics flourished intimately with trees of frosty regions.

By the time Norbourne had changed, Don Gonzalo had come to take him to see the *casa de campo* of his relatives. Their fortune in the new world had been founded two centuries ago by a shipowning ancestor who transported merchandise and mail between Jamaica and the Colombian coast and thence by river boat to Medellín. The department of Antioquia of which Medellín was the capital had subsequently become rich in coffee and gold and cattle, and the family had managed to husband and increase the fortune divided often among much progeny. So Don Gonzalo was able to point from the roof of the hotel to many estates of his kinsfolk dotting terraced slopes of the foothills above the amphitheatre of the city. Norbourne selected this one and that one from among them, and they drove out to see the places.

Like ivory towers poised between earth and sky, the country houses of Medellín hang just far enough above the town's activities to give a feeling of serenity and just far enough beneath the green glory of the mountain tops to call to mind the vanity of human riches. Unlike most Spanish houses they possess both verandah and patio. Like those of post-war houses in the southern United States the verandahs surround both sides of the houses as well as the front. They are broad and inviting, but without upper galleries or formal Grecian columns.

Norbourne was taken first to La Concha, the home of one of Don Gonzalo's sisters. The great drawing room was entered directly from the centre of the front verandah. It extended to the series of French doors giving on the patio which sloped upward with the hills and looked upon the mountains. The patio was laid out formally with pavements of round white pebbles and flowering plants; the galleries of the two side wings were festooned with vines and climbing roses. A fountain of blue marble shot a slender column of water high into the air. Shimmering white egrets were parading with their broods about the fountain's edge, and, Narcissus-like, regarding their reflection lovingly in the pool's mirror. Beyond the fountain, reached by a short flight of stone stairs cut into a green embankment, a Moorish gate broke a white brick wall. Beyond the gate was a rose garden, with Japanese plum trees in the four corners and mauve orchids massed thickly on the wall's flat top. In the centre of the plot a Moorish bath of cream-coloured tiles sank into the ground in the shape of a keyhole. Nine narrow steps descended to the bottom. Here the six young ladies of the household come for cold baths in the sunshine. Locking the garden gate behind them, they have no apprehensions in unmasking their beauty to the rose trees.

"Would you like to see the orchard and the vegetable garden?" asked the only son of the family, who with his beautiful, smartly-dressed wife had just dropped in to see how his mother and aunts and six unmarried sisters were getting along. He had been educated at Starkville, Mississippi, where he had elected to study agriculture. He was just as American in his manner and address as his wife, who had gone to school in Paris and London, was French in dress and English in accent. Don Gonzalo proudly told Norbourne sotto voce that the young man managed the family affairs with great acumen and had developed into a skilful business man as well as a scientific planter.

Through a cool grove of towering shade trees they passed along a broad mossy walk, where marble seats were half concealed in shallow green alcoves. Winding tributary paths led up to the higher terraces of the orchard and the cutting and kitchen gardens. In the mellowing sunshine the atmosphere was fragrant with the odour of orange blossom, guava, lemon, spice, and globular golden melons. Flowers grew in borders around the edges of fruit tree plots; old fashioned temperate garden varieties blossomed beside exotic tropical specimens. Carnation, petunia, heliotrope blended their scents with those of fruits. Espaliered apple trees, trellises, and arcades varied the pattern of the vast kitchen garden.

"It is spacious enough to feed a regiment," Norbourne commented, regarding the bounty and the beauty with delight. It was as if La Concha lay at the mouth of a horn of plenty which rested on the mountain's curve and poured out its fruits and flowers and sustaining vegetables in an unending fullness.

In the long dining room where whiskey and soda was set out among resplendent crystal and silver on a richly carved sideboard, Norbourne had a distinct shock. Around an antique dining room table fit for a king a dozen Grand Rapids golden oak chairs—the sort Negroes in the Southern states buy on the instalment plan for their cabins—stood incongruously cheap and vulgar, like uninvited guests. Norbourne stared at the chairs, looked at his hosts and hostesses, expectant of explanation. But they only seemed puzzled by his quizzical expression and asked if he would like more soda in his whiskey. Six weeks later he left South America without solving the puzzle.

At the *casa de campo* of another sister, three hundred varieties of orchids flamed along an avenue of ancient mango trees that led from the back of the house to another Moorish bath set in a bower of ferns just where the mountain broke into steep ascent. Vines heavy with orchid blooms clung to the bark of the trees and ran along the ground in a matted border six feet wide. As varied in intricate design as snowflakes under a magnifying glass, the orchids were of every conceivable colour. Some were pale and ethereal in texture like Indian pipes; some flamboyantly, fleshily magnificent. The mistress of the place bore the romantic name of Zoraida. She was a commanding large woman with the assured gracious air of a duchess. Her heavy-lidded dark eyes were as Moorish as her name. In rough English tweeds and elaborately arranged grey hair, she strode among her orchids, snipping off rare specimens to show Norbourne differences at close range.

"This is called the Death Mask orchid," she said, holding up a blossom that looked like a cluster of enormous orange-coloured grapes with small purple polka dots. It appeared to have been dusted heavily with cream-coloured powder. From within the half-open hull of each grape, as if carved out of ivory or bone, leered a tiny human skull. Madame Zoraida handed Norbourne the flower to feel its lead-like weight. It was heavier than a bunch of Malaga grapes. "The Indians say the ghost of their ancestors murdered by the conquistadors come back in these orchids to haunt us." The odour was sickeningly sweet; so overpowering that a single blossom might provide incense for a cathedral.

"Apparently orchids do not require more nursing here than dandelions do with us," Norbourne said.

"No, the woods are full for the picking. It's only when I import new specimens from Brazil that we pamper them. I have them brought in by aeroplane, you know. But they quickly take to their new surroundings here. Orchids thrive in this climate like all parasites." She paused at the sound of a motor horn. "Here are my sons back from polo," she said, with a shade of significance, indicating a car rounding a curving garden wall which was dotted with small apricot-coloured orchids. "They were both educated abroad. I spent eleven years in Europe with them. They ended up at Cambridge and Oxford, one at each. I lived in London between them. Even with all this"—her eyes swept her acres, her house, her flowers, the azure sky—"would you believe I am often nostalgic for London and its fogs? But the boys were educated, so there was no excuse to stay longer."

"And what do they do here now? Coffee? Gold? Diplomacy?"

Madame Zoraida smiled with a *femme du monde* shrug. "They play polo and bet on the races."

Lessons

The Viennese aerodrome manager came for Norbourne in his roadster that afternoon at two to drive him out to some of the neighbouring villages. In the rumble seat Hermann's police dog took the air with them. They drove out past the country club and the last of the *casas de campo* into the real country. The sun shone. The air was inspiriting as wine. The fat acres were green with plenty. The neat cottages of the peons were embowered in banana plants and crêpe myrtle bushes. Petunias garnished window boxes. Birds whistled in the hedges. The whole department of Antioquia up to the coffee *fincas* on the higher ridges seemed like a vast irregular garden. The road twisted, circled, and turned up new pleasing prospects at the top of each hill, at the bottom of each valley.

In the little plazas of the hamlets the wares of the Sunday markets were spread out under the sky's blue canopy. Peons sauntered socially among the patches of produce, piece goods, harness, knick-knacks, cheeses, cheap jewellery, and *al fresco* charcoal restaurants. Dangling from the belt in front in the manner of a Scotch Highlander's sporran the men invariably wore a kind of lady's shopping bag made of goat skin. Here they carried their money, tobacco, lunch, pocket handkerchiefs, and oddments. When asked directions they were courteous, somewhat grave, but agreeable to exchange a smile. One fellow who had had a few extra drinks unsteadily dismounted from his mule to tell the way to Machado. While he pointed the direction he kept his gaze thoughtfully on the dog in the rumble seat. As the car drove off, he remarked to a friend, "I think it is better to be born a rich dog than a poor man." No malice, no resentment in his tone, just a philosophical observation in a land where the division between the classes is sharp.

"Though ignorant," said Hermann, "the peons here are self-respecting and respected. In many factories, workers, when summoned to assemble, are addressed as 'gentlemen.' The Latins, from top to bottom, desire to be respected above all things."

At one village they stopped at a bodega on the plaza to have a beer. They sat at a table on the sidewalk, watched the slow flow of humanity and talked of this and that.

An old hag with a cheroot in her mouth and a twinkle in her eye, hobbled by, paused to look at the parked car and at the two foreigners. She took her cigar from between her gums and said she would like to have a ride in an atuomobile and have the fun foreigners had. Hermann smilingly told her she was asking too much of life, that she was old and by the look in her eye she had had her fun. She looked at him for a long moment with a kind of disdain for his callow understanding. "Well, at any rate," she said, "I'm happy to keep the cage, even if the bird has flown away. I wonder if you will be."

She hobbled off, puffing with relish at her cheroot. The men smiled, acknowledging the thrust.

"And you never know where you're going to learn a lesson," Hermann remarked. His eyes became reminiscent. "I remember once in Vienna after the war, there were no jobs, many of us went back to school. In my class there were twenty-eight students. Twenty-five of them had been officers or petty officers. We couldn't afford to buy civilian clothes, so we were permitted to wear our uniforms, but not our caps. We wore any old thing on our heads we could borrow or beg. All stars and bars and insignia of rank had to be ripped off our tunics. The first day the class met, a man with three stars torn from his shoulder entered the classroom. Over his right eye he wore a black monocle on a black silk ribbon. The class rose. He announced that he was Herr So-and-so, our instructor in calculus, and asked us to be seated. He sat down at his desk and began to arrange his papers. We remarked the affectation of the black monocle, exchanged scornful winks. One fellow took out his watch, unscrewed the crystal, inserted it over his right eye and assumed a supercilious expression. Another followed suit. Soon all the crystals from pocket watches and wrist watches were unscrewed and stuck on faces. We smirked at each other and looked very proud. We would teach this ex-captain a lesson!

"At length the professor-captain rose to begin his lecture. He stared at us in astonishment. He turned red, then very pale. There was dead silence. We held our mocking expressions. At length the professor said tensely, 'Very well, gentlemen, you have asked for it.' He reached up and let his black monocle dangle on its ribbon. There was no eye behind the monocle. Even the lids were slashed and seared."

Hermann paused, and Norbourne let out a sympathetic "Hum-m," surprised and touched by the twist in the story.

"We were speechless with mortification," Hermann went on. "We bowed our heads and took out the watch crystals. We began screwing them back in the proper places. It was a dreadful sound,

I can tell you, that screwing of the little crystals into the watches. Then one redheaded chap got up and went to the desk and mumbled an apology. One man after another did the same thing. The professor smiled with understanding forgiveness. 'Just a little misapprehension, gentlemen,' he said in a low voice. 'We are prone to distrust what we do not understand.' He took up a piece of chalk and turned to the blackboard. 'Now we shall begin the study of calculus.' "

Norbourne couldn't think of just the right thing to say, so he lit a cigarette.

"That's partly why nations fight," the Austrian said after a moment. "They distrust and fear because they don't understand each other. Your country is being so wise now in trying to understand Latin America, to have these republics understand you. And they are beginning to lose their distrust."

"I hope so," said Norbourne. "We've got to stick together. If the rest of the world goes to pot and cuts each other's throats, we could manage happily enough among ourselves on this side of the world."

On the way back to Medellín, a rain cloud sprang up from behind a hill where corn was ripening. The shower came quickly, thick and blinding. They stopped the car on the roadside. Norbourne was delighted with the rain, with the green landscape washed in grey.

"I have never got to like rain," Hermann said. "I was at the front for three years. But here in Medellín at least it is never cold rain."

"What do you think of Remarque?" It was a question Norbourne liked to ask Germans and Austrians.

The lines about Hermann's mouth tightened. "He forgot only on thing——"

"And that?"

"The winter. Winter in the trenches. It is something to remember the rest of your life."

Treasure Trove

On the flight to Cali, where Norbourne was to take a train to Buenaventura because there was no air service, they passed over hundreds of coffee plantations and then went high over the mountains. Mountainside fields were so steep they were like meadows trying to turn somersaults and so thick with yellow daisies they looked as though a fleet of treasure planes had dropped millions of gold coins for largesse. It was in a more wooded part of this vicinity that a private aeroplane bearing two hundred and fifty thousand dollars in gold had crashed four years previously. For a fortnight rescuing government planes had vainly searched for the wreck. When at last all hope had been abandoned, a party of treasure hunters travelling by mule back, unaware of the accident, stumbled upon the lost fortune. And alongside the quarter of a million dollars in scattered coins lay the ruins of an aeroplane. In the bushes close by they found a man unconscious. He was the American manager of a platinum mine, named Marshall. Because he had been too badly hurt by the fall to get away, he had stayed by the plane while the three other passengers and the pilot and co-pilot had gone off into the forest one by one to find help. None ever came back. Evidently all five died dismally in the wilds, killed by savage beasts or exhausted by starvation. Marshall had sustained life on a box of a dozen chocolates and a thermos bottle of water. With fortitude and foresight he had rationed himself to one chocolate a day and two swallows of water. When the providential treasure hunters had appeared all the chocolates were gone and he was existing chameleon-like on the air. Whatever bitter twinges may have racked the amazed treasure seekers' breasts, they turned heroically to life-saving.

Colombian Trains and Japanese Talent

The train journey from Cali to Buenaventura was six hours of discomfort over a winding, mountainous route composed largely of switchbacks. Buenaventura with a population of 25,000, overwhelmingly Negro, is Colombia's third most important port and the terminus of the Pacific Railway System. Coffee, platinum, and gold are exported. In the dry seasons when the Magdalena River becomes coy and unpredictable, the Pacific port takes on a fevered activity because it gets much of the commerce that logically belongs to Barranquilla and Cartagena on the Caribbean. The seven coaches were so crowded that many passengers stood up or sat on their baggage in the aisles. There was no Pullman car, no observation car. But four young ladies were forced to observe from the platform of the back coach, sitting on the floor and hanging their legs over the edge. An exhausted, sensitive-looking fellow whose melancholy black eyes revealed his Jewish nationality plopped on an up-ended suitcase, his thin, nervous body drooped in abject contempt of his environment. He looked like a musician and turned out to be a shoe salesman from Boston, as Norbourne learned in the restaurant car when they sat at the same table.

The restaurant car, in the middle of the train, was negotiated by a leap of two feet from one open vestibule to the other, the train swaying and lurching full tilt. Within, it was like an old-fashioned guard's van turned into a fourth-rate lunch waggon. Cramped from sharing a seat with a broadbeamed *mestizo* matron, whose family had arrived early and taken half the window side seats on one side of the coach, Norbourne leaped every other hour to the restaurant car and lingered over a small coffee. The shoe salesman said he had lost fifteen pounds in the past three months. He loathed Colombia. When his car broke down in the country, which was often, he had had to sleep in Negro huts and eat bread fried in lard. His digestion was ruined. Now he could scarcely eat anything. He felt sure he had stomach ulcers.

"Why don't you travel by train?" Norbourne asked him.

"Only a few of the trains go anywhere," he answered despairingly. "There are railway lines here and there, but they are not end to end. The lines of one system resent crossing the boundary of the next department. For all practical purposes most of them might be non-existent. Many fair-sized places have no connection except by mule back with the outside world. You wouldn't believe how backward and illogical the people are. And the people of the coasts know as little about the people of the high plateau as Hottentots know of Vermonters." He sighed profoundly. "I'm going back now to resign. I can't stand the smell."

He confessed it was the smell of the Negro villages that undid him. His sense of smell was so abnormally acute, he said, that he selected his friends and enemies by scent. He fell in love by scent. He had fallen in love with a Scotch-Irish girl in Boston because her scent was overpowering to him. "If a duchess came into this restaurant car," he maintained, "drenched in Caron's most alluring odour I could smell right through to the elemental woman. The perfume would merely add to or detract from her natural odour which either attracted or repelled me." He shook his head dolefully and sniffed the air about him.

At a station called Dagûa, Norbourne got off to stretch his legs. There on the platform he saw Burton Holmes, the prince of travel commentators, with his camera to his eye, snapping pretty girls and looking fresh as a daisy. A Negress was offering for sale the hugest bananas Norbourne had ever beheld. They had burst their skins in the fullness of their maturity. He would have bought some if train ashes had not lurked in the crevices.

The train crept and creaked with the movement of a measuring worm travelling on its side instead of its belly. At last it plunged into the fœtid flats that was Buenaventura. No place ever more ironically belied its name. There is, however, a certain picturesque squalor in the bamboo shacks with the hideous corrugated iron roofs streaked with rust, in the half-naked old Negresses with disgusting skin diseases who sit in dank doorways searching for lice in the woolly heads of naked potbellied children. The welcome lies in the swarm of black boys who chase the train and hang on to the car windows and scream like wild monkeys for your luggage. Outside, despite your own yells of frantic protestation and dire threat, some of your luggage goes one way and some another. Norbourne tried to chase his two bags both ways at once and resigned himself to fate like the tragic Jew with the sensitive nose. But somehow at the Hotel Estación both suitcases were finally assembled. In a hullabaloo of howls for rooms, Norbourne got the privilege of sharing the last vacant room in the place with a squint-eyed Rumanian Jew, who sold women's dresses from New York, but who still spoke little English. However, he knew enough words to say, "Pretty different from Park Avenue this, isn't it?"

After he had sponged off to the waist and changed his shirt, Norbourne took a turn about the hotel. It was a maze of galleries and open corridors with an octagonal inner court. Perfectly constructed for the tropics, it lacked somewhat in privacy, because the tops of the dividing walls between the rooms were open for air circulation and one heard every private sound from whispering and teeth-washing to turning over in bed resoundingly re-echoed, and whenever a light was turned on in the room on either side, a great flood of illumination gushed over the top.

Downstairs he saw the last two bathers crawl out of an outdoor swimming pool, as the sun went down like a globe of liquid fire into the Pacific. A distinguished-looking gentleman with sharp pointed grey beard was taking photographs at his side. Norbourne introduced himself to Burton Holmes. They dined together. At dinner Holmes opened a can of *pâté de fois gras* which he had brought back on the maiden voyage of the *Normandie*. His wife had insisted on adding this luxury to his aeroplane allotment of luggage, assuring him that it would cheer him in some uncivilized predicament. He was in one now, because he could not get a room before midnight when the Spanish boat sailed for Panama. He had got into a somewhat similar predicament in Tokio once, he confessed. While he was attending a garden party for the Prince of Wales, the Imperial Hotel burned down with all his clothes in it. In formal attire and top hat he cruised about Tokio in rickshaws for three hours hunting a sleeping place. Every hotel and lodging house was full to the billiard tables and hallways.

"So I said, 'Well, I know one place in Japan where they know how to treat gentlemen and not let them wander the streets all night.' I went to a house of hospitable young ladies. I made it very clear to the mistress of the place that I had come only to sleep, but the young lady whose room I had to share thought of course I was joking. She had a talent for imitating animal sounds. She could laugh like a hyena, crow like a cock, bray like a jackass. All night she entertained me. Every time I dozed off she would poke me and give a new imitation, squeak like a mouse or trumpet like an elephant. I pleaded for mercy. She thought I was playing a game and she would laugh a gay girlish laugh and then grunt like a rooting hog. I never spent such a fatiguing night. In my morning coat and top hat I escaped at first dawn, leaving the young lady tremendously perplexed."

Someone at the next table re-echoed in consternation the news that the Spanish boat might not arrive at all that night.

Holmes looked a bit dashed. "Really," he said, smiling uncertainly, "I don't know what Buenaventura has to offer. I wasn't exactly favourably impressed by those rusty corrugated-iron roofs. However——"

Equatorial Appetite

The flying boat arrived from Cristobal at ten-thirty. In those few early hours of daylight it had already flown 466 miles. It was named the *Santa Maria* after Columbus's flagship, that most famous of all ships, which opened the original trade route between the hemispheres.

On board, with his wife and seventeen-year-old son, was the cartoonist, John T. McCutcheon, who plunged into fame when a youngster by sending back the first detailed report of Dewey's destruction of the Spanish fleet—he had happened to arrive at Manila Bay on a pleasure trip just as the shooting began. This brother of the creator of *Graustark* was carrying out a journey as incredible as that mythical kingdom. Within six weeks he was to visit some dozen capitals in three different continents and twice cross the Atlantic. He had left Chicago only three days before. He was to traverse the west coast of South America to Santiago, fly over the Andes into Argentina, and up the east coast to Rio de Janeiro. From Rio he would take the Graf Zeppelin to Germany, spend six days inspecting European zoos, and return on the *Normandie* in time to preside as toast-master at a Fraternity convention in Chicago on September 1st.

When Norbourne heard of this project, they were five thousand feet above the world finishing luncheon with a dessert of fresh peaches and chocolate cake which had been baked and iced the day before in the Canal Zone some 550 miles away. Below them lay the Island of Gorgona, where Pizarro had made his epic decision to push on to Peru in the face of obstacles that would have staggered any but a superhumanly stout heart. Having awaited for many dreary months the co-conqueror Almagro's return from Panama, blistered by incessant tropical rains, half crazed by the plague of mosquitoes and starvation rations, most of the men were more than willing to obey the Governor of Panama's orders to abandon the foolhardy enterprise when a ship at last arrived to take them back. But Pizarro dramatically whipped out his sword and traced a thin line in the sand. "On this side lie Panama and security," he said; "on that side lie hardship, adventure, riches, Peru. Who will join me?" He stepped across the line from north to south and waited. He made no rhetorical harangue. Such eloquence as belonged to the bastard swineherd lay in the stark force of his character. Few moments have been more pregnant with destiny, as Pizarro waited. Thirteen men followed the leader across the line in the direction of Peru. Their decisive step determined the course of history.

Norbourne, looking down from five thousand feet, wondered what Pizarro's shade hovering about the island must have thought to see human beings up there in the air flying in comfort faster than the fleetest birds. He wondered if four centuries hence men might not just as conceivably be shooting in rockets to other planets in similar agreeable ease and companionship. The one would be scarcely more miraculous than the other.

Shortly before one o'clock the plane slowed down and circled once or twice about the town of Tumaco built on an island in Tumaco Bay. They docked at the air-float at one-five. "The siesta hour here," Captain Dunn explained with a canny grin as the passengers got out for a smoke, "is eleven to one. If the ship arrives before one, the port workers charge extra for having their siesta disturbed. So we delay until a few minutes past one."

A new landing float was being constructed. The young man in charge of construction was named Legare. Norbourne had a cigarette with him on the discarded float alongside the half-completed new one. "Are you one of the South Carolina Legares?" he asked with casual challenge.

"Are there any others?" the young man answered laconically.

Norbourne laughed. It was the answer he had rather expected. "What's the town like?"

"Mainly bamboo and corrugated iron. It has a big export trade in cacao, copper, vegetables and tobacco. But the climate's the lousiest—damp and sticky. Plenty of fever and dysentery. Plenty of mosquitoes too. Great business in Flit. No use to use mosquito nets. They melt. What this place cries out for is a General Gorgas."

"How about the people?"

"I'm the only American in the thirty thousand inhabitants. Tumaco's all right for one night. Will Rogers found it amusing. He spent a night here."

A coal black dwarf with an enormous head and tiny arms that reached only half way to his waist crawled out of one of the carpenter's boats and approached them. He wanted to show Norbourne some tricks with sticks. Legare shooed him away.

"How did you happen to come to South America?"

Legare glanced towards the island and smiled ironically. "For adventure, fun. I walked across the Argentine for the exercise. Got tired of walking and helped construct the flying-boat runway at Mendoza. Built the aerodrome at Tacna, Peru. Kept on working ever since. I like to build things. Graduated in naval engineering from Annapolis."

"What do you do for amusement at night here?"

"Get in bed and read *These Eventful Years.*" Legare smiled again with sly grimness, like a man caught in a trap of his own make and choice. "There's absolutely nothing else to do. It's a big book and should last me some time yet," he added encouragingly.

From the rank tropical growth of the mainland, dugouts manned by Negroes and Indians naked to the waist had eased into the bay and were gliding silently up to the float. They offered native fruits for sale. In the bow of one dugout a black woman with long breasts ate bananas lazily in prodigious bites. In her lap a lusty two-year-old straddled her, his legs clinging about her middle as if he were riding a hobby horse, With his little fists he held the two dugs close together and sucked on both teats at once.

"Equatorial appetite," Legare observed.

II

ECUADOR

"*The chief value of a trip to South America is that it teaches some North Americans to shrink their heads a little.*"

Christopher Morley

ECUADOR

Rainbow Round the Thunderbird

"Entered by Turbo and left by Tumaco," Norbourne wrote in his note book, when they were in the air. It reminded him of a line in a Tunisian handbook: "One reaches Gafsa by way of Sfax." Within an hour after taking off from Tumaco the plane passed into Ecuador, the country that took its name from the equator and has its capital straddling the line at an elevation of 9,300 feet. Within another hour they flew over the town called Esmeraldas where the Spaniards saw their first emeralds. Up to the tops of the mountains the landscape was the colour of the precious stone, as prodigally green as tropical humidity could make it. The flimsy bamboo houses built high on piles looked as if the soil's fertility had made even the dwellings shoot up into the air. There were no lower stories, only upper stories or lofts reached by outside ladders. The houses made Norbourne think of the Diego Riveras' twin studios at Mexico; though the artists' houses were the quintessence of the modernistic style and these were as primitive as China.

It began to get cool in the plane. The passengers put on their great coats. Sea travellers going south from Panama are invariably surprised to find the weather colder as they approach the equator. On passenger liners the room stewards lay blankets on the beds and often receive requests for extra ones. The cold weather at sea lasts all the way to Cape Horn. From the icy Antarctic regions, the Humboldt current carries a great breadth of cold water along the western shore and cools the atmosphere of the sea and the coastal region, just as the Gulf Stream in converse manner sweeps across the Atlantic and warms the British Isles and western Europe.

A pencilled message from the co-pilot, marked precisely "15.07 p.m. July 23rd," was sent back to be passed among the passengers. "This point, Salinas, extending directly out to sea, was the cause of many wrecks to old pirate vessels, as they would run directly into it. These ships carried loot of gold and silver coins which were valued according to weight, being merely chopped off in order to have correct values and then stamped. These coins are still found on the beach at certain extreme low tides. Treasure hunters have the point in mind as one yet unexplored. There is oil in the ground here so near the surface that they only need to dig ten-foot holes; then they bail the oil out. The district around these oil locations contains many bones of prehistoric monsters. These I have seen myself." The message was signed "John H. Miller." A postscript added, "We shall cross the equator in twenty minutes."

"This is like a personally-conducted tour," commented one of the passengers.

At exactly twenty-seven minutes past three Captain Dunn sent word by the steward that they had crossed the equator at 8,000 feet. It was colder than Bogotá. Those who had never crossed the earth's middle before instinctively looked down as if to behold some vague demarcation on the rim of the world. But instead of a thin red line like those on library globes they beheld the shapely black shadow of the *Santa Maria* flying in the centre of a full-circled rainbow like a blackbird in a ring of varicoloured flames. It was fantastically beautiful. Norbourne had never seen a complete rainbow before, nor one lying parallel with the earth. And though he was to behold many similar ones in the next fortnight, he knew he would remember his first crossing of the equator by that symbolic circle of heavenly light curled like a vast halo around the thunderbird's accompanying shadow.

A Hat for a King

At four, while they were having tea, they passed west of Montecristi where the world's finest panama hats are made. The misnomer originated during the California gold rush days, when prospectors, returning to the eastern United States by way of Panama because the journey was easier than crossing the Rockies, called the straw hats after the place in which they were purchased instead of Ecuador where they were made. But Ecuador was the original producer of those hats, and it continues to be more or less their exclusive producer. For half a century, however, panamas were considered merely as quaint novelties or dress-up hats for farmers. And then one morning early in the 1900's in a Bohemian spa, Edward VII of England took the air in a Montecristi panama and the image in the glass of fashion was reflected around the entire globe. Today straw hats rank third on the list of Ecuadorian exports, being topped only by cacao and petroleum.

The Ecuadorian littoral was rankly rich with the graceful fan-shaped, plume-like ferns (*Carludovica palmata*) which furnish the straw for the weaving. The process of gathering the leaves and stripping off their outer filaments just as they ripen, of bleaching to make the sprouts shrivel to light compact cords, is complicated and exacting. The preparation of the raw material is done by men, but Indian women and children make the most nimble and expert weavers.

The weaving is a cruel, tedious, backbreaking process. On the floors of the lofts, they sit on wooden saddles and stretch forward and down to the wooden frames about which they are fashioning the straw. The strands must be constantly damped from a basin of water. With brief intervals of rest from the cramped position they work from dawn to dark and receive about twenty cents a day for their labour. Performing with the skill of a virtuoso some twelve hours a day, the most dexterous take about six weeks to make one of the finer hats, which retail in the world's smartest shops for a hundred or two hundred dollars. The main profit is divided between exporter, broker, and retailer.

"You know how the straw hat industry started?" asked Mr. McCutcheon. "As an occupation for prison inmates to take their minds off their sorrows. But now the free women and children work at it harder than prisoners. It's about as cruel an example of slave labour as exists today."

"Chimborazo!" called the steward excitedly and pointed to the east.

The distant snowcapped volcano, twenty thousand feet high, gleamed faintly in the afternoon sun like a distant peak in a delicate Japanese print. Captain Dunn was as pleased as an impresario after a success. "In five years' flying," he sent word back to the passengers, "I have seen Chimborazo only twice before." From Prescott, who wrote *The Conquest of Peru* without ever going there, one gets the idea that Chimborazo's "celestial diadem" produces its impression of "higher sublimity" on any day's sail along the coast.

At sunset the thunderbird circled over the chief port and largest city of Ecuador. Guayaquil stands on the broad estuary of the Guayas River forty miles from the Pacific and just below the equator. Like an elongated rectangle the city proper spreads over a swampy plain hardly four feet above high tide, which rises a dozen feet in the harbour. Northward a range of hills three hundred feet high forms the background of the city, and from here the fruitful earth rises in uneven terraces until it reaches its climax in Chimborazo's icy crown which can be seen from the river promenade on clear days.

Norbourne was well aware of the city's former unsavoury reputation. Like Belém and Singapore, two other important ports situated close to the equatorial line, it was long shunned as a pest hole. Innocent passengers on ships between Callao and Panama were hustled into the restrictions of quarantine for the reason that they had merely stepped ashore at Guayaquil. Fumigation was one of the minor inconveniences inflicted on sailors and passengers after a cargo-shifting at the Ecuadorian port. To send a foreign consular agent here for a term of years was regarded as issuing his death warrant. Then less than two decades ago General Gorgas came. He and the Japanese sanitary engineer, Noguchi, aided by the Rockefeller Foundation, routed yellow fever and other contagious diseases. An entirely new water supply and sewerage system was installed to make the arteries and veins of Guayaquil's body function with healthy, unclogged rhythms. The port was transformed to a pleasant tropical city.

The *Santa Maria* swooped to rest on the jungle-fringed river. The copper-coloured water, shot with the polished vermilion and gold of a tropical sunset, was smooth as lacquer. A flotilla of gondolas hewn from logs, miniature sailboats, and little *balsas*—rafts thatched with bamboo like those of the Chinese rivers—glided downstream to the markets and boat-loading centres of the city. They were laden with pineapples, tomatoes, oranges, *chiri-moyas*, and melons that gleamed richly gold and red, like daubs of thick oils on the bright lacquered palette of the river. Indians, the colour of wet clay, and Negroes, the colour of black prairie mud, sat in loin-clothed freedom among their brilliant fruits, unaware that the picturesque quality of themselves and their commerce had a market value in attraction to tourists. Silently they regarded the miraculous bird with the vast silver wings. Methods of navigation separated by a thousand years looked each other in the face. Only the chatter of parrots darting among the river craft broke the strange animated quiet of evening.

A ramp for the docking of seaplanes was being constructed on the shore northeast of the city. Not far away, an international airport for land planes, with three hangars, offices, dining room, sleeping quarters for overnight passengers, and a separate dwelling for an airport staff of twenty officials and pilots, was nearing completion. After passing the simple customs and health formalities the passengers boarded the bus which was to take them into the place formerly known as "a mouth to hell."

The gravel road led through a flimsy suburb constructed of cane and bamboo, those favourite building materials of the tropical Orient, and plunged without warning or hint into a city of stone and plaster with paved streets. It was as if a Spanish colonial town had been lifted from one hemisphere and set down in the heart of a vast slum district in China. The division where the cane stopped and the stone began was as sharp as the difference between the seaplane and the gondolas hewn from logs.

At the Hotel Ritz, when the other passengers had been served, the last room left was not as inviting as Norbourne would have desired. Dunn invited him to spend the night and "pass the breeze" with the airmen. They had private lodgings down the street with an Ecuadorian family—two enormous rooms with seven beds and extra hammocks and the privilege of using the guest room whenever there were guests.

Norbourne was introduced to a taciturn, poker-faced Irishman in a striped sateen pyjama jacket who sat in a jalousied window nook playing cards with three young men. This was Captain Lloyd Moore, familiarly known as "Dinty." He had flown the Atlantic in the N.C.5 boat on the first trans-Atlantic non-stop flight to Europe, eight years before Lindbergh's famous solo hop.

Norbourne was impressed by the fact that there was nothing outwardly impressive about this man who had earned his place in fame's chronicle. He looked at the other five or six airmen in the room. They were all younger than Moore—in their twenties or very early thirties—and all in their most casual, off-duty, undress attitude. One of the charming things about aviation, Paul Morand has remarked, is that everybody connected with it is so young. Doing an epoch-making work, these young Americans were as natural and unromantic in appearance as the sixteenth century Spanish conquerors were flamboyant and swaggering. These keen, steady fellows were the new conquistadors. They were helping to write a new history of Latin America. Great changes had been wrought by the sixteenth century conquerors, changes detrimental and hurtful to the peoples of the countries they had overrun, changes achieved by indignities and sword thrusts. Today the conquistadors, slashing only the invulnerable air, were ushering in another new epoch in South America, one fraught with benefits and blessings.

Bootleg Human Heads

After a shower and a change of linen, Norbourne went out to stretch his legs on the arcaded pavements. He ran into a fellow air passenger named Cobb whose business brought him often to Ecuador and Peru. They stopped to poke about in a dim-lit curio shop full of indigenous wares. Cobb asked pleasantly to see some human heads, please. The proprietor with a frightened start darkly denied that he had any. He offered instead heads of heroes carved in vegetable ivory.

"He most likely has some hid away," Cobb said, "but it's tricky business. If a shrunken head is found in your possession, purchaser or seller, the penalty is a fine of 500 *sucres* and six months in jail. The government had to pass the law, because if the Indians ever twigged that heads have value in the white man's market they would depopulate the Montaña. They *can* be bought—bootleg, of course. I know an American college professor who bought two for $15 apiece less than a month ago here in Guayaquil. In London they sell for as much as £25. There's plenty of them in the interior. The Indians will trade them for guns and things. But you're apt to end up a shrunken head yourself if you go into some of that country."

Norbourne recalled the story of a Captain Davis who went up the Amazon to buy a human head to hang in his pub in Belém to attract custom. He disappeared and turned up two years later as a wizened head the size of a cricket ball. He had been bought by an unsuspecting Yankee engineer. His friends recognized him instantly: the features were distinct and the wart over his left eye unmistakable.

Cobb picked up a long Indian blow-gun taller than a man. "They shoot you with these, when they haven't got old breech-loading rifles, and then whack off your head." The highly-polished instrument was made from the hard outer husk of the *chonta* palm. The mouthpiece was of jaguar bone. In a quiver that went with the outfit were splinter-like bamboo darts. There was the gourd, too, full of tree cotton to twirl wisps about the dart to get air compression. But the little gourd for the *jambi*, the mortal black poison of the jungle, was empty.

"The Jivaros—the head hunters—don't mind explaining the secret of their art. They'll tell you about it if you make friends with them before they shoot you. It's a complicated process. Know how they do it? After they get back home from the raid in enemy territory with the head, they sew the lips together with cotton cord and split the skin from the nape to the crown. Then they take out the skull entire and leave only the flesh and skin—a noddle without brain or bone. It's like a deboned chicken you buy in cans. They sew the skin up again and dip the bag in an extract made of aromatic herbs or spice. The mixture stains it darkish blue and acts as a preservative. Next the bag is filled with searing hot pebbles. These are removed and then hot sand is poured in to mould out contours. The head is continually turned round and round, so that the shrinkage shall be uniform. When the sand cools, more hot sand is poured in. With each refilling the head shrinks a bit more. The process of curing and shrinking may take from two days to two weeks. When it is finished, the head is smaller than that of a new-born baby. Some are hardly any larger than tennis balls. The savages hang them like unlit jack-o'-lanterns for trophies from the roof top of their thatch. The smoke from the family cooking-fire cures them still further." Cobb set the blow-gun back in the corner. "In the Montaña they cure heads instead of hams."

"And that too is Ecuador," Norbourne thought, taking from the proprietor a sculptured head of Bolívar, the Venezuelan liberator who had freed the country from Spain more than a century ago. About the size of a ping-pong ball, it was carved out of a tagua nut, a fine hard-grained white composition that looked and felt remarkably like genuine ivory. There were hundreds of similar hand-carved heads in the glass display shelves. The proprietor pointed to a calendar on the wall behind the counter. In the square for Wednesday, July twenty-fourth, the hero's profile filled the space. So tomorrow would be Bolívar's birthday. And two days later, on July twenty-sixth, fell the hundred and thirteenth anniversary of his famous meeting in Guayaquil with San Martín, the liberator from the Argentine. It was the first and only time South America's two greatest heroes ever met. The question as to whether the freed countries should be republics or monarchies was settled within a few hundred yards of where Norbourne was standing. Bolívar insisted on republics. San Martín wanted monarchies, constitutional monarchies like England's. He felt it was their responsibility to act as guardians of an infant people. Bolívar maintained that monarchies would condemn the people to perpetual childhood. "Let them be infants," he said, "let them grow up by whatever hard knocks of experience, but with the ultimate heritage of manhood ever held before them. South America will have to suffer the chaos of birth. A hundred years of chaos perhaps—and all the agony of transition. There will be a metamorphosis of the physical life, until all the races are recast and there is a unity of the people."

One hundred and thirteen years ago he had talked in Guayaquil of unity. How long had he thought it would take? He hinted at three generations. In 1935 little of the eastern territory of Ecuador had been explored by white men. Whole tribes out there had never set eyes on a white face. The government did not know whether the population was a million and a half or two millions; no exact census had ever been taken. Less than half the inhabitants could speak the official language of the country. Certainly not more than a fifth could read or write it. And in those unexplored trans-Andean regions untamed savages still killed with blow-guns and shrank their victim's heads with hot sand

and spices, just as they did centuries before Pizarro's lieutenants marched triumphantly into Quito in 1534. A bootleg traffic in human heads still went on in Ecuador's largest city a century and a decade after Bolívar met with San Martín and presaged the unifying of the people.

Norbourne turned the Liberator's head about in his hand. Lying there in his half-closed fist, carved by a novice in fake ivory, none of the dynamic authority of the irregular-featured face was lost. This was the head of a conquistador, one as blind to obstacles as Pizarro. The sensual full-lipped mouth, at once ruthless and generous, was made for rhetoric and for command. The nose, large and sharp, was inquisitive, aggressive, daring, dominant. Those heavy-lidded eyes belonged to a creative artist whose plots were romantically heroic, transcending the contemporary, flinging far into the future. They protruded with execution and prophecy.

Norbourne bought half a dozen heads of Bolívar in honour of his birthday.

"Don't you want a Sucre too," urged the shopkeeper. "He's the real hero of Guayaquil, he won the battle here."

So Norbourne bought a head of Sucre on Avenida Sucre and paid for it in *sucres*. Not only avenues, schools, theatres, hospitals, plazas and commercial buildings were named after the general, but even the coinage of the republic commemorated his fame. The face of the third ranking hero of South America was that of quite a young man, as it should have been, for Sucre's career was among the most meteoric in history. At fifteen, while still an engineering student in Venezuela, he entered the ranks of the liberating forces. At nineteen he was made a lieutenant-colonel. At twenty-four Bolívar elevated him to the rank of brigadier-general; the next year he became General Chief of Staff of the Liberating Army. His victory in May 1822 assured the independence of Ecuador, and he became its first governor. Before thirty he had tasted his greatest glory.

As they left the shop, the proprietor whispered darkly that "he knew a man who knew a man who was thought to have——." They didn't wait to hear him finish.

From behind the pillar of the portico emerged a *café con leche* girl in her early teens. She made an alluring gesture with half-professional, half-natural shyness and followed them down the parked avenue toward the Malecon. Weaving in and out of the pageantry of the palm trees and the drowsy-scented tropical blossoms of flowering shrubs, she appeared before them, disappeared and reappeared with as light a grace as if blown by the capricious evening breeze. "A more familiar kind of man-hunter," Cobb said. "I'll bet her darts are poisoned too."

The last glimmer of sun was gone now. The tide was out. The river shone like black patent leather, reflecting the red lamps of the anchored river boats in sharp javelins of light. They stood for a few minutes at the parapet watching the tropical stars prick the dark water with mercury. Then they walked briskly back to dinner.

When Norbourne came in, the men had begun the first course. Moore presided with poker-faced dignity. The atmosphere was relaxed—frank, free, hearty. The food was excellent and bountiful. Norbourne felt good, all warm inside, and cool enough outside. Coffee was served in a small vinegar cruet. You poured a little of the black extract into your cup and the waitress filled it with hot water. At eight-thirty the airmen began to go to bed like boys at boarding school. Dunn was flying back to the Canal Zone tomorrow. Captain Moore was scheduled for Lima. He would call Norbourne at five.

Norbourne, who could sleep on the plane tomorrow if he needed sleep, went out for a nightcap with an Irishman from Brooklyn in the tagua nut export business.

"This fruit of the tagua palm," said the young exporter, as they sauntered down the street, "has proved an excellent substitute for elephant tusks. Fifty million pounds of nuts are exported from Ecuador annually, mostly to the United States and Germany. It's like money on trees, because the trees grow wild from Panama to Peru and one tree bears for a century. Poker chips, umbrella handles, chessmen are made from it. But the bulk of the stuff goes into buttons. You can make a lot of buttons from 25,000 tons of material. Ecuador could button all the garments of the world without the help of animal bones or sea shells."

"Not a bad advertising slogan, that," said Norbourne: "*We button the world.*"

The Booster and the Witch's Broom

At a corner pavement café in the cathedral plaza Norbourne was introduced to a flock of young expatriates, repatriated victims of the witch's broom. They sat there sighing under their native Ecuadorian night sky for the Café de la Paix.

The "witch's broom" is a blight that courses through the cacao trees like wild fire, leaving branches and leaves as if they had been done violence with a rough broom. In its operation, the broom has swept the reluctant absentee landlords home from their villas in France's chateau district and their hotel suites in the Champs Elysées. The wealthy aristocrats of Quito and Guayaquil, out of depleted purse and impending disaster, have been forced to return and take a direct interest in their country's welfare.

These European-reared young gentlemen of Ecuador were beginning to adapt themselves with grace to their enforced environment and to give to the rejuvenated port an air of continental sophistication. Some had gone into business. Some were learning to be overseers of their own estates. Others were preparing for the diplomatic service or studying various branches of engineering suited to the needs of their country. But one and all who had lived abroad refused to pay court to young ladies in the conventional Latin-American way. "I can't be a giraffe," said one blonde Adonis in white linen. "My neck isn't long enough to court girls on high balconies."

"If you won't stand outside the barred windows, how do you meet them?"

"We go to Fortich's to the cocktail dance from twelve to two after Mass on Sunday. Everybody's there. In the afternoon we drive up and down the Ninth of October or the Malecon. It's diverting by way of novelty. Our girls who have stayed at home have not lost the art of saying much without speaking. The exchange of a glance or a furtive hand touch gives them more kick than a kiss does to girls abroad. Those who've lived in Europe say to hell with it, but they're still shy about a rendezvous in the park. They know that at home we revert to type in putting virginity on a pedestal."

He rose and excused himself. "Sorry, but I have a dinner engagement. With my mother. She has sent me a formal invitation. I haven't seen her for a fortnight, so I shouldn't like to let her down. She'd rise to great heights of maternal displeasure.

"No, the bachelors of Guayaquil no longer choose to live under parental roofs. We are following the English fashion of going into diggings — a procedure as revolutionary from a Spanish-American point of view as refusing to stand under balconies and twang guitars."

On his departure, a voluble young man arrived and began to lead the conversation of three neighbouring tables spread under the trees and the stars with as facile a command as if he had been little Alexander Pope sitting crosslegged on a stool holding court in his Twickenham grotto. He was not an Ecuadorian, but the Italian-born son of a Chilean mother and a retired New England opera singer father. He was small, dark, sharp-featured, with eyes piercingly astute at one flash and as naïve as those of a budding genius at the next. He spoke the cosmopolitan English of the English stage. Slightly flushed with preprandial drinking, his words poured out in cascades, spurting into geysers, babbled like a brown brook of his father's New Hampshire. He touched shrewdly on opera, the character of French shopkeepers, modern criticism, the Little Theatre movement (he had himself appeared in one of his own tragedies in Dallas, Texas). He posed questions and, swift as a falcon's descent, made his own answers. Then he soared to praises of life under Ecuadorian skies.

"The alluvial lands of the Guayas river system hereabout grow the finest quality of cacao in the world," he proclaimed. "Cacao, you know, is indigenous to the tropical Americas. At the time of the Spanish conquest, chocolate was a favoured drink with the Aztecs in Mexico and the Incas in Peru. Today the cacao trees still flourish wild, untended and unexploited, in the forests of the Amazon and Orinoco basins." The native-born gentlemen regarded the alien booster with affectionate, lackadaisical admiration.

"Despite large planted acreage in Ecuador, many times that area is yet waiting to be brought under cultivation. We need immigration here. Coffee culture ranks second among our important cultivated crops. But we could grow fifty times as much as we do. Fortunes are to be made in coffee—but we haven't the labourers. There are only six to ten people to the square mile—whereas Italy and Germany have about four hundred."

"What do you pay your peons?"

"Ten cents a day. But," he added quickly, "by a national decree Ecuador has recently abolished peonage. The peon's debts have been cancelled. Today he may work for whom he pleases, come and go at will."

"How far can he go on ten cents a day?"

"Far enough. The Indians' wants are few. You see, Ecuador is in the transitional state—this happy removal of feudal restrictions comes opportunely as we face a new era. And we are facing a new era. So much rich land going to waste for lack of man-power to develop it! And the mineral deposits of the mountains have been only scratched. There's gold, silver, copper, mercury, and lead too, waiting—waiting." He took a swallow of a drink one of his friends with playful solicitation thrust out to him like a chairman at a country meeting giving succour to his candidate.

"Guayaquil is growing fast and right," he went on, holding his glass out of the other man's reach. "The rejuvenation began with the opening of the Panama Canal, which placed the coast of Ecuador on the international highway of maritime traffic. Then a spirit-stirring boom came in 1931 when the Panagra Airways made Guayaquil one of its over-night stops and provided quick mail and express facilities to the northern continent. Now we feel for the first time really in direct contact with the pulse of progress." He tilted the glass and took a swallow quickly.

A clock began to strike ten. Norbourne got up. "Since I'm flying at dawn——," he began, speaking to the party at large.

The alien booster was on his feet in an instant. "Come, you must dine with me," he said.

Norbourne explained that he had dined two hours before and since he was flying at——

"Then you must sit with me while I dine." The young man fixed him with an eye more commanding than the Ancient Mariner's. "You are here for one night only and what do you know of Ecuador? Come!"

Norbourne was beguiled to an Italian restaurant, where culinary fumes curled like a fog about the dusky habitués. Through a combination bar and kitchen that was open to the avenue they wound their way to a semi-private dining room. Before they were seated the opera singer's son had begun to crowd the honours of his country into an impassioned monologue of boosting.

"I have lived in Italy, France, England, New England, New York, Ohio, and Texas, but I have never known contentment until I settled in Guayaquil," the young man chanted over his dish of eggs *à la Russe*. "There is no other place where one may make so much on small resources—where the *ambiente* is so congenial to culture and charm. I am a clerk for a local export firm. My salary is $50 a month. I live like a prince. You see this excellent dinner I am eating, course after course of superior Italian cooking. For my board here, dinner and luncheon, I pay $9.50 a month. Imagine! For breakfast at another place I pay $1.50 a month. And that includes the newspaper!" It was like listening to an aria in which the ecstatic singer proclaims that he has found the Holy Grail.

Picking at the meat course, the young man went on. "Five of

us bachelors live in a flat with a terrace in the tallest apartment house in Guayaquil. A lodging for twenty dollars a month—four dollars apiece. Our house boy—perfectly trained: butler, valet, everything—costs three dollars a month. Recently thirty of the young bachelors gave a party to sixty-five married people who had often entertained us. With an orchestra until three o'clock and a most elaborate banquet, the party cost only a hundred and five dollars. Imagine! And for the very highest social set in Guayaquil—I assure you, the very highest. One of the gentlemen you met this evening was a direct descendant of the Borgias. We gave the party at our place. Characteristically, people who weren't invited said we had given the party to get the husbands drunk so that we could seduce their wives. But I assure you that was not the truth. And that sort of malice, as you know, is the way of the world and is not only a local commodity."

The cosmopolite began the salad course. "And Guayaquil is dearer than the small places. I sent for my parents, found them a place of several acres near Cayambe four hours from Quito. There they live on the edge of a 2,000 foot precipice, facing stupendously beautiful scenery. Peace and magnanimity all about them! The Indians of the valley are gentle and kind and live in an almost unearthly serenity weaving their wool and tending their crops. My parents have an income of $35 a month. On this, they can maintain three house servants and three peons—and they keep seven saddle horses! Imagine! On account of the altitude the same horses can't be ridden every day. So we keep a string. Of course they *should* have an automobile to take them to Quito more often. The roads are treacherous though." He paused, and looked in the direction of the bar and kitchen. "If there was a Negro here I would borrow one of his hairs and show you. Put a Negro's kink on a piece of white paper and you have an idea of that road. It curves like a snake about the equator. And think, my parents sleep under four blankets every night right on the equator!" He pushed aside his dessert and got up. "Ah, there's no country like it!

"Come, you must have a nightcap at our place. I want to show you how we live here. And I am writing a novel depicting the psychology of the Galapagos Islands—you know they belong to Ecuador and lie six hundred miles directly west of here. I want you to hear a paragraph or two. I have called the novel *Sometimes the Peace Is Broken.*"

Norbourne protested that he was really in need of sleep.

"It's no distance at all to my place. We shall walk. It will wake you up."

Norbourne was walked twenty blocks down the middle of sleeping arcaded streets. A friend from Tennessee who shared the flat joined them en route. Norbourne's mind had wandered vagrantly to the sleeping airmen, when suddenly from both sides they hustled him out of the way of a careening automobile. "Life here is as cheap as living," the Tennessean spoke up, while the booster caught his breath. "For killing a pedestrian the fine is 100 *sucres,* about $10, and ten days in jail. If the driver of a car is injured in the accident in which he kills a man, he goes to the hospital and a policeman stays in the room with him ten days. That is considered his jail sentence."

The lights in the apartment house building had all been extinguished. They negotiated the five flights of medieval stairs in Stygian blackness. The men guided his footsteps, rallied his progress. "Ours is the tallest apartment house in Guayaquil," the booster said proudly. Adding cheerfully, "Quite a climb, isn't it? But the view of the stars on the river is inspiring enough to be worth it."

The flat white roofs of the slumbering city, the clear sky glittering with unaccustomed constellations was very nice, but Norbourne saw it vaguely as if through mist. The living room of the flat which opened into the booster's bedroom through an uncovered arch, was austerely monk-like with home-made tables, chairs, and book shelves. It was ornamented with antique treasures of ecclesiastical art, intricately moulded silver candlesticks, carved wooden crucifixes and painted triptychs. The ornaments had been selected with an infallible discrimination and bought for a song. "For that priceless sixteenth century saint there I paid a dollar and a half at Quito."

The host's companion handed him a brandy as Norbourne roused himself from rapturous appreciation of the statuette.

"Now sit there." The booster indicated a low couch-bed in the corner. Norbourne sank down with relaxed heaviness. The impact shivered his backbone, as if he had mistaken iron for eiderdown. He got up confused. A thin matress had been spread on wide wooden boards narrowly spaced. "It's not the fashion of Guayaquil for the beds to have springs," the host explained defensively. "Boards and thin mattresses are much cooler." Norbourne sat down again with caution and drank what brandy had'nt been spilled.

"Imagine!" said the booster, surveying his domain, "my entire room was furnished on $17—museum pieces and all. Where could you do so well on so little?"

Norbourne admitted he couldn't say. He wondered what a wife would cost. "Are you going to marry here?" he asked.

"When my salary is raised to $60 a month, I shall marry," he answered promptly. "I'm now making $50 a month. I shouldn't want my wife to do without certain luxuries."

He moved directly to the centre of the room, stood there, and unfurled a sheaf of manuscript. Clearing his throat as a conductor taps his baton on a music rack for attention, he began to read, "Sometimes the Peace Is Broken. Chapter I——"

At two a.m. Norbourne's feet were lighted down the treacherous black staircase by flickering matches struck one after the other by the friends like a chorus of strophes and antistrophes. "Who knows," he thought drowsily, "the youth may be a genius—but there's no doubt he's a salesman."

The alien booster had "sold" his adopted country in one evening better than a whole brigade of tourist agencies and chambers of commerce could have done it in a month. If Norbourne were a youngster he'd look into the scratchily-developed mineral ores—and the cacao, coffee, petroleum. Or perhaps he'd gather those ivory nuts growing wild and rotting, instead of buttoning the world.

Funeral Ribbons

In the bus the next morning, Holmes and McCutcheon and a gentleman from Quito going to Lima to buy diamonds were buttoned to the chin in their overcoats. Though the thermometer would probably stand at ninety by noon, the early morning atmosphere at 2° from the equator was refreshingly cool. On the way to the airport, in the bamboo and cane section of the city, they passed a funeral, then another funeral, and one more yet. In each case the cortège consisted of a string of six or seven *mestizos* in their shirt sleeves, walking single file. On the shoulder of the most forward man—whether father or lesser relative, Norbourne did not know—was borne an infant's casket draped with an imitation cloth-of-silver pall and tied about with a bow of blue ribbon like a box of bonbons. "They bury them before the heat of the day sets in," said the diamond merchant. "The cloth and the ribbon will be returned to the undertaker."

The cemetery lay beyond on the fair hillside exposed to all the cleansing breezes that blew. The living had built their houses in the flat swamps. Mrs. McCutcheon logically wanted to know why. The gentleman from Quito smiled philosophically; no, that he could not explain.

The sun was not yet shining on Bolívar's birthday when they took off into the grey morning in a tri-motored Ford. They would not be out of sight of land now until they reached Lima. They flew down the river, cut corners across the Gulf of Guayaquil, skimmed along the vegetation-confused coast where alligators lazed on the river banks, and passed over the town of Tumbes where Pizarro first set his mailed foot on the country that is now known as Peru. Here the conquistador was confronted by ingenuous subjects of the Incas, who very nearly embarrassed him by inquiring with engaging simplicity why he had not remained at home to cultivate his own soil.

III

PERU

"In those early days any Spaniard, even the poorest soldier, thought the whole of Peru was little for himself alone."

Gomara

PERU

Prelude to Lima

Suddenly, sharply, as if the curtain had fallen at the end of an act of opera and risen immediately on a set depicting some far-removed portion of the globe, the oozing Ecuadorian jungle had vanished and the rocky Peruvian desert stretched southward, dry as mummy dust, unmitigated, mysterious, disenchanted. For more than twenty-five hundred miles, from Tumbes, the northernmost town in Peru, to Coquimbo in Chile, the coastal strip that lies between the Andes and the ocean is rainless sand and unproductive rock except where intersected by rare river valleys. Pizarro seeking El Dorado had first dieted his gold-hungry eyes on this vast yellowish desolation—a desert as long as the distance between New York and Los Angeles. From his celestial vantage point in the aeroplane Norbourne regarded the wasteland with compelled fascination. Despite all he had read, he was not prepared for this prelude to Peru, for the immensity of this barrenness. The Pacific too had lost every trace of lively blue. Its still surface was the milky green colour of olive oil—as if the world's supply of the commodity had been dumped off Peruvian shores. Both land and sea seemed as silent as during the æon before the creation of any living thing.

The coastal desert, which averages forty to a hundred or more miles in width, is one of the three distinct regions into which Peru is divided topographically. The Cordilleras of the Andes in three ranges traverse the middle territory in a north and south direction, with two separate high plateaus or tablelands lying like broad furrows between rows of ploughed red earth. East of the mountains, descending into valleys crisscrossed with feeders of the Amazon, is the sparsely-populated tropical district inhabited only by semi-savages and a few storekeepers and rubber planters of Spanish descent. In this abundant lush Montaña, where the density of the population is not more than one person to three square miles, millions of immigrants could earn a goodly living if the region were more accessible.

But it is easier to reach the Atlantic by the Amazon, a distance of 2,500 miles, than it is to traverse the 500 miles to the Pacific. A mule back journey across Peru takes three weeks under excellent conditions. Now a Douglas plane can fly this distance in half a morning. The late President Leguía, shrewdly aware of the strategic and economic necessity of bringing isolated districts into closer unity with the capital, used his stimulating persuasion to make his people air-minded. The present chief executive, President Penavides, also vigorously endorses every plan to further aeronautical development.

When the plane landed on the sands of a busy petroleum port at nine-fifteen, the Indian oil employees took no more notice of it than they would of an oil tanker appearing on the sea, so accustomed had they grown to the air transports. Talara is the westernmost town in the subcontinent, and the outlet for three oil stations. Some three hundred and fifty whites, mostly English and Canadians, employees of the International Oil Company, have encamped there with the same objective as Pizarro—to draw gold from the soil—in this case, liquid gold. As in colonial days when Peru was regarded as a place to live in but not to die in, the white men of Talara, even those who had remained a decade or more, had temporary, here-today-and-gone-tomorrow expressions on their faces. But they have made themselves at home in British fashion as Britishers do the world over. They cheer themselves with polo and boast of three polo grounds. The married men have built bungalows with hopeful patches of irrigated green gardens for their wives and children.

"The women are more contented since the aeroplane came," a

father said to Mrs. McCutcheon. "If the children get very sick they can fly with them to Lima. And most of them fly to the American hospital in the Canal Zone to have their babies. The coming and going of the planes has relieved that trapped feeling that some of them used to complain of."

At the neat little concrete airport a miniature front door garden with shrubs and periwinkles had been laid out. In one of the beds the airport manager was trying an experiment of grass-growing: Bermuda grass and nut grass. Nut grass was Norbourne's particular *bête noir* among garden pests. Now he looked with downright affection on the sharp little spears struggling to relieve the sand's monotony in a place where it rains about half an hour a year.

"Talara never has more than a couple of good rains a century," the manager said. "The south-easterly trade winds expend their moisture on the other side of the Andes, and the Humboldt current creeping up from the Antarctic cools the sea-breeze and prevents precipitation on the sea-side of the Cordilleras. So, except for some freak in nature like the cloudburst of 1925 which nearly washed us into the sea, raincoats are as unnecessary as central heating."

The gong sounded twice and the thunderbird was off to Piura, the first town Pizarro founded in the New World in 1532. Beyond the Piura Valley, where cotton is intensively cultivated, the plane turned from the coast and flew over the vast tract known as the Desierto de Sechura. Dry sand stretched out on both sides now fifty miles and more to east, fifty miles or more to west—an interminable, waving sea of sand, with rocks covered with sand drift and engraved by the winds with crescent designs. The only vegetation was some low greenish-black scrub bushes which looked like dried droppings of prehistoric monsters that had passed that way into extinction. There was something terrifying about that desert. Stupendous with silence, it seemed hungry for flesh, ardent to bleach bones.

The plane shot upward through a ceiling of cloud and the earth was blotted out. "It's like crashing heaven's pearly gates," said the Bromo Quinine representative from St. Louis. For mile after mile now they flew over a buoyant sea of opalescent foam. Before, behind, there was nothing but this enchanted creamy lake. Above, the heavens were palest blue, like a Bellini Madonna's veil. Far away to the left the flame-tinged outline of the icy Andes shone unearthly like some archangel's abode.

"No matter how high the lark soars, he must come down to earth for his dinner." Though the saying is not necessarily true for thunderbirds, which generally carry their dinner with them on long flights, today the plane came down through the clouds and landed near the desert town of Chiclayo. Under striped canvas awnings of orange and cream stretched on the yellow sands like Arabian pavilions, the passengers enjoyed a hot meal. Norbourne had found it good to eat dates and cheese and drink Algerian wine on a brief excursion into the Sahara. But to have a tasty herb soup, fillet of fish, breaded veal cutlet, and fresh limes, fresh green peas and French beans set before him in a wilderness was hardly to be expected. He thought again of Pizarro and the worse-than-Spartan training his men must have given their bellies on their painful march to cities of the high plateau.

Just a hundred miles east of Chiclayo lay Cajamaraca, the fateful city where the conquistador met Atahualpa, the Inca emperor. By a perfidious trick in one half-hour of late afternoon the Spaniard slaughtered thousands of unarmed Indians, got possession of the royal personage, and won for Spain a kingdom as rich as avaricious dreams. It was there that the captive emperor made his fabulous offer to win his freedom by filling the room in which he was confined with gold to the height of his upstretched arm. Pizarro promised him his freedom for the ransom. The Inca sent forth commands. Day after day files of his subjects arrived from every part of the kingdom bearing on their backs finely-wrought objects of the precious metal, which had no monetary value for the Indians. From hundreds of miles distant they came, trotting over the cold mountain trails. At last before the incredulous eyes of the Spaniards, the room was actually filled. For several weeks Indian goldsmiths were forced to melt down and cast in bars the supreme handiwork of royal artisans—vessels, platters, ornaments. And when the ransom was acknowledged as being paid in full, instead of letting his captive go according to his bond, Pizarro, with characteristic unscrupulousness, cooked up a charge of treason against him and in a mock trial had him condemned to be burned alive. At the last minute the dismayed emperor was offered strangulation instead of burning if he accepted Christianity. He submitted to acknowledge the white man's God and received baptism at the stake. Before the trickle of holy water had had time to dry on his brow, the ruler of a quarter of a continent breathed no more.

At one-thirty the thunderbird circled over the ruins of Chan-Chan, great capital of the Chimú Empire, which was conquered by the Incas a hundred years before Columbus landed in the Bahamas. From the air the ruined city looked like a modernistic cemetery. Eleven square miles of geometric patterns: foundations of temples and palaces with jagged relics of walls; straight lines of canals, avenues; intricate formalities of chalky gardens. Here among the windowless dried mud houses, the burglar's tools were said to be only a sponge and waterpail—he would wash his way in. From Chan-Chan alone the Spaniards boasted of carrying away four million dollars' worth of gold and silver ornaments. Treasure seekers still poke about hopefully among the crumbling adobe walls. But they glean little except wasp stings, for wasps have appropriated the bleached skeleton of ancient grandeur and resent human intrusion.

A few minutes by plane east of the ruins, on the Moche River, lies Trujillo, namesake of Pizarro's birthplace in Estremadura. It is the third city of commercial importance in Peru. The extension of copper mining has augmented its prosperity. Cocaine for the Japanese market is manufactured from the mountain-grown coca plant. Half of Peru's sugar cane is grown in the neighbouring river valleys. Beyond the mosque-domed churches and the roofs trailing magenta bougainvillea lie the irrigated acres.

At the aerodrome another airport garden is well under way. From a rubber hose water plays economically at the bases of feathery pepper trees. Periwinkles bloom and shoots of young bougainvillea climb new-made trellises. In a back garden, across a deep irrigation ditch, an Indian boy is ploughing with a yoke of magnificent black bulls. The plough is fashioned with a single handle like the gearshift of an automobile. The boy holds it in his left hand. In his right is a venomous-looking cowhide whip longer than any ever used on slaves. The beasts do not lower their heads like oxen but throw them back high in the air in splendid scorn. Just beyond the white-washed garden wall, a young brown man and a girl with their arms about each other's waists stand in the doorway of a house made of sugar cane—a house out of Grimm's *Fairy Tales*. Silently regarding the passengers from the plane who are strolling about, they stand motionless as figures caught in a spell of enchantment. The black whip snakes hissingly through the coolness, the bell signals, and the passengers stamp the dust of Trujillo from their feet. In their unsubstantial house of sugar cane built on the shifting sands, the Indian couple in the doorway remain utterly still, as if they had been there for ever, and would stay there unchanged through eternity.

The plane flew out over the sea again, flirting with the coastal edges, skimming headlands. It passed over the open roadstead and port of Salaverry, where ships were discharging cargoes into lighters and cotton was being packed off to England. The lighters looked like split black cigars floating in olive oil. A long pier shot out to sea, a pier which the Mapa de Ruta says makes possible the loading of a thousand tons of produce daily. The settlement of Salaverry has no other function but to connect the irrigated valley with the sea. Since there are no continuous railway lines between the valleys, the sea is the great transportation trunk line. Unless one flies, every time one goes inland into Peru one has to come back to the sea to go anywhere else. As trade depends on the headlands and the piers, so all life in the coastal regions depends upon the river. If there were no river there would be no irrigation, no patchwork of cultivated fields, no houses, no people. Wherever the last thread of irrigation ditch stops, the desert assumes its old negation and creeps off to the feet of the sharp-edged Andes under whose mauve and bronze-coloured walls is buried Peru's inassessable mineral wealth.

Looking down with a bird's-eye perspective, Norbourne realized that in this one day's flight from Guayaquil to Lima he was getting an intense impression of the physical background of one of the world's most interesting vanished civilizations, as well as a slight grasp of the geographical forces that help to mould the modern nation that has supplanted it. He could not have got so clear an impression otherwise except by months of uncomfortable travel. By ocean steamer one can see next to nothing. But here in the air, flying over these barren regions with their occasional fertile river valleys, the most casual observer can get an idea of the fundamental economy of the nation. He grasps at once that the agriculture is intensive rather than extensive, that every square inch of soil that can be watered must be made to grow something, that each precious drop must be rigorously husbanded to make it do its task of moistening the parched earth. He can understand why Peru's best engineers constantly seek for new means of utilizing the rivers' flow. He can realize why laws governing the conservation and distribution of water are of prime importance to the valley people. Their very life depends on it.

And some of the country's history stares him in the face, as the plane flies over Inca burying grounds and little glory-stripped towns that once rang with the spurs of Pizarro and his brothers in conquest. He looks down on the laboriously-terraced hillsides of the Indians with their miniature fields now dust-dry, because the Spaniards destroyed the elaborate irrigation works which watered them and also destroyed the socio-economic system under which these fields were cultivated and their products distributed.

The plane returned to the sea's edge, where sculptured sandhills descended to the water and joined the sprawling salt-sprayed rocks. The mountains idling behind them—beige, champagne, furry cream, chalky fawn with black rock rips sticking up like ears—looked like a convocation of gigantic Siamese cats taking siesta.

Norbourne was considering a siesta himself, when suddenly the air was full of waterbirds. Petrels, gulls, pelicans, and albatross seemed rained down from heaven. The *Santa Maria* was nearing the famous guano islands. Beneath, for a dozen leagues or more, the sea was so prodigiously thick with fish near the surface of the water that one could have walked on a pavement of fish scales. One might have thought that some marvel similar to that Jesus of Nazareth performed to feed the multitude had gone on for ever because the miracle worker had neglected to check its operation. The birds would swoop to their feast and rise together forming a flying carpet woven in black and silver. Then they would burst apart like a shower of sparks in a pyrotechnical display and trace lacy patterns against the sky. Where the current bore the fish out to sea, a legion of guanayes, pelicans, and blue-footed booby-birds would follow with the furious zest of falcons. They are well-disciplined birds. They have their leaders; they fly in perfect formation; they flap their wings with the uniformity of racing crews swinging their oars.

Like opaque icebergs the white guano islands shone yellow and blue in the afternoon light. Here were domes of pearl and turrets of turquoise, bastions and colonnades of streaked marble, sculptured by wind and ocean spray out of bird manure. It clung to the jagged rocks and hardened like incrustations of coloured enamels. In these fairy palaces fashioned from their own droppings, birds slept, mated, hatched their young. For countless generations these winged creatures that have never seen trees, never pecked at straw, never ruffled their feathers in rain, have swept up and down Peru's waters. For ages to come, as long as the Humboldt current brings them anchovies from the south, they will haunt the coast. Billions of fish to feed millions of birds. Their territory is protected by law. They have been protected since the days of the Incas, who knew their value. These are the sacred money-birds of Peru.

Much of Lima's cultural aristocracy owes its wealth and position to the operations of seabirds' bowels. Many noble fortunes have been sustained for generations because certain families held guano concessions. Guano built palaces in Lima where few below the rank of archbishop were received. Guano hung ropes of pearls about titled dowagers' proud necks. Guano educated their amorous-eyed, chaste daughters in Belgian convents. Guano instructed their downy-cheeked sons to dally in the best manner of the Paris boulevards. Guano buried their noble spouses in mausoleums of surpassing splendour. Strangely enough it is all due to left-handed Providence. For if Providence had not withheld rain from the region, the guano would have washed idly into the sea.

Every two and a half years, under the regulations of government monopoly, four or five hundred Indians come to clean house for the birds. They scrape off the ornamentation, store the booty in gunny-sacks, and load it into boats. During these four months of manure-gathering they sleep in rock crevices wrapped in gunny sacking in the midst of the consecrated disgusting stench. The first time a load of Peruvian bird manure entered a foreign port—Southampton in 1839—the stench was so overpowering that the harbour master ordered the entire cargo to be dumped overboard. But the world soon realized guano's value as the supreme natural fertilizer and for three-quarters of a century the Peruvian government has maintained itself richly on the product which has been piling up for countless centuries. The market demand for guano is still so considerable that the supply falls far short of it. Only the excess beyond Peruvian agricultural needs is exported.

As the afternoon advanced, birds returning from feasting began to settle on the pale islands like dark clouds. Some islets they covered as completely as if a pall had been spread over a bloated emperor's bier. One island at the very gateway of Lima has been denied the birds for nesting. It is reserved for Peruvian prisoners and is called "The Island of Dead Men."

Jewel in Fog

Norbourne had read of Lima's magnificence when first seen from the air—a flowering oasis in a desert, with parks and plazas, spacious boulevards, houses and palaces built around patios in full bloom. But on Bolívar's birthday the dripping fog of winter blurred the vision. The airport at Miraflores, the suburb named for its thousand flowers, was enshrouded in mist. One might have been landing on fog-bound Scottish moors. Customs officers, airport officials, friends to greet guests were wrapped in burly greatcoats like men at a football game in sleety November. It was not raining; it never rains in Lima—at least not more than once in thirty years—but the thick blanket of cold cloud was unquestionably wetting.

Norbourne was totally unprepared for this first chilly view of New Spain's jewelled capital, which lies ten degrees nearer the equator than sun-hot Havana. Exactly four hundred years ago, in 1535, on the banks of the rocky Rimac, Pizarro had founded the city one sunny summer's day in January. He had called it "The City of the Kings" in honour of the Feast of Epiphany which commemorates the visit of the gift-bearing wise-men to the Bethlehem manger. Perhaps he did not know that mist would engulf his capital for six months of the year. Perhaps if he had, he would have laid it at Chosica, thirty miles farther away, up in the highlands, above the limit of the coastal fogs, where there is eternal sunshine. On the other hand, he was doubtless guided in his choice of situation by its strategic position. If Indians came out of the mountains behind him in massed attack, he could gallop in twenty minutes to his anchored ships at Callao. After all the inconveniences his troops had suffered, a few months of fog were as insignificant compared to military discretion as dew to the rushing Rimac, from which Lima took its more popular name.

Her Greatest Tragedy

The American Ambassador, Mr. Dearing, who had come to the airport to meet the McCutcheons, invited Burton Holmes and Norbourne to stop with them at the Embassy for tea. They went on just as they were without driving into the city to drop their luggage at the hotel. A mysterious greyness silvered the suburbs. A road twisting about Miraflores wound its way through a series of misty Corot canvases. In the lamp-lit drawing-room of the Embassy an informal group of Peruvians and Americans were chatting about a crackling log fire. The fireplace was an inspired innovation of Mrs. Dearing's. Its construction had added a chimney to the city's chimneyless architecture and unwonted cheer to winter afternoons in Lima.

Norbourne found himself seated by a Peruvian lady with gorgeous eyes enhanced by long lashes and a Parisian nose veil. She nibbled at a lettuce sandwich while he warmed his inside with cups of hot tea. Up to the last two years she had been living abroad. The fall in the rate of exchange had sent her home.

"Tell me," Norbourne said, "has the Mediterranean attitude towards women in Peru changed radically during your absence?"

The lady smiled ruefully. "For all the brave talk, I think it has changed scarcely at all. Our men are still Moors to the hilt."

"But there is the country club and golf," he suggested.

"Yes, yes, of course—golf and the country club! And we have a very beautiful country club in Lima. It is very nice indeed. It has everything—like all the beautiful country clubs the world over." Her words trailed off in imperceptible mockery.

Norbourne laughed. "I only wanted to see what value you set on—your new privilege."

"Ah, yes. Our men believe we should be in an ecstasy of liberation—because they allow us to swing a golf club in public. There is virtually nothing else—except marriage, and that means nothing but—marriage. We don't vote. We can't get divorced—unless we do it in Paris, as I did. Here a wife's whole morning is spent getting ready for the husband's luncheon. Peruvian business men always come home for luncheon. But since I no longer have a husband I haven't even the preparation of his menus to stimulate my days." She smiled, glanced down at her exquisite feet and high-bred ankles, and put on an expression of philosophical ennui.

"But don't you lunch with gentlemen friends at restaurants?"

She raised her eyebrows in mock horror. "That would be unspeakable. Every respectable door in Lima would henceforth be closed in my face." Norbourne struck a match for the long thin cigarette she had extracted from a black enamelled case. "Here I am a widow with a fourteen-year-old son. I've lived in France for years. But to dine in Lima in public unchaperoned with a gentleman would finish me." She made a helpless little gesture with her hands, indicating they were bound by thongs.

"So naturally Paris spells paradise to South American women."

"Well," she drew her brows together slightly, "it is a place where you can feel you are a person, not a mollusc. Of course, if you've known nothing else, it's not quite so deadly." She leaned forward as if to impart a secret. "Do you know, the average woman's life in Lima is so uneventful that her greatest tragedy is failure to secure a fourth woman for bridge."

The Late Leguía

The hostess brought over a handsome young man with thoughtful black eyes. "You said you wanted to get a Peruvian opinion of Leguía. Here's someone who will tell you without bias. Señor Galván."

She took the lady away, murmuring, "I know you don't want to listen to politics, my dear——"

The two men seated themselves with whiskeys-and-soda. Galván came of a line of diplomats and landholders. His father had been Minister to Belgium; his uncle, the senior diplomat in Washington. After completing his education in Germany, he was now working for a steamship company.

To Norbourne, the recently dead President Leguía was, along with the peon Gómez of Venezuela, the most interesting South American dictator of the twentieth century. From the position of representative of a New York life insurance company, Leguía, who came of good family which had little prominence and no influence, rose by his innate cleverness to the presidency of Peru in 1909. In 1919 he was elected to a second term, and thereafter for the next eleven years he held power by a velvet-gloved iron fist until a financial collapse following the world depression forced him to resign. He was called saviour of his country by his friends, highwayman by his enemies. Leguía was ruthless, but a masterly organizer and builder. He had a plan. For the average Latin American military dictator to have much more than bombastic sentiments is unusual. The aristocrats hated Leguía because he taxed them heavily and curtailed their exploitation of the Indians. But they enjoyed his roads, the splendid new parks and boulevards, the sanitation which was improved fifty per cent under his régime.

Norbourne indicated the composite picture he had formed of Leguía from all he had read. "What you say is true—so far," Galván admitted. "Leguía was the shrewdest man in Peruvian politics for a century. He was uncannily clever. When you went to him with a petition, with a plan which was only vaguely formulated, in a quarter of an hour Leguía would know your scheme better than yourself, see the whole thing through to its completion and point out ways in which you could improve it. His intuition was as feminine as his notoriously beautiful hands. He was a very little man, you know, only about five feet two, very dapper, well-turned-out, a home-loving family man, with an eye that caught the ladies' imagination. He could charm anybody he wanted to. He was as fearless as a lion, too—went about dangerously as if some kingly divinity protected him. When an assassin looked Leguía in the eye—and there were plenty out to get him—he couldn't pull the trigger or thrust the knife." There was an overtone of admiration in the young man's voice, as he paused to light a cigarette.

"Well, what was wrong?"

Señor Galván inhaled gently and blew out the smoke. "Leguía had every quality a statesman should have, except—honesty. His government went to pieces because he took for ministers people of dark origin, clever men, who had been at universities, but who were socially hopeless and inherently corrupt."

"Why did he?"

"When people asked him that—why he had such inferior ministers—do you know what he would answer? He would look at them with whimsical weariness and say, 'When a carpenter has something to build and can't get good material, he makes use of whatever wood he can get, does he not?' "

"But why wouldn't your better men be his ministers?"

"First, the cabinet officers were mere tools of Leguía. His was the only law. The constitution was utterly disregarded if it stood in his way. A man of the upper classes couldn't afford to link up with him. He would have been caught in a tissue of dishonest dealings. And it would have been like—like betraying your class. Leguía was definitely on the side of the people. No one had ever before tried to help the illiterate Indians as he did."

"Well, why not?" said Norbourne.

"To be sure, why not? Now that he is gone many of the younger generation that opposed him are asking that question again. If he had stayed in power——" He paused and turned accusing eyes on Norbourne. "Do you know what really brought about his downfall? Your United States bankers. They had a lot of surplus money in the 1920's and they wanted to lend it. They bribed Leguía's ministers and close relations with half million dollar 'fees' to persuade him to borrow vast sums. Against his better judgment he was over-persuaded. His prime weakness lay in not being able to say no to his children and partisans. He borrowed too heavily. The depression came. Business went to pieces. When there was no more money to pay interest with, and no plums for the politicians, the men he had raised from nothing turned against him and betrayed him. A man who had been his stable boy and whom he elevated to be President of the Senate was one of the chief leaders against him."

He paused abruptly, grasped Norbourne's hand as he struck a safety match against its box. "What kind of matches are those?"

Norbourne looked at the box in surprise. "Why, I don't know. Some I picked up in Guayaquil, I believe."

"Well, if you don't want to sample our Peruvian jails or pay a $25 fine, better chuck them in the fire. It's against the law to use any but Peruvian matches. You know we irrigate our crops with matches."

"What's the catch?" Norbourne asked, lighting his cigarette.

"You see, the irrigation projects are very expensive. And the government decided that the smokers should finance the work. So they gave a concession to a Swedish match company to run for twenty years at $800,000 a year—granting them exclusive manufacture and right to sell matches in Peru. You know the desert of Peru could feed the whole of South America if it could be brought into complete cultivation. Irrigation was another of Leguía's pet projects."

He handed Norbourne a tiny box. "Here, stick these in your pocket and don't use any other kind when you're out of your room. Many a scoundrel supports himself and his family by informing on foreigners with contraband matches."

"You really don't think so badly of Leguía, do you?" Norbourne said, remarking the white llama silhouetted on the sky blue ground of the match box.

"He had a certain genius," Galván answered somewhat grudgingly. "But to me, any kind of dictator is intolerable. And yet we are far from being past the state of dictators. Even Bolívar, you know, changed his ideas at the end. He saw he had had too much faith in the people. All the twenty Latin American nations have adopted the republican form of government, but in politics on the whole they are uncompromising and intolerant of their opponents. Often the only way to get a new party in power is by revolution. We shall always have dictators, mild or tyrannical, until public opinion is allowed real freedom of expression. Yet we almost always smash the dictatorships we set up, because fundamentally we hate domination.—We're still so young in government in this ancient land."

"What's going to happen now?"

Galván made a wide gesture of interrogation. "Some of my friends have gone Bolshevik, but I'm not sure they know what they're about. They have vague ideals, but I doubt if their ideas are workable. Peru is not an industrialized capitalistic country. It has peasants, but virtually no proletariat like Russia, England, or the United States, where there are many factories. The empire of the Incas was communistic in an agrarian sense, not in an industrial sense. The Aprista, the National Socialistic Party, think they have a plan. They propose to protect the small landholder and raise the status of the Indian. They are not nearly so violent as the Communists. Its members oppose bloodshed and aim at a gradual and cautious ending of man's exploitation of man. But who can say what will come? Frankly, we're all rather in confusion about the future. But so does the rest of the world seem to be just now."

"Quite so," Norbourne assented, as the hostess came up hesitatingly.

The two men rose guiltily as though caught in a social error. The McCutcheons were saying good-bye to the host. The party was breaking up.

Full of Future

Out in the hall where the footman was helping them into their coats the Ambassador introduced Norbourne to Captain Harold Harris, who directed the flying activities of Pan American

Grace Airways on the West Coast and across the Andes. He was a powerfully built dark man with a determined face and black hair curly as a wig. He looked like an ex-football star and more like a Peruvian than a Californian. Harris had flown with the Italian forces during the war. When he left the army in 1925 he held ten world's records. He had commanded the first American flight across the Alps from Milan to Paris, and was the first army officer to save his life with a parachute when the plane he was testing became unmanageable.

Harris offered to drop Norbourne by his hotel.

Outside the grey mist had blended with the darkness. There was nothing to be seen except the weird shimmer of automobile and street lights. Norbourne urged Harris to tell him how and why he came to Peru. "I came to dust cotton," he said succinctly.

Late in 1926 Harris, as representative of a New York firm, brought five crop-dusting planes to rout the insects. During the growing seasons of 1926 and '27, while flying over various parts of Peru, he became impressed with the tremendous distances between populated centres. He came to appreciate forcibly at first hand the lack of rapid transport for people, mail, and spare parts between U.S. headquarters and the South American base. "If you've waited three weeks for a spare part after you've sent an expensive cable and then it comes wrong and you have to send a second cable twice as long and wait another three weeks, well, it's hell," he said feelingly.

"On May 19, 1929," Harris said, "the first air mail from the States arrived in Lima, the day before the first air mail left Lima for Miami. By November tenth, air mail left Montevideo for the United States. Ground and flight facilities were constantly improved and we soon began doing a passenger business. Up to October of last year with more than 6,500,000 miles of Panagra operation only one fatal accident had occurred and one sack of U.S. mail weighing five pounds had been lost."

"How do the powers-that-be treat you here?" Norbourne asked.

"We've passed through a war and several revolutions without

being molested in any way. In fact all sides have been exceedingly courteous, whichever way the tide turns."

"You like it here, then?"

"Exceedingly. Living is not expensive. Life is not too crowded. And our business is full of future."

Norbourne turned the phrase over in his mind. "Full of future." And was not that somewhat incorrect but meaningful phrase the most impressive quality of the South American situation?

Mr. Morley's Way

The façade of the Grand Hotel Bolívar gave on the imposing Plaza San Martín. The edifice is built of white stone in modified Renaissance style and occupies a whole block. It was erected by the government in 1924 to provide lodging for distinguished guests at the centenary celebration of Peru's independence. The furniture and fixtures for the two hundred rooms and two hundred baths were imported complete from England. A dozen years ago in all Peru there were no hotel rooms with private baths, Norbourne was told. But though he was grateful for the hot water, he was utterly unimpressed by Lima's boasted hostelry. It lacked even a soupçon of "atmosphere." In the round central lobby of conventional gilt and pink marble and ferns, a cosmopolitan clientèle sat enjoying the "vermouth," the hour of the appetizer, which lasted from six to seven or eight or nine. Most of the women had on fur coats. In the room behind the lobby a tiny fireplace, bare as Mother Hubbard's cupboard, gaped inhospitably. Lima needs open fireplaces as much as Bogotá.

After a flavourless American *table d'hôte* dinner in the dining room, where the service was halting and indifferent, Norbourne went out for a brisk walk. The corrugated iron curtains of the shops were fastened down. There was no sound of music or gaiety anywhere. Men with unreasonably-padded shoulders paced the pavements in the fog. The only bright spot of colour was the crimson lining of the policemen's blue capes thrown back over their shoulders as they stood at the street corners, wooden and unsmiling as cigar store Indians.

Stopping in at the bar for a warming nightcap, Norbourne met the young Lima representative of a Bolivian tin concern. He had been graduated from Harvard business school and was named Mason. Mist blew in gusts from the street entrance. Everybody except the bar boys wore overcoats glistening with moisture.

"From a tourist's viewpoint Lima is perfect," Mason said, sipping his pisco sour as they sat alone at one of the round heavy oak tables. "But three days to a week is enough. Your first impressions are best. I've never seen a place that makes a more charming impression and then lets you down so utterly. To me at first it all seemed too good to be true—as indeed it was. Then you wake up one morning a few weeks later to find that instead of inhabiting a world capital, you are lodged in a gilded Indian camp. But to the traveller it is too wonderful to be missed, especially in summer —October to May. Of course, you are seeing it at its midwinter worst. But, mind you, in fog or sun, summer or winter, the impression of contemporary Lima is sure to be confused. The divergent vital elements of the country as a whole—a country fundamentally discordant in race, topography, economy and spirit—have not fused harmoniously as they have, say, in quick-stepping, materialistic Argentina."

Back in his vast room with its commonplace highly-varnished furniture and peculiarly stingy illumination, Norbourne sat up in bed in his dressing gown and read Christopher Morley's impression of Lima in a delightful little book called *Hasta la Vista*, which Holmes lent him. He took feeling pleasure in the genial author's recipe for keeping warm and cheerful during the evenings in Lima. "I always completed the emotions of the day," Morley wrote, "by pulling a Waring and Gillow armchair into our bathroom (not to keep Titania awake with a light), putting on an overcoat and sitting chastely among white tile to read Somerset Maugham."

Sun in Winter

Out of the gloom of the evening before, Norbourne awoke to rare fortune. In one of her unaccountable caprices Nature had chosen to give Lima sunshine in the foggy season. Façades and cornices, tiled pavements, arcades, statues and stained glass were dusted with golden light. Roof tops blazed with potted flowers, varicoloured rugs and cushions; and turkeys, tethered there according to the Peruvian custom, gobbled with gusto as they preened their feathers. The Japanese florists' windows sparkled with colour. Society girls out on a charitable mission collected coins in their shining boxes with facile magnetism. Chauffeurs radiated cheer that was spontaneous and not a trick of custom.

Norbourne set out early for a day of sight-seeing. He went first to the Quinta de Presa, the Palace of the Perricholi. Micaela Villegas, the actress called La Perricholi, was Peru's most glamorous woman. In the golden decades of the eighteenth century she was the mistress of Lima's greatest viceroy, Don Manuel de Amat. Thornton Wilder has made her one of the central figures in *The Bridge of San Luis Rey*.

Officers and privates of the police guard loitered about the paved courtyard behind the gates beyond the bridge. Front side wings had been added to the main building and transformed into a police station. A trim smart-moustachioed officer came up courteously, challenged Norbourne, and then conducted him across the flagstones.

The baroque palace rose like a confectioner's triumph in sugar and chocolate. The walls were cream plaster, the columns and pilasters of chocolate-coloured stone. A broad staircase with wide, shallow steps, easy for an old man's climbing, turned left and, accompanying a carved oaken balustrade, wound to an upper gallery, where a waxen Christ agonized on a wooden cross in a golden shrine. If the courtesan did not really set up housekeeping here, as many claimed she never did, tradition told a better story than history, for she should have dwelt in these walls and gardens. They were made for a lover's rendezvous. It was a perfect pattern of a palace a septuagenarian lover might provide for a sparkling young mistress.

"Both the actress and the viceroy were excessively devout," the officer commented, as he waved his fingers towards the diminutive altar.

On the top of the palace, which seemed all galleries, roof gardens, and stairs, was a belvedere where the lovers dined by moonlight. Norbourne looked down on the deserted garden spread out below. Yellow trumpet vines running about unrestrained in venturesome trails proclaimed with a thousand little golden blasts that here once upon a time love in fantastic triumph sat. In a concrete conduit, which had been constructed of silver in the viceroy's time, a branch of the Rimac flashed through the garden, making melodious music. Birds intoxicated with the sunshine fluttered among the orange trees and sang spring songs in midwinter. Beyond the garden wall, a slab of the Andes, iridescent mauve and violet, looked soft as a pigeon's breast in the morning's light. Behind them, facing the toy palace, the city of Lima, with its towers and spires, its pastel house walls and glimpses of green convent patios, breathed an antique aroma.

As they walked to the end of the garden, they paused before the Moorish summerhouse topped with a birdhouse built in the shape of a crescent. "Here in the afternoons the viceroy would refresh himself by watching the actress and her maids bathe in the pool beneath," went on the officer-guard. "You know why she was called the *perra-chola*—'the half-caste bitch'? Her protector gave her the name one night when she so far forgot her manners as to box her leading man's ears in a fury on the stage. She came of exceedingly humble parentage, Indian and Spanish with perhaps a bit of Negro in her. The people took up the opprobious *perra-chola*. Though she was their idol, they often yelled it after her in the streets for sport. The Limeños, punctilious with their saints, have always been irreverent with mortals and quick to lampoon the mighty. She changed the nickname to Perricholi to give it an Italian flavour and thus ease the sting." He stretched his arm out in front of him. "There she is now standing at the end of the arbour."

On a slender pedestal stood the marble bust of the young Micaela. The viceroy had had it done by a Genoese sculptor. The meagre boyish breasts of the courtesan did not accord with the roguishness of her eye or the vine leaves wound in her hair. The officer touched the figure lightly and made a scornful face. "But you never can tell——. And this girl won the Louis Quatorze of Peru. After he was recalled to Spain she put the finishing touch to her life by forsaking the stage and entering a convent. Even in their pranks Peruvian women keep their peace with heaven."

They passed back through the courtyard. "Do you think the Perricholi ever really lived here?" Norbourne asked.

"There is doubt," said the officer. "The house she is known for certain to have wantoned in was shaken down by an earthquake. A stinking tannery stands in the place. Only the entrance gates are left, but you can still imagine the gilded coaches and gay throng of pleasure lovers that went in and out. The eighteenth century was our Golden Age. Life was lived in those days. Everyone was rich; the cost of living low. The theatre was a blazing triumph. Today we have lost our zest. Lima is no longer joyful. We study politics and frown. It is better to laugh and make love."

Norbourne paused briefly at the National Library. During the Chilean occupation of Lima in the war of the 1870's the National Library was used as a barracks by the Chilean soldiers. In indifferent ignorance of the value of the priceless volumes and documents among which they were quartered, the soldiers proceeded to play havoc with the library. They rough-housed with the books, swapped them for drink in bodegas, used them for currency in brothels. They lighted their cook fires with ancient manuscripts, ripped out pages for cleaning their guns, tore off priceless sheets for toilet amenities. All but 8,000 of the 60,000 volumes were destroyed, when the victors sailed back to Chile. An interlude in a petty war had ruined six decades of painstaking labour. Ricardo Palma, the beloved librarian not long dead, gave his life to retrieving the devastation Chilean soldiers had made. Today the library has more than 100,000 volumes.

In 1821, immediately after Spain's yoke was broken, San Martín had founded the library as a first essential step to bring sweetness and light to the new nation which had been smothered under the vice-regal administration. "The Spanish government," he declared, "convinced that ignorance is the strongest pillar to support despotism, forbade anything that might lead to the spread of education. Our aim is to create an educated citizenship, because education is the very negation of despotism."

But the government has not always followed the gleam of San Martín's enlightenment. The University of San Marco, the oldest university on the continent, has been closed again and again, because the students rebel against the medieval ideas and methods of instruction. Norbourne wandered about the fresh green, ancient courtyards of the university. It was a pleasing spot, sequestered and yet airy—ideal for the studious, if they were allowed a modernized curriculum. A new basketball court in the college of the lawyers was promising. But there were no students about—only grizzled guides, a professor or two, and occasional soldiers. "A university empty of students is not healthful for the nation," said the guide who showed Norbourne the collection of stuffed animals.

The Torre-Tagle Palace is the most beautiful example of Spanish Colonial domestic architecture extant in the Western Hemisphere. The façade of mellow stone is broken by two long-windowed Moorish balconies screened by a black lacy filigree of carved wood from which the ladies of the family unobserved watched the world go by.

José de Tagle, the first owner of the house, was sent to the New World by Philip V to fight pirates. As a reward for his success in capturing raiders, the emperor gave him the title of marquis and a plot of land in the very heart of the capital. In 1730, settling down to the life of a cultured gentleman, Tagle began to build a castle that was to be a home and pleasure palace. It was completed in 1735, two hundred and two years ago and exactly two hundred years after Pizarro laid the cornerstone of the cathedral. For the materials he drew the best that he could find in various parts of the world. The stone came from Panama, the wood for the timbered ceilings from Costa Rica, the wood for the balustrades from Guayaquil, the tile from Seville. The house was furnished by the foremost European cabinet makers. Rugs, silks, tapestries, vases, clocks, tooled leather, silverware and delicate glass came from Persia, China, France, Florence, Venice. Tagle, with an innate sense of taste and a passion for harmony as strong as his zest for pirate chasing, achieved a masterpiece of its kind which no Peruvian artist, poet, or musician ever surpassed.

The inside is a symphonic poem of Moorish courtyards with embracing galleries, arcades, flights of stairs winding about walls or tile glazed with all the fresh colours of a summer garden. On the second floor one wanders about bedrooms, retiring rooms, alcoves, terraces, a generous ballroom. One is shown an ornate chapel with an altar front sumptuously decorated with relief work in pure gold. Much of the original furniture is in place. Family portraits and original old masters adorn the walls. Although today the palace is occupied by the Foreign Office (which uses only the rooms surrounding a back courtyard for its business) nowhere can one better experience an evocation of past glory.

At the Inca Museum the *huacos*, or funeral vases, were of terra cotta, beige and blue—the colours of the Andes, the desert sands and the sky. The Indians had worked with the colours with which they were most at home. The decorations were of formal motifs, geometric, suggesting both Egypt and Greece. Sometimes mythological monsters, gods with unreasonable numbers of members were portrayed. Generally the drawings were of the daily life of the people: women baking, children supping, men playing ball or fighting to the death. The *huacos* suggested that everything carried on in this earthly life would be pursued in the unearthly one. And in a private room forbidden to minors were representations in pottery that made the obscene perversions of Pompeii seem restrained and dignified. The Inca potters had moulded them with an extravagant and wicked sense of humour.

In long glass cases there were mummies swathed regally in cloaks of green feathers. They squatted dismally with their hands across their eyes as if shutting out the vision of the future they had been so magnificently prepared to greet. For a long time Norbourne regarded those travesties of former high estate with repugnant pity.

As he drove to the Maury for luncheon, he was thinking that Peru had perhaps lived too long with her past, like a bereaved widow who draws the blinds and communes with musty shadows. Only in the last two decades had the country begun to open up the windows, air the rugs, and look up to the sky and the future, instead of keeping eyes lowered on the historic earth.

The restaurant of Hotel Maury claims to be one hundred and nine years old. With its long mirrors heavily framed in gold leaf and its festoons of vines and cages of song birds it was reminiscent of the French quarter of New Orleans, except that there were no women in the place. After a pisco sour for an appetizer Norbourne feasted on *camarones*, cray-fish, with mayonnaise served in avacado pears, followed by the house's specialty, *suprême de pollo Milanese*. It was the best food he had tasted on the whole trip.

After luncheon, with no set purpose, but merely to get a general impression of the city, Norbourne drove about for a couple of hours. Mason was quite right about the confusion: the essence of Lima is hard to catch. It is a medley of contrasts and surprises. It reminded Norbourne not merely of different cities and countries, but different continents. The sun-baked mud walls that bordered the roads between the modern seaport of Callao and the capital called to mind Biskra and date orchards of Algeria. The cotton fields irrigated with melted Andean snow might have been those of Alabama. The suburbs, where most of the American and English colony and the newly-married generation of well-to-do Limeños live in bungalows and villas of mauve, green, azure, and cream, with flowering trees and fenceless lawns, recalled both Southern California and the Riviera. An ancient grove of gnarled olive trees planted in 1560 might have been an Italian landscape near Sorrento. Plazas, churches, and convents, with tiled gardens breathing old Spain from every stone, were within sight of modernistic ferro-concrete apartment houses in the process of construction. Pastry shops and flower shops were presided over by Japanese. Before the forty-two cinemas of Lima were placarded the faces and figures of ubiquitous Hollywood stars. And while he was watching from the road a few minutes of a chukker on the polo grounds of the most luxurious country club on the continent, a new V-8 Ford passed with three Chunchos, savages from the trans-Andean region, in the back seat, their faces streaked tribally with blood-red paint, their heads adorned with bandeaux of parrot feathers. By their expressions they seemed quite taken with the odd amenities of civilization.

"Anywhere the Llama Goes"

Like an Oriental beauty who has granted the favour of a season by lifting her veil once, Lima the next morning was again muffled in mist. But the city is blessed with both summer and winter resorts at her front and back gates. In summer, her citizens visit the bathing beaches. In winter they visit sunny Chosica. No matter how dismally the capital is choked with fog, there is escape by train or motor or horseback within an hour more or less. At an elevation of almost three thousand feet, thirty miles up the Rimac valley, lies Chosica in perpetual sunshine, gay as a Swiss village.

Norbourne drove to Chosica for luncheon with a former Minister of Public Works he had met at the Embassy. "In twenty minutes we shall be in the sun," the ex-minister said as they left the Bolívar. On one side of the road a corps of treasure hunters were disrupting a hill. On the other, bordered by adobe walls, cotton fields extended for unbroken miles. Across the road lay a demarcation of sunshine, as if the paving contract of one company had stopped and that of another which used different materials had begun. Norbourne looked at his watch. They had driven for twenty minutes. Then began the steeper climb to Chosica.

The station was the first stop from Lima on the line officially called the Central Railway, but sentimentally called The Railway to the Moon. Beyond Chosica lies one of the wealthiest mountain areas in the world, but little development could be achieved until transportation facilities made possible the removal of the great mineral deposits to the international steamers by means other than the backs of asses and llamas. There lay the precious ores: silver, gold, copper, vanadium. There were the mines and smelters, waiting for the engineer to bring facilities for marketing the products. It was this railway to the moon, built by a North American named Meigs, which had been the first step in the development.

Henry Meigs, a Yankee adventurer with an indomitable faith in his abilities, came to Peru to escape some trouble he had got into in California. He confronted the most difficult engineering problem man had yet tackled: to take a railway up to a height of nearly three miles over a prodigiously tricky stretch of topography. When the staggering difficulties he would face were detailed to him by the Peruvian government, Meigs replied with coolest confidence: "Anywhere the llama goes I can take a train." And though he died before his superhuman task was quite complete, build the railway he did, not only overcoming the stubborn and treacherous obstacles of nature, but the abysmal difficulties of a depleted treasury. When the money for paying wages gave out, Meigs raised the money himself, offered up the last cent of his private fortune to the achievement, and when everything was gone, by the force of dynamic personality, persuaded the men to work on for virtually no wage.

Rising to a height of over 15,800 feet between Ticlio and Morococha, the highest point of any standard gauge railway in the world, the line passes through sixty-one mountain tunnels, over forty-one bridges, and negotiates thirteen switchbacks. One bridge, the Verrugas Viaduct, hangs in the air like threads of a spider's web, five hundred and seventy feet long and two hundred and fifty feet from the valley floor. Through tunnels, over bridges, along canyons, by the edge of yawning precipices and under cliffs running wild in savage abandon, Meigs threw his rails over the mountains and constructed his epic poem of the triumph of man's wits over nature's Herculean hostility.

New Transport Era

"There is no question about the incalculable benefits the North American engineers have conferred on this continent," said the ex-minister. "When Latin Americans criticize North Americans for their aggressive ways, they forget where they would be without them. And today we need more than anything else your engineers, civil, mining, mechanical, electrical, hydraulic—every sort.

"As an example of what American capital and up-to-date methods have done for Peru, take one example: copper." The ex-minister went on talking, as they passed over a bridge beneath which some naked youngsters were splashing about in the cold stream direct from the mountains. "Shortly after the completion of the Central Railway to Oroya in 1893, an American engineer named Van Slotten went to New York with a rosy tale about mining possibilities. With Yankee alacrity Cerro de Pasco Copper Corporation was organized with a moderate capital of ten million dollars. The company soon bought up 730 mining claims covering nearly 6,000 acres, and by 1904 it had built a railway extension from Oroya to the mines, thus connecting the output directly with the port of Callao. Now see the result. Peruvian copper production in bars jumped from one ton in 1904 to 8,778 tons in

1907, to 24,770 in 1914 and to 53,017 tons in 1929—I have the figures all in my head because it was my business once to get them. Almost all of this came from the American-owned Cerro de Pasco territory. Despite the howls against foreign exploitation, United States initiative helped significantly to bring prosperity to Peru. It gave employment to thousands and in its varied ramifications brought increased business in hundreds of ways. Best of all, it taught us the value of our own resources, which we were too careless or disinterested to develop. And now that we have been properly stirred from our lethargic state by the tonic of North American vigour and initiative, we are beginning to strike out for ourselves."

The chauffeur stopped the car before a green gate in a high brick wall. The men got out. A gentleman with a monocle was instructing a little girl on horseback in jumping hurdles. Norbourne was introduced to him. They watched the performance for a moment and then entered the gate and climbed the series of steps to the house. "He's first cousin to the King of Portugal. His fortune's gone and he has become a fashionable riding master here. Charming fellow. He was Portugal's most noted amateur bull fighter."

Though there are ten bedrooms at the hostelry at Chosica, it seems to consist of sun-rooms and flower gardens on different levels and a long paved terrace dotted with beach umbrellas and deck chairs. The bar-room at the end of the terrace is rigged out like a woodsman's hut. Here the proprietress—an American widow born in the apple country of Virginia and noted locally for accompanying her spouse on a two thousand mile muleback journey through the Hell-hole of the Chaco—mixed the Bronx cocktails herself, and left the men to their talk.

They settled themselves comfortably in deck-chairs and the ex-minister took up the thread of his talk. "And this latest development—aeronautical engineering—Peru owes the United States a great deal for that. Besides the obvious benefits, it is making possible certain mining developments which would be an utter impossibility without the aeroplane. For example, three years ago I was among a group of Peruvians who took over an old gold mine at Cochasayhuas in the heart of the Andes, which had proved unprofitable because of its inaccessibility. It had been worked to some extent in conquistador days. The meagre machinery was transported by Indian back and the output carried into Cuzco by the same slave labour. They had quaint ways of driving the Indians. They chained them together with iron collars around their necks. When the slaves fell dead on the trail from exhaustion, the goaders wouldn't take time to slip their collars—they would just whack off their heads and leave them where they fell." He paused to offer Norbourne a cigarette from a straw case. He did not smoke himself. "Well, we wanted to open up that mine, and we realized it would only be profitable if we had the most modern machinery. The job of getting it to the mine seemed impossible. From Cuzco to the mine site, the sixty kilometre trip over the intervening mountain ordinarily requires from ten to twenty days. The trail is narrow and dangerous. The cost of building a road was prohibitive. And mules haven't been born yet that can carry a tenth of the weight of some of the pieces. Panagra Airways came to the rescue in June 1933, and transported 55 tons of mining machinery.

"Later when 660 additional tons of still heavier machinery were needed, one of the multi-motored passenger planes, the *San Fernando*, was converted into a cargo ship by removing all the cabin seats and opening a hatch in the top of the fuselage. The windows were blocked with sheet aluminium. The plane was loaded by a boom and gin pole with double hand-winches.

"This aerial freighting was conducted with one hundred per cent success under conditions far from ideal. Take-offs and landings at the high altitudes are much faster than at sea level. High winds and various atmospheric disturbances have to be considered constantly. Ground radio stations were installed at Cuzco and Huanacopampa. The standard two-way PAA system radio apparatus kept the plane and the ground in constant communication. An average of four flights a day was made. In addition to a complete hydro-electric plant, a crushing, milling, amalgamating and cyaniding gold plant, capable of treating 150 tons of ore every twenty-four hours, was borne over impassable terrain. Some of the individual pieces of freight weighed as much as two tons——"

At this point the hostess returned to insist that they should come in at once before the soufflé fell. Norbourne heard the rest of the story during luncheon. "What did the Indians think of such goings-on—gigantic birds shuttling back and forth over their mountains?" he asked, remembering the story of the chief who wanted to hatch thunderbird eggs.

"Well, they were about as amazed as ever an Indian allows himself to be. The news of the wonder spread to distant regions. Indians from the banks of the sacred Lake Titicaca, with a bag full of food and a pouch of coca leaves to give them strength, trotted for eighteen days over tortuous mountain trails to get a view of the plane. And when they arrived and saw the silver-winged creature descend from the sky and light upon the ground, they were struck dumb with awe. Some of the old ones dropped on their rusty brown knees in mute reverence.

"On the day before the last load was carried the Indians arranged a fiesta, and celebrated the achievement of the marvellous mechanical bird and its young white masters. They decked themselves out in their native finery, blazing with colour as if at some religious ceremony. At the conclusion they brought forth gifts for the young men who lived inside the bird and ruled its speed and directions. Pottery jugs, coca, flowers, bright-dyed ponchos woven of alpaca wool, and food enough to satisfy the thunderbird itself: corn cakes, frozen potatoes, mutton, piquant sauces, and an indignant black ram that did not appreciate the flight back to Lima."

"How many trips in all?"

"The four hundred and twenty-first round trip was completed on October thirty-first, 1934. At three-thirty in the afternoon the

Lima radio operator received the message: 'Last Trip—Cargo Finished.' It marked a triumph of a new transport era."

"Without benefit of aeroplane, then——" began Norbourne, as they went back to the terrace for coffee.

"Our gold mine would have remained as useless as a boat without a bottom," the ex-minister finished the sentence. "And that is but the beginning," he went on as they sat on the balustrade of the terrace and drank their coffee. "Already the exploitation of other mines is under way. New sources of untapped riches are looming up." He waved his hand to the east and the mountain heights. "One of the few virgin frontiers left to big business."

Industries

That afternoon back in Lima at the National Industrial Exhibition, Norbourne learned more of Peru's potential agricultural and mineral wealth and the use local manufacturers are beginning to make of her national resources. Mason went with him and explained things. Unlike the great European manufacturing countries, England, Italy, Germany, which depend largely on other countries for raw materials, Peru is supplied within her own domain with everything for her mills except wheat and steel. She has cotton and wool in superabundance for piece-goods, thread, tweeds, ponchos, blankets. Her modern buildings are being constructed of Peruvian cement. From the Amazon district come the finest cabinet woods for her furniture factories. Peruvian tanneries prepare the leather for her new and growing industry of bootmaking. The vineyards and brandies of Pisco are famous. Her mineral springs supply her with abundant mineral water. Up to 1931 a heavy importer of Chinese rice, she now raises more than enough for local needs and exports some to Chile. She raises her own tobacco. She grows many of the ingredients for her medicines: quinine, castor oil, and coca leaf, from which cocaine is manufactured in three cities. Though her automobiles are imported, they are fuelled with petrol and oil produced in her north coastal departments. The flour mills still have to depend largely on imported wheat, but factors are at work to improve the quality and output of this Peruvian commodity.

Despite the fact that Peru ranks fourth as the largest producer of silver in the world, and that the Cerro de Pasco Copper Corporation is reported to have an investment of some $70,000,000, oil is the most valuable of all Peru's exports and accounts for about one-third of the total. Cotton ranks after copper, and sugar and silver follow close behind. These five products far outstrip wool and vanadium, of which latter Peru provides 80 per cent of the world's supply.

Throughout the years the United States has brought something more than a third of Peru's total exports. During the last decade the United States sold Peru almost three times as much as Great Britain, its nearest competitor, and more than four times as much as Germany.

"The United States has been able to cope with the European markets well enough," said Mason. "It's the Japanese that they haven't taken sufficiently into account. Ever since the World War, Japanese exporting business to Latin American republics has been going up and up. In Peru in 1933 Japan jumped to fifth place in the leading nations Peru imported from—passing France and Italy, Belgium and the Netherlands. And while imports from the United States, England, and Germany declined in value woefully from 1929 to 1933, Peruvian imports from Japan in the same four-year period increased more than one hundred per cent."

"How was that?" said Norbourne. "Can they undersell other nations because of their low labour costs?"

"That's part of it. But it's not all. There are fifty times as many Orientals in Lima and Callao as there are Americans, twenty-five times as many as English. They have wormed their subtle way in by small methods—starting hole-in-the-wall retail shops for the Indian consumers of cheap goods, then branching out. Besides dominating, within a few years, the small retail businesses—the clothes and novelties—they have assumed control of the sweet shops and the florists. Because they deal in retail they come into direct contact with the proletariat and the lower middle class, which the American residents, who are generally representatives of large corporations, never do. They get their fingers on the pulse of the masses, and they make the appeal of kinship. They spread the theory that the Incas and the Japanese were once one people and that they should stick together against the white race. Compare them in feature, complexion, size, and strength, and they do seem strangely akin. They are doing everything they can to gain sympathy for Japan and they spread a subtle propaganda against the United States. They cater to the needs of the indigenous population. They ingratiate themselves by offering for sale what they have previously ascertained is precisely what the natives want. They are too shrewd to follow the old Yankee way of merely trying to dump their surplus on Latin America."

"And is the Japanese influence spreading likewise in the non-Indian East Coast republics?"

"Japan's exports to Argentina in 1933 increased 80 per cent over the previous year—and in Brazil more than 100 per cent."

"And the first steps for us to take to stem the Oriental tide——"

"Would be for the United States business man to admit his own traditional obtuseness fairly and squarely—to get the little consumer's point of view."

Parade

On the grey Sunday noon of the nation's chief fiesta Norbourne paused by the beautiful ancient fountain in the Plaza Mayor, where the world seemed elbowing for position in an endeavour to get opposite the Presidential Palace. With a wise eye, Pizarro himself had laid out that square. At the time when there were only sixty-nine rude houses in "The City of the Kings," he had foreseen its growth by providing a plaza worthy of the capital four centuries hence. Some say that he spread his plaza with such abundant proportions in order that he might enjoy bullfights from his palace windows. In Panama during intervals of conquest he had won the epithet of the Fearless Toreador for his valour in the ring, and the legend went that once he had conquered a particularly fierce bull by pronouncing the magic word "Jesus." Up to 1768, when the Arco stadium was built, bull runs were commonly held here in the central plaza. As many as two hundred beasts were sometimes slaughtered to make a single holiday. Here too the Inquisition finished off its human victims with dramatic and pyrotechnical *autos-da-fé* for the edification and delight of the populace. But today the houses of Lima had emptied their people into the ghost-thronged square for no more Roman attraction than a martial parade.

Norbourne looked at the faces of the crowd. Except for the few Spaniards of ancient lineage who have kept their white blood unmixed, the people were a conglomerate mass with complexions of various shadings of Indian red, brown, deep sallow, olive, sour cream. Some pigment was pure Mongolian yellow, some black as the heart of Africa. Both the Quecha and Aymara Indians look like cousins of Mongolians at best, and now that the natives have cohabited with emigrated Chinese and Japanese the younger generation looked surprisingly Oriental. The policemen with their red-lined blue capes were not Mongol, not Indian, not Spanish. In blood, stature, physiognomy, and temperament they were a cocktail; the proportions seeming to be one jigger Chinese or Japanese, one jigger Spanish, two jiggers Indian. Peru, Norbourne knew, remained predominantly Indian. Out of the estimated six million population of Peru, less than half a million are white. About a million are of mixed blood or Mongolian in origin. Speculating vaguely on the composite face of Peru a century hence, Norbourne began manœuvres to get through the crowd across the square to the pavement facing the Palace.

On the carved wooden gallery the bareheaded, wide-girthed President Benavides and his bareheaded, wide-girthed cabinet, all in evening clothes, were reviewing Peru's military strength.

Red satin ribbons cut diagonal slashes across their dazzling white shirt fronts like gaping sabre wounds. For two hours they had been reviewing and saluting. The infantry had gone by with expressions as grim as if they were to do battle at the end of the street. The bronze Aymara Indians from the mountains have strong, compact, enduring physiques, bodies that can stand phenomenal punishment, privation, and freezing. They are said to make enthusiastic fighters, and are much fiercer than the Quechas who prefer to farm in peace. The cavalry pranced by, very smart, debonair. The navy, the marine corps, the Red Cross with stretchers and spanking new medicine chests on wheels passed in pageant.

Now ear-blasting bands pass, blending the fury of Indian war dances with the Congo's ritualistic violence and sad relentless rhythms of the Spanish plateau. A great black savage, a full head taller than his musical comrades, pounds his drums with terrific wrist twists as if he were trying to split it to pieces. His chin sticks out in hard lines, pushing the atmosphere out of his way. Staring hypnotically on some inner vision, the whites of his eyes gleam wildly in the blue-black skin. His legs move superbly with animal vigour, the steel muscles bulging under the tight cloth of his trousers. Sweat swirls from his forehead and cheeks. His nostrils dilate and his inflated chest almost bursts the buttons off his tunic. Rigours pass over his frame like those attacking neophytes in religious ecstasy. He is terrifying and magnificent, a lost savage king with small mentality and mammoth dreams. A Frankenstein creature who could crush the skulls of his comrades between his bare fists like walnuts. He looks as if he were cunningly aware of the power of his brute strength, as he steps in exaggerated rhythms and beats his drum furiously for the glory of Peru.

Behind this band with the black drummer, the company of little sailors pass, twelve-, ten-, eight-year-olds from the naval academy, fair or brunette, with blue or olive-coloured eyes and blood of purest Castilian stock. They are very smart in their expertly tailored uniforms. But after hours of marching over music they are pale with fatigue now, these future Admirals of Peru.

End of Conquest

High Mass was in progress in the grey twin-towered cathedral when Norbourne entered. Pizarro with his own devout, thieving hands had laid its foundation stones. Women of all classes were kneeling, whispering their shortcomings to the Virgin. Most of them wore the plain black *manto*, that head-covering fashioned like the blue scarf the Mother of God wears in Renaissance pictures. A few high-bred faces were framed in beauty-enhancing mantillas of rare old lace, heirlooms in which their noble ancestresses had offered their proud devotion. Only one or two modern young women and a few foreigners were defiantly brazen enough to wear small Parisian hats. The ecclesiastics of Peru still frowned severely on ladies' hats within the church. A *chola* in her early teens, without *manto*, had spread a tiny yellow handkerchief on top of her black hair, and held it with her little fingernail stuck like a hat-pin into the middle of her top-knot, while she asked some saint for what her heart desired. In this wise she obeyed St. Paul's admonition of twenty centuries past that no female should enter Christ's temple with uncovered head.

The organ music throbbed an accompaniment to the pious muttering. The ritual was bathed in the odour of incense. Late canons trudged in to take their places—a set of elderly, grey-haired gentlemen attired in black gowns and little purple capes tipped with ermine, not unlike a coterie of paunchy greengrocers dressed up for masquerade. Puffing, they clambered up the altar steps and wedged themselves in the exquisitely carved seventeenth century stalls. Switching on little individual electric bulbs like those in Pullman berths, they started mumbling their prayers. From time to time they paused to look up at the gold-encrusted pillars. Occasionally one or another stooped to spit at one of the neat individual white enamel cuspidors from Akron, Ohio, that dotted the purple plush carpet before each stall, like white poker chips on a gaming table.

An eager, unctuous guide beckoned Norbourne to the chapel at the right of the main entrance. He tiptoed with exaggerated precaution, as if to beware of awakening a sleeper. In the shadowy, windowless gloom on a supported shelf some six feet from the floor lay a long glass coffin. The guide struck a match and held the flickering flame close to the dusty glass. Within, like rotting bundles of greenish parchment, lay the mortal remains of the conqueror of Peru. The long frame with the shrivelled legs extended over six feet—taller in death than his fellow Christians, as he had been in life. The guide pointed out in the mummy's shoulder and neck the marks of the fatal wounds that Almagro's bastard had given him. The conqueror's head was mended with wire. Clutching, bony fingers made a gesture of hiding the body's abject nakedness. Of course, it may not have been Pizarro at all on whom so much curiosity and tribute were showered, but some foisted unknown substitute. Yet as Norbourne regarded this starkly impotent figure, which was the dead colour of last year's wasps' nests, it seemed to possess some incorruptible dignity, to exude a subtle macabre overtone of former high estate. And although he had rarely believed in authentic bones of crypted saints, he was quite inclined to believe that this desiccated empty breast had once heaved with the indomitable spirit that belonged peculiarly to Piazarro and to no other.

Perpetual Life

Leaving the cathedral, Norbourne went to the palace to see Pizarro's famous fig tree. Signor Bustamente, the President's private secretary himself, offered to show him about. One had to get within the palace to realize its great size. It was like a series of buildings within buildings, a group of houses within high city walls. Parts of it suggested a barracks, a fortress, a château, a series of business offices. It was forbiddingly austere here, overdecorated there. Norbourne saw little to delight him except the proportions of Pizarro's garden, the great patio in which reconstructed wings separated by centuries formed the boundaries. In one corner, huddled against a gallery, crouched the fig tree planted by the conquistador. With only a few dusty leaves left on its twisted branches it looked as senile as the coffined mummy that gave it life. A breeze rustled the dry branches and the joints creaked as with ague.

"Yes, she is tired," said Bustamente. "Nearly four centuries of fruit-bearing. But each spring she takes heart again and puts out fresh leaves and little figs."

"Keeping Pizarro's memory green," said Norbourne, as they descended a brief flight of stairs into the garden. The vegetation was wilted and bloomless, as if the palace gardener had no love for flowers. Only the blue fountain and the high-backed seats of tile that had been made to bloom in Seville were lustrous with colour.

Bustamente spread his fingers out to touch the sparkling fountain spray. "Do you know Mr. Waldo Frank?" he said. "Brilliant fellow, very brilliant. Too bad he's a Communist—sees everything he looks at through Communistic spectacles. But very brilliant.

"And here is where Pizarro was killed." Bustamente paused under the roof of the one-storied section at the back and indicated a spot on the coloured pavement. It may not have been the spot, but it served just as well for evoking the dramatic ghosts.

Norbourne recalled how the jealous and greed-cankered Pizarro had allowed his son to execute Almagro, his old coadjutor, without uttering a syllable to save him. And Almagro's ruined friends who had been stripped to poverty got their revenge. They attacked the marquis in his own house. Hearing their blood-curdling whoops reverberating along the passage, he just had time to seize a sword when the gang fell upon him. He fought stoutly, but a thrust in the throat brought him to his knees. Like a hero in a Lope de Vega drama he died in the grand manner. Dipping a forefinger in his own blood, he traced the sign of the cross on the pavement and fell on his face to kiss it, giving up the ghost with God's name on his shrewd lips.

Within a very few years everyone of importance connected with the conquest of Peru had come to a violent end. The ruthlessness and treachery that had made them great for conquering had unfitted them for living at peace among themselves. Pizarro lived in his new capital only six years. But the old conquistador's spirit still pervades the place after four hundred years have stalked into the past.

"In modern Peru today," Norbourne said to the secretary as they shook hands good-bye, "one feels Pizarro infinitely more than one feels Cortes in Mexico."

Thick as Water Hyacinths

As Norbourne drove in the Panagra bus through dim dawn-lit Lima to take the plane for Arequipa, mist hung intimately like portières about the doorways of the narrow streets where many of the colonial families still live. Yes, Norbourne thought, Lima, like its climate, is half sun, half mist. Old Lima seems very tired; new Lima very, very young. The tawdry and the new make grating music against the seasoned and traditional. It is in the throes of economic and spiritual rebirth. It lacks direction and reasonable unanimity. The nation's four or five million pure Indians munch their wads of thought-drugging coca, aim to keep out of the white man's affairs. The more wealthy darlings of the nation play polo, while other youths babble communism and paste seditious posters on church walls. As Mason had said, quoting someone: "The paradoxes of the capital thumb their noses at the social and political theorists."

Before a bright blue villa in the suburbs the bus stopped for "Dinty" Moore. With the casual gait of a prime minister he sauntered out of his rose-embowered front gate, cool, detached, without one unnecessary muscle movement. He sat in the empty seat by Norbourne and showed him snapshots of his Peruvian wife and two handsome dark-eyed offsprings. He seemed already as much at home in his alien environment as Ambrose O'Higgins, the runaway Irish peasant, who rose to become viceroy of Peru at the age of eighty in 1796.

The *San Pablo* flew over the turtleback sand dunes where tawny offshoots of the Andes came down to dip their feet in the lapping sea foam. The guano islands were deserted. The birds had gone hunting. Sometimes they stretched across the surface of the sea like unending caravans. Sometimes they crowded thickly together and formed black acres on the water. Billions of jelly fish, whitish, pulpy, bulbular, disgusting, lay floating near the olive-drab surface, thick as water hyacinths in Louisiana bayous.

At Pisco, where the famous brandy is made from the fruit of near-by vineyards, they stopped for ten minutes. After Nazca, the mountains became welted, ridged and fuzzy with woody scrubs. From the air they looked like old rhinoceros hides.

At one o'clock they landed on the new field at Arequipa, the city that is proud to salaam before three magnificent volcanoes bearing the fascinating names of El Misti, Chachani and Pichu-Pichu.

"Anodyne for Jangled Nerves"

The Quecha name, "Arequipa," means "Here we rest," just as "Alabama" does in another Indian language. Although the town was refounded by Pizarro on the Day of the Assumption, 1540, it had been known for centuries as a rest station for runners rushing fresh fish to tables of the Incas in their highland capital. With a population of 60,000, the second largest city of Peru lies in a fertile valley 7,500 feet above sea level and 107 rail miles from the seaport of Mollendo on the Southern Railway of Peru which terminates at Cuzco. Blessed with an invigorating climate of eternal early spring, the place is healthy despite the picturesque squalor of its side streets. Though more than half the population seen on the streets today is Indian, towards the end of Spanish vice-royalty, Arequipa had the greatest white population of all the South American cities under Spanish dominion. Today, like Lima and Bogotá, Arequipa prides itself on its aristocratic background. Except for tramcars and automobiles, modernity has not outwardly disturbed its traditional spirit. It is intensely independent, intensely religious, intensely patriotic.

An antique city of oyster-white spread under a clear blue firmament, Arequipa is all of a piece. Here, unlike Lima, the composite essence of the place seems as nicely welded as its solid architecture. Like Bermuda, it is its unique building material that gives it much of its outer distinction. While the island's houses are constructed from white coral limestone, Arequipa is reared from petrified volcanic ash or lava, called *sillar*. The fact that the citizens live in walls fashioned from the fruit of volcanoes may account for that strange mercurial vitality that agitates Arequipan breasts. For its people, more virile than the Limeños, are quick to flare into love, quick to hate, to forgive, to ridicule, to dance, to fight, to revel, to take Holy Orders.

For all the electricity in the air, for all the change in daily temperature—thirty degrees difference between the brilliant sun-warmed days and cool nights—Norbourne found Arequipa the haven of rest that bore out the significance of its name's meaning. But the feeling was largely due to Mrs. Bates and her Quinta, where she provided comfort for a limited number of paying guests.

The house was a long rambling structure built high off the ground, with a dozen additions of rooms, nooks, sun parlours, baths, all on slightly different levels, and pent houses like cabins perched on the roof and reached by narrow flights of stairs appearing in unexpected places. In the wood-panelled dining room one ate at tables for two or four or eight in a veritable museum of art treasures and paintings of the El Greco school. One had whiskey and soda in a library hung with priceless Inca tapestries and an odd trio of affectionately autographed photographs of General Pershing, Premier Venizelos, and Noel Coward. In the drawing room in the evenings one played bridge in an atmosphere warmed by a brazier and scented with an aroma of eucalyptus leaves simmering in a brass finger bowl.

Norbourne was sitting at breakfast on the roof garden of Quinta Bates facing the glory of El Misti's symmetry. An immaculate diadem of snow crowned the volcano's serene proportions. Like two less beautiful Sister Fates, the bulk of Pichu-Pichu hovered in the right background and the purplish mass of Chachani lounged at the left. Rising nineteen thousand feet above sea level against a luminous sky bluer than Sicily's above Etna, Misti seemed as near as a morning's stroll.

Sunshine splashed on the orange cone of the volcano, poured over the tiled floor of the terrace roof, spattered on the climbing geraniums twisting about the green wooden balustrade, on the breakfast dishes, on Norbourne's face and hands and body, on the brindled bulldog lying companionably at his feet. He finished the last crumb of his breakfast and stretched out in a deck chair, luxuriating in an abandon of relaxation. The air was like dry champagne. He had slept profoundly under soft, fawn-coloured vicuña skins; he had dressed briskly in an atmosphere as crisp as early morning in the Adirondacks; and now, basking in the sun's golden elixir and gazing steadfastly on El Misti, he felt his breathing become delightfully equable. Majestically aloof, yet stirringly intimate, the volcano mutely preached the beauty of tranquillity. From the alleyway behind the house came the strange, thin music of some passing Indian playing snatches of native melody on a reed pipe. Birds sang in the topmost branches of the mimosa and eucalyptus trees. There was nothing he had to do, no one he had to see, no statistics to set down in his note-book. "This," he said, "is the quintessence of contentment."

The wife of an English commercial traveller, coming up for her tea and marmalade, said in passing, "To open that garden gate and walk up the flowery path to the long verandah is like entering Paradise. This is like no hotel, no boarding house on earth. It's like a country mansion house party where every guest is independent."

Everyone feels that way about Quinta Bates. Harassed business men from Lima, dog-weary diplomats, mining engineers from the interior starved for a taste of civilization, exhausted tourists, pause at Quinta Bates to refresh themselves in body and spirit. People come for a day, stay for a week, a month, stay until their hostess puts them out to make room for others. Noel Coward was so enchanted with the place that he composed a three-page poem in octosyllabics extolling its virtues and the personality of its presiding deity.

Her name is plainly Mrs. Bates
(A strange capricious whim of Fate's
To crown with such banality
So strong a personality).

Though for half a century her name has been Mrs. Bates (acquired from her dead English husband) she was born Ana Montieth in the New York village of Bath-on-Hudson. Her girlhood was spent in Chile, her young married life in copper-mining towns of Bolivia, where often for years at a time she was the only white woman. A pioneer in comfort, she has mothered two generations of mining engineers, prospectors, homesick clerks. Everybody calls her *Tia*—Spanish for "aunt." Famous from Cristobal to the Straits of Magellan, she is undoubtedly the best-known woman on the subcontinent. Legends have grown up about her in her lifetime.

"How do you achieve such contentment in your guests?" Norbourne asked the hostess, intercepting her at the foot of the stairs when he came down from breakfast. She had paused to give some crisp orders to servants.

"My prescription is very simple. I give them good American food with enough native dishes to remind them they are globetrotters. I keep the beds soft and the water hot. And I let them feel at home." She spoke in forthright, direct manner, while humour played about the corners of eyes that were as keenly azure as Dean Swift's.

"That's all there is to it?"

"That's all. Misti does the rest. They go up on my roof garden and stretch out in deck chairs and look at the volcano. Misti casts a spell over them."

She waved Norbourne to take a seat in the out-of-doors lobby as if she had a few minutes to give him if he liked. She sat down, grateful to snatch a brief rest herself. The lobby was an open verandah connecting the dining room with the main building. Against the walls stood chests brought over by the conquistadors. On the centre table were strewn the latest English, American, and Spanish magazines. Hummingbirds flashed like jewels among the trellised morning-glories.

"I have just returned from a wedding breakfast"—Tia explained her costume with a grimace. She was in gala attire. She wore a black dinner dress and a black lace mantilla was caught about her snow-white hair. "The weddings of the poor take place at four-thirty a.m. Only at that hour will the church make honest women of them free of charge." Mrs. Bates had arisen from her bed in the dark chill of the early morning because the Indian groom was a former gardener in her employ and his feelings would have been hurt if she had not attended his wedding. "I think he wanted my moral support," she said, her eyes twinkling. "He's only a little fellow and his inamorata looks like a virago. During the ceremony he swayed and turned green. I thought he was going to faint. But the bride, a large dirty creature in white, slanted an executive eye at him, reached in his pocket, pulled out a cigarette, twisted it in two and shoved it under his nose. 'Here, sniff this,' she commanded. He sniffed and recovered."

"You're fond of these Indians, aren't you?"

"Sometimes. Sometimes I want to slay them. They are exasperating creatures. But they know I am their friend and they seem grateful. At least they didn't slaughter me when they were in slaughtering mood. I went through several bloody uprisings of the Corocoro Indians in Bolivia. My white friends were massacred, beaten to death with iron rods, their bodies left on the pampa for dogs to eat. I remember being wakened once at three o'clock in the morning. In the moonlight the hills seemed to be moving, they were so thick with the black ponchos of the Indians. That time I was apprehensive, because some of the fellows came from a distant district. We took the children and hid in an abandoned mine. I had to spend the night sitting in a puddle of water. I was so uncomfortable that when daylight came I said to my husband, 'Hell, I'm going home. I prefer massacre to this'—and home we went."

She laughed and got up. "Now I must get out of this idiotic garb. I have to put a new room-boy through his paces. And there are some rose trees to be set out."

"I hear you've been god-mother to five thousand of their infants," Norbourne said, hoping to detain her in conversation.

"Well, a thousand or so at any rate," she modified, straightening the periodicals on the table. "They choose me because they say I have the *bueno mano*, or lucky hand. The Indians believe it good fortune if their children die in infancy, for then they go straight to heaven. In hard reality they reckon it a blessing to escape life—their lot is pretty hard, you know. Because the proportion of my god-children who die is great, they say I have the lucky touch. As god-mother I provide a tiny shroud and a wooden coffin. Often the parents ask me to furnish a yard of white ribbon. They fasten it to the baby's shroud and let it hang out of the coffin. When I asked the reason they said, 'Why, Tia, it is to pull the god-mother up to heaven.' " She smiled over their touching naïveté, and yanked off her mantilla.

"Yes, I'm coming," she called to the Chinese-Indian cook, who stuck an inquiring face through a screen of vines and withdrew quickly like a conjurer's apparition. "She's a perfect devil, that cook. I fire her and rehire her. We part in rages and weep on each other's necks when I take her back. She may keep me out of heaven yet. I'll need my god-children's ribbons."

As she went off with regal tread to interview the cook, she turned to say: "Francisco is your room-boy. Look on him as your personal valet. There are no bells. But he's supposed to anticipate your wishes. Join me for an appetizer before luncheon in my little room."

"An amazing woman. She has imperial stuff in her." A lawyer from Lima had joined Norbourne as Mrs. Bates disappeared and he had turned to look at the garden. The lawyer had come to examine a concession given to a Swiss to search for treasure which the Jesuits were supposed to have hidden at the foot of Chachani. The approximate hiding place had been revealed by an old paralytic in a hypnotic trance induced by a German butter broker. "Your country couldn't have sent us a better unofficial ambassador," he went on. "For decades she's taught manners to American and British prospectors. Half of Arequipa comes to her for advice. Her head's as full of sense as her heart is of kindness." He pointed out into the garden. "You see those little detached houses over there in the corner behind the pomegranate trees. I'm staying in the one she built for her husband. He deserted her, and twenty years later asked her to take him back to die. She built that house for him and let him come. Then she nursed him until he died. . . . I have to go to the office. Would you care to walk with me?"

Little Brothers of the Camel

Out of the Quinta's green double gate they walked right into a herd of fourteen llamas in the narrow, walled street called Calle Jerusalem. Their Indian owner and his round-faced male offspring followed them on bare feet. Part sheep, part camel, with faces like pretty, inquisitive spinsters, the llamas stepped precisely, shyly. Their alert pointed ears, standing perpetually erect, were pierced for the adornment of gaily coloured tufts of dyed yarn. On their backs they bore panniers of charcoal and coils of rope made from their own wool. They were not all grey or dun-coloured: two were smoke-blue and three were salmon pink. At the sight of strangers they sidled to the other side of the street and whined like newborn babies—it is the only sound they can make. Their master whistled to them soothingly. By various soft whistlings he directs them. They are the gentlest of beasts. No one would dream of whipping a llama. No one dares to overload them. Set a burden on their backs they consider a kilogram too heavy, and they protest by lying down quietly with inflexible determination.

The men walked beside the herd. Norbourne reached out to pat a salmon pink one. His companion grabbed his arm. "Don't. He might spit in your eye. They won't bite or kick, but if you anger them they spit. Their saliva is said to be full of germs: a certain kind of syphilis. The disease doesn't affect the llama. He has it constitutionally. Just as yellow fever germs kill men but do not hurt the mosquitoes who transmit the disease. Bolivia has a law prohibiting a man from driving a herd of llamas over the mountain unless a woman accompanies him. Your United States government won't permit llamas to enter the country for fear of contamination."

At the master's whisper-like whistle, the animals turned left down the street with the tram-car tracks which led to the market place. The men stopped to watch them. Fascinating little brothers of the camels, as distinctive as white peacocks on parade or cream-coloured pumas relaxed in siesta before their cavern lairs! Once or twice they glanced back at Norbourne and his companion curiously, the expression of their eyes virginal, docile, full of eternal wonderment. Their little feet tapped the lava cobblestones demurely, like the sound of silver striking on a muted gong. They stretched their erect heads on elongated necks as far towards the heavens as they were able—six, sometimes seven, feet from the ground. "Like ascetic astronomers the beasts are most content when nearest to the unencumbered stars," the lawyer said.

At the furious honking of an approaching automobile, the Indian did not yell or strike at the llamas; he whispered to them and waved his hands reassuringly. One confused beast he took in his arms and shoved gently out of the way.

"Like the Indians of the high plateau, llamas thrive on privations, dieting on the scant grass of cold climates in rarefied air. The lushness of coastal valleys brings them both to ruin. Between the Indian and the llama a mystic bond exists. The beast bears some of the Indian's burdens; his wool furnishes material for his master's poncho; his dried dung provides his fuel. In famine his flesh saves him from starvation. Inseparable earthly companions, the tie lingers beyond death. When the llama passes into realms of rest, the Indian holds communion with the beast's spirit by making music on a flute fashioned from his friend's thigh bone."

At the next corner the men paused to let pass a flock of nuns with black-aproned charges from one of the numerous orphanages. The children turned longing eyes on the painted push cart of an ice cream seller who jingled his string of bells tantalizingly. The ice cream carts of Arequipa are fashioned after seventeenth century sedan chairs which Spanish grandees once imported for their wives and mistresses. The sides of the vehicle are garishly decorated with scenes of court folk at play in palace gardens.

In front of a cinema advertising James Cagney in bellicose pose, two Indians were glowering so intently in argument that the lawyer and Norbourne had to step off the sidewalk on to the cobblestones. "If they were drunk or angry enough to fight," said the lawyer, "you'd see a sight. They are better than gamecocks and quick as cats. They fight with their bare feet. They aim vicious kicks at each other's vulnerable spot. Many a man has lost his manhood in a foot fight."

The pink and white colonnades of the rectangular Plaza reminded Norbourne of St. Mark's in Venice. Its long, low, oyster-white cathedral, with the graceful twin bell towers pointing the way to heaven, occupied one complete side. Between the towers like some inspired architectural adornment loomed the dazzling distant cone of Misti. The men paused to have a cigarette on a bench among the palm trees and sat facing the snow of the mountain peak.

"Every town should have its volcano," Norbourne said.

"And its Quinta Bates," the Peruvian added.

When a clock boomed ten the lawyer strolled off to his work and Norbourne poked about the near-by curio shops. He wandered to the open-air market that was redolent with dirty-faced Indians clad in gay ponchos, multi-coloured skirts, bright shawls. He paused before the forbidding gates of numerous monasteries and convents. In almost any direction he went, after a few squares, he ran into the slums. The twisting by-roads and alleyways with their low, flat-roofed houses were as paintable as streets in Biskra—and as smelly.

Red Flags

Just before luncheon while Norbourne and some of the guests were drinking Cinzano in Tia's glassed-in verandah nook, where Dr. Korff, the Finnish nobleman scientist, was discoursing by demand on the cosmic rays he had come to study, two lady guests from Boston came gasping up the brick walk. Dismay fluttered from every joint and feature. At the steps they began yelling at a gaping servant polishing a window: "*Aqua caliente!* Disinfectant!" They thrust their umbrellas against the balustrade (heaven knows why they had taken them), shook themselves like wet dogs, vigorously stamped the dust from their feet. "*Aqua caliente*. Quick. Hurry. *Aqua caliente!*"

Tia emerged solicitously, but with the cool reasonableness she reserved for excitable females. The women waved her back with gestures of Edwardian melodrama. "Don't come near us," they warned her, their schoolmarm features transfigured into distorted masks of terror. "Don't come near us! Have you disinfectants? Lots of *aqua caliente!* We got caught in the smallpox district."

In the excitement the bulldog sprang up, bared his teeth in a snarl and barred their way.

"Nonsense." Tia spoke authoritatively. "There's no smallpox district. The paper says there are only three cases in the whole town."

"Oh, we know better." The ladies waggled their heads. "Every few houses had little red flags hanging over their doors. We tried to get out, and we got lost. We turned up this street and down that. We ran into more and more of them. It was like a labyrinth—we thought we'd never get out."

Tia laughed heartily. "Those were only *picanterias*, little restaurants."

"No. They were disinfecting. We saw pots smoking on the floor. It smelt queer."

"They were cooking—cooking meat and vegetable marrow with peppers and spice. The red flag is the restaurant's sign, like the barber's coloured pole."

The ladies from Boston swayed slightly. The Finnish searcher into cosmic rays quickly poured out two drinks. "Have a spot of appetizer!" he offered.

Four servants with dilating black eyes dashed from the dining room and the kitchen hallway bearing steaming jugs and pots. "Take the hot water and give Misti a good bath," Mrs. Bates ordered.

"Misti!" shrilled one of the ladies in confusion.

"Misti's the name of that bulldog laughing at you there," said Tia.

Regard for Indians

One morning Norbourne played golf with the keen, amusing son-in-law of a local politician-millionaire, who, people hinted, might be the next President of Peru. The young Peruvian, now manager of a mineral water bottling works, had had the distinction, as he laughingly said, of failing for his degree at California's five leading colleges and winning five separate letters in athletics. That afternoon Norbourne went for a motor ride with him and his Iowan brother-in-law, stationed in Arequipa in the alpaca wool business. (Wool is Arequipa's most important commodity.) They did the honours of their town most agreeably, showed Norbourne the bull ring, the race track, the Thermal Baths of Jesus on the slopes of Pichu-Pichu, the Harvard Observatory clinging to the side of Misti, the neighbouring villages.

Wherever the roads close to the town followed the small streams, large-bodied trees grew and shaded the grey hovels of the peasants, giving them a tolerable relief from their bare poverty. But in the higher waterless districts, as donkeys laden with bundles of produce trundled by or automobiles whizzed past in a fury, volcanic dust from ever-dry roads swirled about windowless baked-mud huts and made the habitations of the humble seem intolerably pathetic. Near the edge of a grassless precipice the men stopped the car and got out to look across the gorge at a new view of Misti. A typical hut stood within twenty feet of the edge and some twenty from the road. It boasted the addition of a lean-to built of poles and corrugated tin. A bent old woman, her face wrinkled like a discarded dish mop, crouched over a fire of llama dung, stirring a stew. She reminded Norbourne of the old Arab women at Biskra for ever cooking *couscous*. A brown baby tethered to a pole by a dirty string crawled about the bare ground. Scurrying around like a member of the family, a dusty white guinea pig paused to shoot a suspicious glance from its pink eyes at the strangers, and then ran to hide among the baby's rags. The place was begrimed with the smoke of a thousand smouldering cooking fires and stank from utter lack of hygiene.

The men tried to exchange some pleasantries with the old woman, who scarcely raised her head. But the baby regarded them with wide-eyed interest and curiosity.

"The housing conditions are pretty deplorable, aren't they?" Norbourne said as they got back in the car.

"Yes, the Indians are filthy folk," said the happy-hearted Iowan.

"I wonder," said Norbourne with a speculative malice, "if they were before the Spaniards came."

"It's in the breed," said the Peruvian, "but they were better off then. The Incas made their subjects work, but they took care they didn't go hungry or ill-clothed. The state provided for the old and infirm. My ancestors worked them to the limit, and let them go to hell when they couldn't work."

"But they're a lousy lot," said the Iowan. "They don't do anything to better themselves. Look at that fellow driving the donkey with the hay on its back—see his jaw working? He's chewing coca. That's all they do—drug themselves with coca."

"Perhaps he's walked far," suggested Norbourne. "Coca gives them endurance, doesn't it?"

"Yes, those beggars can run all day on an empty stomach if you give them a wad of coca."

"Is it true that a certain amount of coca is part of their weekly rations at the mines and on the farms?"

"They wouldn't sign a contract without it."

"I don't much blame them," Norbourne said. "It keeps them from thinking."

"They don't think anyhow."

The Iowan leaned forward in the back seat with his head thrust between Norbourne's and his brother-in-law's shoulders. "You know, I've got a scheme to make a pile of money quick if I just had the capital to begin with. You see these donkeys everywhere on the road. Well, they are indispensable to the Indians. They can't do a thing without them. I'm thinking of cornering the market."

The Peruvian laughed at the absurdity of the idea. "How?"

"I'd offer to pay a man slightly more than the regular price for his animal. He'd contract to sell, thinking he could buy one from his neighbour and make a little money by the transaction. I'd arrange individually with each man to bring me his donkey on a certain day to a corral, or say to certain corrals—maybe in three or four different villages would be better. They'd all bring them. I'd pay them, and own all the donkeys. Then when they tried to buy others to replace them they wouldn't find them because I'd have them all. They'd be helpless. They couldn't work their crops, gather them, or bring their produce to market. So they'd have to buy them at my price. I could make a profit of two or three hundred per cent."

"But how could they pay for them?" Norbourne demanded indignantly.

"They'd find a way. They'd sell their implements, or I could take mortgages on their houses, which would mean owning them."

"And why not take their ponchos and their stewpots?" Norbourne said with cold passion. "Why not," he added, "their lives? You could make bone meal for fertilizer from their bones."

The Iowan laughed out of the corner of his mouth. "Don't take me too seriously," he said.

The Peruvian took it both as a joke and as a dubious speculation. "You'd get stung," he said cheerfully. "You'd find all sorts of unaccounted-for donkeys springing up. You couldn't really corner the market. In the end you might have to sell them for a few *soldi*."

Poor Indians, Norbourne said to himself, begrudged of their miserable poverty. Without the Indians Peru could not exist, yet they were contemptuously considered on a par with beasts of burden or even less. Perhaps the young man from Iowa had not meant to be taken seriously at all. But his attitude and what he had said showed clearly the callous disregard the average foreigner and the average Peruvian had for the race they exploited. They had no animosity to the Indians. They did not enjoy their miserable plight. They merely thought of the profit and shut their minds to any other consideration. If an Indian would work for ten cents a day, why be fool enough to pay him twenty?

Half an hour later at the Peruvian's house for cocktails, Norbourne was unprepared to find that the host's library was made up almost entirely of books on sociology: Karl Marx, Strachey, Waldo Frank, a complete set of Upton Sinclair, a dozen volumes on contemporary Russia, half a hundred of Haldeman Julius's little blue books. "Social reforms for the Indians are embryonic to say the least," the host said with engaging assurance. "But some of us are thinking. Here, read this." He handed Norbourne a marked copy of *The Nation* of several years previous. "See what Mariatequi says."

Norbourne read: "The Republic should have bettered the conditions of the Indian; instead it has increased his poverty, aggravated his subjection, and deepened his misery. The republic has meant the entrenchment of a ruling class which has gradually and systematically absorbed and possessed itself of the land. To a people of tradition, whose very soul is the land, this dispossession has meant material and moral bankruptcy. The land has always been the joy of the Indian; he feels that life comes from the soil and goes back to it. . . . He can maintain indifference to everything, except the loss of the land which his hands and his spirit occupy and make fertile. Peruvian feudalism has been greedier and harsher than Spanish. The Spanish overlord generally had some of the outlook and manners of a nobleman. The Creole landowner has all the defects of the plebeian and none of the virtues of an hidalgo."

"Do you agree?" Norbourne asked, looking up.

"In general, it just about hits the nail on the head."

"What is going to be done?"

"We hope to give much of the land back to the Indians—as painlessly as possible. It takes time. It's such an astoundingly new idea, you see. We don't want to get too excited or fly off half-baked and merely shout noble sentiments from the house tops before we know what we can do."

"Whoever does bring about some lasting reform," Norbourne said, as they joined the others in the drawing room for cocktails, "has a neat chance of making the biggest name since San Martín."

Regret

Norbourne was loath to leave Arequipa. He had spent the last two days in complete *dolce far niente*, basking in the sun on the roof, playing golf, lazing in the garden, chatting with other temporary truants from the pressure of routine. The other guests, too, sighed profoundly at the thought of ever saying good-bye to the contentment of Quinta Bates. They would look at each other with odd, intimate expressions of international cabalists who had been let in on a secret privilege. Often they would quote some of the Coward couplets which they had seen in Tia's guest book. The passage Norbourne liked particularly for its aptness ran thus:

The spirit of the place conserves
An anodyne for jangled nerves.
The water's hot, the beds are soft,
The meals are many a time and oft,
The flowers are sweet, the grass is green,
The toilet is austerely clean,
Which, in this ancient continent,
Occasions vast astonishment.

When he went to pay his absurdly small bill and to thank Mrs. Bates for everything, he found her in the den with Dr. Korff discussing the type of foreign business men that came to South America.

"The average Englishman used to be of much higher type than the American," Mrs. Bates was saying. "I often blushed for my country—some of the engineers and prospectors were so crude. But the American adventurer, as a type, seems to be dying out. The Americans who come down now are for the most part college graduates. The majority today don't come with the grab-as-much-as-you-can-as-quick-as-you-can attitude of their fathers and grandfathers. Of course, there are exceptions. There will always be hogs among men. Teddy Roosevelt was right when he said, 'There is not in the world a more ignoble character than the mere money-getting American bent only on amassing a fortune and putting the money to basest and most selfish uses.' In the old days I used to tell them that in strong language, and they'd take it from me."

"What do the South Americans really think of us these days?" Norbourne asked as they finished their business in the al fresco lobby and walked along the verandah to the steps. He had already said good-bye to the doctor.

"They are having a change of heart about us—make no mistake about that—and much of it is due to Franklin Roosevelt's good neighbour policy. I know little and care little about United States politics. I never voted in my life—I had to be a British subject as long as my husband lived. But Franklin Roosevelt's foreign policy seems to me the only intelligent, as well as decent, one to pursue. And down here he's regarded as an '*hombre simpatico*,' and that counts for something with these emotional people."

"You'll be coming back to the States?" Norbourne said, holding out his hand to say good-bye.

"I'm coming back to die and to have a fling before I die." Tia's face lighted up with anticipation. "I want to stay right in the heart of New York in a one-room apartment and feast on bright lights and bustle, and go out in a whirl of good fun."

"But what will these wandering souls here do without you?"

She sighed reminiscently, shook her head dubiously, and then declared with sudden vigour: "I don't care. Some day I shall say, 'To hell with them; I need a vacation!' and I shall hop on a plane and fly home."

Norbourne raised her hand to his lips. "It was worth coming to South America just to meet you, Tia," he said.

"God bless you," she said. "I'll burn a candle for you."

He paused halfway down the stairs. "Coward expressed it too neatly in doggerel for me to try to thank you in inspired words. But that's the way we all feel—

> "*Of every place I've been to yet*
> *This I shall leave with most regret.*"

INTERLUDE

INTERLUDE

The City Left Unvisited

Mason, the Lima representative of the Bolivia tin concern, was on the plane on his way to La Paz. At Tacna he was to change planes. "You should be shot for not going to La Paz," he said in scornful disapproval of the glaring defect in Norbourne's itinerary. "It's the most picturesque place I know between Cristobal and Montevideo."

Norbourne apologized. He did regret he could not fit La Paz into his schedule. But his limited time and the red tape of the upset government made it impossible. "My consolation," he said, "in leaving some of the best places unvisited is that it serves as an excuse for a future trip." He had missed Quito, and Iquitos on the Peruvian Amazon, and Cuzco, the archæological capital of the continent. But these unseen cities would remain, like certain books he had not found time to read, promises of future delight.

Arriving at Tacna and seeing its amphitheatre of white sand dunes surrounding the landing field, Norbourne was again reminded of Biskra and the Sahara. On the glistening heights above the town one of the bloodiest battles between Chile and the Bolivian-Peruvian allies was fought in 1880 during the War of the Pacific. Chile had won the victory and dictated the peace terms at Ancon, by which she gained her most valuable nitrate fields and took the last strip of Bolivia's sea front. For half a century thereafter the dispute between Peru and Chile over the provinces of Tacna and Arica bored the world's newspaper readers. Not until May 1929 was a settlement effected by which

Peru got back her own Tacna, Chile kept Arica, and Bolivia continued to be deprived of a seaport.

Norbourne got out for a last chat with Mason. They had lemonades at the air station.

"You know, the highest regular air operation in the world lies right here between Tacna and the Bolivian capital," Mason said. "The aerodrome at La Paz is almost as high as Mont Blanc. You don't see the city until you're right on top of it. It sits in a sort of circular valley—almost like a huge pit sunk several hundred feet below the level of the *altiplano*. The view all along the motor road down to the city is superb. The car doesn't slow up for the Indians who may be in the road. The driver just honks his horn and the Indians scamper—looking back with a grin, and then they smile at each other, particularly at the ones who came the closest to being hit. It's a sort of game and they seem to love it." He paused and took a sip of his drink. "Incidentally, I've never seen such naturally cheerful Indians. The Indians in Peru are a stolid and wooden lot who don't seem responsive to anything. But in La Paz if you just catch the eye of an Indian walking along the street she smiles at you."

"Why do you say 'she'?"

"Because you don't see many men, except old ones. The younger ones were all sent off to the Chaco War—to be shot or die of thirst or dysentery. Most of them remain there through eternity, fertilizing the soil thereabout. These Indians haven't even the faintest idea as to what the war is all about."

"Have you?" said Norbourne, who had read the dispatches for three years.

"It's a silly, unnecessary mess all round. Bolivia claims that Paraguay simply walked in and occupied the outer regions of her territory, began to colonize it and plant military forts there. Paraguay says Bolivia's action was merely attempted robbery, that she thought Paraguay wouldn't dare offer armed resistance to her superior numbers and wealth. When matters reached a crisis of dispute in 1932, Bolivia saw a chance to gain a port on the Paraguay River and a free outlet to the Atlantic. Nine-tenths of Bolivia's population is ignorant Indian. They have no reason to be patriotic, God knows, and they're incapable of taking much military training. When they go from the cold plateau down into the humid green hell of the low Chaco, they suffer intensely and sometimes they die within a week merely from the effects of the climate. They say that six hundred out of a thousand of one regiment deliberately threw themselves under motor trucks to get out of their misery. I doubt if it's true. But last year I myself saw Indian women throw themselves on railway tracks to keep the trains loaded with their men from going out. And half of them with babies on their backs. It seemed as though about every other Indian woman was carrying a baby on her back—in a blanket, much like a North American papoose. Some of the women were mere girls, too, and what with the fortunes of war and the general uncertainties of life, you couldn't much blame them for not having treasured their virtue." Mason paused and took a big gulp of lemonade. "Incidentally, the most impressive feature of Bolivia's style of dress is the women's skirts. They wear very full, brightly-coloured skirts—dozens of them. It is said they never take them off, but just add a skirt when they see a nice bright one that takes their fancy. The under ones gradually wear or rot to pieces and eventually drop off. At any rate the general effect makes the street scenes of La Paz colourful, if not gay.

"La Paz, you know, is more like Spain than the other towns over here. It's a lot like the older parts of Madrid or Toledo. Tiled roofs, large patios. I paid a visit in one of those houses where you enter through a courtyard paved with cobblestones. Donkeys were standing there laden with produce which they had just brought in from the farm. The Indian women, who had accompanied the donkeys, were seated on the stairs, and they got up and took off their men's hats and bowed and said '*Buenas tardes*' when we passed—just as if they had been in rural Spain."

"It's ironic," said Norbourne, "that the capital should be called La Paz when a tenth of her man power has just been killed."

"This damned war has been going on since 1932, and has apparently ended in a draw. There are people who fear that even when a peace treaty is signed at last it won't amount to anything but a prolonged armistice. By May both the Paraguayans and Bolivians were exhausted and the armies had to admit a stalemate."

"That's one reason an Inter-American Peace Conference is brewing," Norbourne said, "to forestall these bloody boundary disputes."

"Well," said Mason, with a kind of hard emotion, "when you see the cute little devils carried about on the backs of the women you can't help wishing to God for something. Going along the street in La Paz on my last trip I passed an Indian woman with a year-old baby on her back. I winked at it and it caught my eye and smiled and stuck out a chubby little fist. By the woman's side walked another woman carrying a live turkey to market. The cynical reflection occurred to me that the turkey and the kid were being raised for much the same end. The turkey, with the acute instinct and perception of animals, seemed to sense its immediate fate, and looked sadly resigned. But the little human animal has had its instincts dulled and it didn't even guess and grinned as if the whole world was its friend—even the stinking yellow-bellies."

"What are they?"

"The half-blooded politicians who thought they might profit by a little war."

The second bell sounded. They shook hands, exchanged cheerios. Norbourne turned to board the Douglas for Antofagasta.

"In a few minutes you'll be across the border of Chile," Mason shouted. "You'll like the Chileans. All North Americans do."

IV

CHILE

"The North reflects the South; the Andes elsewhere are called the Rockies, but they are the same mountains."

Paul Morand

CHILE

Desert Wealth

At Arica the passengers disembarked to go through the simple formality of having their passports examined. This northernmost town in Chile lies pleasantly in a vale of oranges and olives under the legendary Morro where so much blood was shed in the fight for the stronghold in 1879 during the War of the Pacific.

"Foreign ships in the harbour made wagers on the number of hours or days it would take the Chileans to capture the fortress from the Peruvians," the bright young purser told Norbourne. "The Chileans threw away their rifles and ran up the hill. With their *corvos*—claw-like knives—they carved their way through walls of human flesh to victory in twenty minutes."

Under a tropical sky of an hour past noon the surrounding fringe of sandhills looked soft as champagne-coloured velveteen. Mauve and green shadows lay gentle and inviting as baskets of fresh figs. The cordial landscape was like a last refreshment offered a traveller before setting out into the desolation of the desert.

Just beyond Arica begin the sulphurous stretches of Tarapacá, a region more terribly destitute than the parched wastelands of Peru. From the high comfort of the aeroplane Norbourne gazed on the sterility. The Four Horsemen of the Apocalypse had apparently passed that way, cursing the land with pestilence. For hundreds of miles the panorama repeats itself with repellent monotony, without one spot of encouraging green, without even a wet ditch to cheer the spirit. The pampas, a thousand to eight thousand feet above the sea, are the colour of plague and death:

bilious yellow and the chalky white of soda sulphate. The flanks of the Andes to the east seem smeared with dried blood.

In this forbidding terrain lies the nitrate wealth of Chile. Here again—as in Peru's arid coast with its guano islands—Nature is compensatory. To make up for robbing northern Chile of every spring of growth, she has given her nitrates with all their commercial value. If the region were not rainless, the nitrates, like the guano, would have washed into the sea. Here potentially is enough explosive material to blow the human race to atoms. But like the slave-with-two-faces of the adage, the power of the nitrogen to deal death is offset by the power to give sustenance to life in the form of nitrate of soda. Doomed to perpetual sterility itself, the Chilean desert provides fertilizer for the gardens of the world. On his quest for gold in 1540, the great Valdivia was much concerned when his mistress Inez, the only lady who went conquering with the conquistadors, was often choked and blinded by the whitish dust their horses scuffled up from the grey *caliche*. But he had no notion that the annoying substance was the world's most remarkable stimulant to plant-growth, and that one day the country he was conquering would glean from this pock-marked region its chief item of income. Nor did he conceive the value of the rich copper deposits that lay on the western slopes of the Andes.

It was in 1809 that the nitrate was discovered. The deposits in the Tarapacá Desert were at first exploited by Peruvians, on a small scale; the products being sent to Callao for use in the manufacture of gunpowder. Only after 1830 did nitrate begin to figure in commerce as a fertilizer. The European countries which were gradually reaching great population density were the first to use this fertilizer scientifically. The discovery of deposits in 1867 at the head of the Quebrada, just behind what is now Antofagasta, led to the War of the Pacific. After the Chileans had won and taken control of the pampas, the English became interested and introduced the Shanks process, which greatly facilitated the removal of impurities from the nitrate as well as the crystallization which left the product in a form suitable for shipping as fertilizer.

In 1922 the Guggenheims entered the field and evolved a new process for the extraction of the salts. As a result of their mass handling of the compounds and their use of machinery, the cost has been reduced to one-fifth of that of old methods. This has made possible an intensive commercial competition with the existing synthetic processes and the maintenance of Chilean nitrate in the world's markets.

Chile has proved to be the chief mining country in South America, producing about two-thirds of the entire continent's output of metals and minerals. Possessing not only the most valuable deposits of nitrate of sodium on the face of the earth, she is also the world's second copper-producing nation, and she supplies ninety per cent of the world's consumption of iodine, a by-product of the nitrate works. For many years the considerable output of copper was produced from little better than holes in the ground, worked in the most primitive manner. The fact that most of the mines had been previously discovered and exploited to some extent by the Indians and Spaniards simplified the task of modern engineers in finding the ore. The famous El Teniente mine of the Braden Company was located in the eighteenth century by a fugitive Spanish officer, who bought his freedom with the proceeds of ore shipments. The Spanish colonists mined the high-grade ore intermittently until 1908 when the Guggenheim brothers purchased the interests. The original company was formed with a capital of $625,000 and equipment to exploit 250 tons of ore a day. From this modest beginning the capacity of the reduction plant has grown to 25,000 tons per day, and $50,000,000 has been invested.

The Braden Company is only one of the three huge Guggenheim establishments which dominate the copper industry in Chile. Americans are responsible for ninety per cent of Chile's copper output. In 1919 the owners turned toward the vast potential sources of the metal in the northern desert at Chuquicamata.

At these deposits, eighty miles from the sea and at 9,500 feet elevation, they have triumphed in large-scale engineering. The finest copper in the world is here extracted by the electrolytic process.

Twenty years ago Chile controlled the world's market for pure nitrogen. For half a century the export tax on nitrate paid for almost half the government's expenditures. During the World War, when Germany was blockaded from her nitrate supply, necessity forced her to produce synthetic nitrogen. The result was that Chile's production of 75 per cent of the world's nitrogenous fertilizers in 1916 dropped to a mere 10 per cent in 1932. In that year copper supplanted nitrogen as the nation's leading exploited commodity. But the world surplus of copper lowered the price to such an extent that the small profits from copper could do little to help the country's financial condition. Her export trade dropped from $278,000,000 in 1925 to $43,000,000 in 1932—an 85 per cent slump.

Chile suffered more acutely from the economic landslip in the world depression than any other important nation, because she was already having her own acute individual one before the world depression began. She is said to be staging a phenomenal comeback.

Leaning his head back against the seat's soft headrest, Norbourne began speculating about what these economic factors had meant to the Chileans whom, as Mason and a dozen others had told him, North Americans always liked. Had they lost some of their cultural heritage along with their economic independence? What kind of lives had they built for themselves out of these shifting sands of economic change? He was eager to meet and understand these people, their leaders, their women, their young men. In a land where lie millions of tons of material which can bring either devastation or fertility, the character of its people seems a matter of prime importance. He was glad there was little of archæological or historical interest that he would feel compelled to see in Santiago. In Peru, the country and the past had seemed more important than the people; in Chile, the people came first. Instead of doing a round of churches, museums, public buildings, he would endeavour to spend most of his time seeing the country through the eyes of its own countrymen.

Sword-shaped

Norbourne contemplated the map the purser had brought him along with a luncheon set out on a chromium tray that fitted conveniently on the arms of his seat. Shaped strangely like a wavy two-edged sword, Chile extends nearly three thousand miles from the tropics to the tip of Cape Horn, where the land breaks up into a glacial archipelago. Her narrow width compressed between the Andes and the Pacific averages only about a hundred miles. If laid across the face of Europe, the Chilean sword would reach from Portugal to Moscow, or it would leave a scar from Nova Scotia to lower California if slashed diagonally across the United States. "The warlike shape of Chile," Norbourne said to himself, "may be a symbolical warning that no one attacks her with impunity."

Like ancient Gaul, Chile is divided into three parts: the northern desert with the nitrates, copper and iodine; the dense southern forest with volcanoes and fiords and lakes "where it rains thirteen months of the year"; and the delightful central valley with its fertile soil and excellent climate and well-disciplined rainfall. The northern part is uninhabited except where people scratch out nitrate or copper from the soil and other people on the coast pack it into foreign ships. Semi-savage Indians wander about the wet southern woods. The central portion is the real Chile, where most of the people live. With an area of 290,000 square miles, about equal to the combined areas of Italy and Germany, Chile's entire population is no more than 4,500,000. The scant density of 15 persons a square mile is striking when compared with Italy's 400 or Bermuda's 1,400. With half the territory discounted as incapable of cultivation or habitation, experts estimate that Chile could easily support a population of thirty million.

Norbourne finished his luncheon, laid aside his map, and looked down on the dry, cracked land where the wealth lay on the surface or was embedded only a few feet in the *caliche*. *Oficinas*, abandoned or belching puffs of smoke, crouched sullenly on the arid pampas, their smoke-stacks rigid in the sun's fierce glare. From the plane the rail-tracks connecting the plants with the sea looked like telegraph wires that had dropped on the ground. Men appeared smaller than insects crossing a sun-hot concrete road.

"What are the men who work down there like?" Norbourne asked the purser, whose name he had learned was Jorge Elliott—one of those odd combinations of Spanish Christian names and British or German surnames that abound in Chile. Elliott's father was English, his mother Chilean. He was an intelligent youth with black eyes that glistened alertly behind thick-lensed, horn-rimmed spectacles. He had been educated at the naval academy, wrote verse and essays, and was acquainted with almost everybody worth knowing in the country.

"The *pampinos* are a stern and sturdy breed," he said, "hard of muscle, tough of heart. Many of them have the blood of Araucanian Indians in them—those fierce aborigines of Chile that were never really conquered by the conquistadors."

"Their characters harmonize with their work and the landscape," suggested Norbourne.

"Precisely. As labourers they are unsurpassed if you keep alcohol away from them. Drunk, they can be beasts. They can think up devilish vengeance, too. In 1922, when I was a little boy, they had a rebellion. My father was then the assistant manager of one of the nitrate *oficinas*, but he happened to be in Iquique. They captured four *carabineros*—mounted police—sent to calm them. They tied them each between two mules, sliced their middles open, lashed the mules into a fury and sent them galloping over the pampas with the men's entrails hanging out. Mr.

Jones, the English manager, was a close friend of our family—the kindest man in the world. I called him Uncle—often rode horseback on his foot. He didn't dream they would harm him. But can you imagine what those devils did to him? They crucified him between two flag poles, one flying the Chilean flag and the other the British. They dug out his eyes and stuck long candles in the sockets and lighted them. They joined hands and danced around the pole by the candlelight. I tell you, they're a savage lot when aroused."

"After all," Norbourne commented, "it takes a hardy folk to stand the strain of living among dynamite explosions, in a region deprived of everything necessary to human life."

"There's good in them, too," Elliott added, not without sympathy and admiration. "They have the defects of their qualities. They can stand terrific hardship. They're as strong as lions, and they ask nothing of any man. They'd fight for Chile to the last breath."

To the right, clinging to the hills to keep from sliding into the sea, was the port of Iquique from which the nitrates and iodine were shipped. A Grace Line passenger steamer, one of the famous fleet that plies between New York and South America's West Coast, was heading south to Valparaiso.

"In Iquique and Antofagasta," Elliott said, "everyone lives to get to Santiago."

"Just as in Santiago perhaps," Norbourne suggested, "—like Bogotá, Guayaquil and Lima—they live to get to Paris."

"Well, not quite so much so, I think," he replied with a show of patriotism. "Besides, many of our Chileans would prefer London, and"—with an ingratiating smile—"some of us would be most happy to see New York and Washington. You know the world calls us the 'Yankees of South America.' "

Yes, Norbourne knew that. "Why?" he asked.

"Because of our initiative," Elliott replied promptly, "our eagerness for the new. You will see it in the energy of the people. When Chile's independence was consolidated, we organized the first navy in South America and went to help Peru gain independence. We had the first technical school and the first National Musical Academy. Ours was the first Agricultural Society on the continent. Our best newspaper *El Mercurio* is the oldest in the Spanish language still published today—third in the world after the London *Morning Post* and *Times*. In 1850 the first railway in South America was built here—by one of your Yankee engineers. Not long after, State Railways were being constructed all over the country. For a long time we were one of the few countries to have such an institution. We were the first to establish a Stock Exchange; the first to organize and equip a well-trained army. We have the finest navy in South America. Today we employ German instructors in our army and English instructors in our navy. Incidentally and consequently, Germans and English gain thereby in prestige. While we have an especial admiration for the British—partly because so many of us have British blood in our veins—we are glad we caught the germ of Yankee efficiency. But I regret the skyscrapers of Santiago. They spoil the harmony of our low-roofed skyline. They were built to show off. Too much Yankee is not altogether good—do you think?"

"Just enough is much better," Norbourne agreed.

Pampino's End

In the late afternoon the thunderbird swooped to its evening's resting place. The passengers alighted in a cloud of desert dust and rode in the company bus several jolty miles. They passed the garrison headquarters where Chilean cavalrymen were dashing like Cossacks in exciting manœuvres and kicking up such a screen of yellow powder one could hardly see the ocean. At length they reached the asphalted streets of modern Antofagasta, as harsh and charmless and up-to-date as any new town in the Kansas prairie. A block off O'Higgins Street, the principal thoroughfare, the bus stopped at a Swiss chalet pension behind a wooden fence with a small garden plot and two window boxes of geraniums. The aviation company, unimpressed with the service offered in the local hotels for the price, had established its own inn for overnight passengers. The German proprictor, holding a sheet of paper with the list of guests—sent by radio—assigned them to their rooms as they entered. Dinner would be at seven. What did each take for breakfast? Breakfast would be sent to their rooms at six-thirty. The bus would pick them up at seven. All very neat, very simple, very relaxing. The beds were comfortable, the dinner excellent.

After dinner a local newspaper man, a few years out of school, came news-gathering. Norbourne turned the tables and asked him questions. The youth was homesick for the south where he had been born. "People come from the south to the north only when they have lost their money," he said. "My father ekes out a living here by giving piano lessons. . . . No, we are not happy. How can people be cheerful when they have to decorate their homes with paper flowers? We are serious, because the little green we look at is all artificial. I think I could make love to a shower of rain. The water we drink and wash in comes from San Pedro, a hundred and ninety miles away. They say that in the old days when a visitor asked for a glass of water in the *oficinas* they gave him champagne. It was cheaper. Water was the supreme luxury. . . . Yes, conditions here depress the people's characters. There is no great attraction in living. Yesterday a *pampino* killed himself in one of the local banks. He did it in characteristic manner. He asked the bankers for help in some difficulty—he owed them money. They refused. 'You must pay a little bit now,'' they said. The *pampino* had a sense of humour. 'Very well,' he said. He went away and came back. 'I will pay you all,' he said. 'You can scramble for the bits.' He stuck a shell of dynamite in his mouth, and struck a match to it."

The next day, as if to get over the unlovely region as quickly as possible, the Douglas did not stop until it reached Ovalle in the luxuriant vale of Chile, where rain fell in season. Here fruit and honey abounded, and sheep fattened on green hillsides. The passengers' eyes feasted gratefully once more on verdure.

At ten minutes past one the purser announced the first sight of Aconcagua, where the Andes reach their climax in a heaven-kissing peak more than twenty-three thousand feet high, eternally immaculate with snow. Within half an hour the thunderbird had landed at Santiago.

Happy Landing

The sparkling new airport at Santiago bespoke energy and that "full of future" aspect. Its chromium and its brasses shone modernistically. Its spaciousness hinted at the expansion of air traffic the coming years would bring. There was a smartness, an alertness in the clerks and officials, a pleasant, unflurried radiation of efficiency and good humour, a kind of spontaneous international intimacy that made Norbourne feel as much at home as if he had been set down in Baltimore or Louisville. He felt far less a stranger here than he did on arriving at the docks of Southampton. The Chileans put him immediately at his ease.

After Rio de Janeiro, Santiago de Chile is famed for the most thrilling natural setting of any city in the Western World. In his first glimpse of the capital from the ground, Norbourne's eyes turned straightway to the icy heights of the Andes that glistened like a wall of fretted crystal against the azure sky. "The incomparable Rio hasn't that," Elliott said, as the passengers got into the bus.

The car turned into the Alameda, the Avenida de las Delicias, which extends for almost three straight miles, slicing the city into halves as if it were a piece of ripe fruit. The unusually broad boulevard with its façades of clubs, public buildings and the town houses of the wealthy is divided into three parts. Four rows of French poplars troop in parade marking off the sections. The wide middle portion with its flower beds, grass plots and palm trees, is reserved for pedestrians. Here children were playing in the shadows of statues of Chile's national heroes.

"There," said Elliott, indicating the marbles and bronzes, "the infants get their first lessons in history and patriotism. We call it our open air Hall of Fame."

"I am sorry it is not the blossoming season of the Japanese plum trees," he added. "Then our Alameda is truly an avenue of delight."

Even though the Hotel Crillon faced a narrow business street and had no view and did not furnish soup, Norbourne found it the most pleasing city hotel on the West Coast. From the dull gold hangings in his room and the Circassian walnut furniture to the stationery and the hall carpets, everything was in the best of taste. In the dining room, although the luncheon hour was just over, they served Norbourne and another man who had been on the plane—Alden Swift, vice-president of the packing company. The string quartet in the eighteenth-century gallery continued to play for the two of them until the dessert. The cuisine was excellent, the vegetables perfectly cooked, the little oysters marvels of flavour and seasoning. They ordered a bottle of the best dry white wine, Undurraga, a beautiful, clear, pale amber. A quart cost forty cents.

"Imagine!" said Mr. Swift. "And where outside of France or Italy can you find better? Certainly there's nothing in this hemisphere that can touch it."

As far as his experience went, Norbourne agreed heartily.

The head waiter presented them with a little booklet on Chilean wines and was delighted to answer any questions.

The wines of Chile are made from choice varieties of grapes imported from the Bordeaux region in France. In the manufacture of red wines the predominant varieties are Cabernet, Merlot, and Cot. In that of white wine, Muscatel and Semillon are favourites. The high standard of Chilean wines is in no small measure due to the earnest efforts of the government to improve the varieties of grapes cultivated and to restrict them to the choicest types. A Board of Control supervises all exports and permits only the highest quality of wines to be shipped abroad.

Within a decade after the founding of Santiago (1541), several good-sized vineyards flourished around the city. To no soil or climate in the New World did the grape respond so joyously. The first export of wines was made in 1857, when small quantities were shipped to the countries along the Pacific coast. In 1930 there were 209,950 acres of vines under active cultivation in Chile. The capital invested in the industry is about $135,000,000, and it furnishes employment to some 200,000 men.

Norbourne was considerably surprised to learn that almost 80 per cent of the exported Chilean wines go to Europe. Curiously enough, for many years Belgium has been by far Chile's best customer, with Germany ranking second. Even more strangely, France ranks third, and Holland fourth. Out of the million and a half gallons exported in 1930, Belgium took about half the output.

Mr. Swift decided to order four dozen cases for his private cellar. "There's a tidy fortune to be made in the United States by importing Chilean wines," he said, holding his wine glass up to let the light shine through the liquid. "In fact," he went on, "there are all sorts of opportunities for new business connexions with South America now that the aeroplane has made it accessible. The saving of time and money to a business man is incalculable. Take my immediate case. This is a particularly busy season with us in Chicago. I ought not to be away. But I'm on an emergency flight, a sad mission; our Argentine manager was killed in a motor accident last week. We have to decide on his successor. Four years ago it would have taken me six weeks to get to Buenos Aires and return by the fastest steamers. Five days ago I was in Chicago. Tomorrow I shall be in Buenos Aires. Neat, isn't it?"

They had become so absorbed in their talk that they had forgotten to order dessert. The waiter made a suggestion. It came—a chocolate soufflé filled with a fruit ice cream, a poem of a concoction, sufficient for four portions. "In Chicago," Swift said, "this dish would cost not less than two dollars." In Santiago it cost fourteen cents.

Norbourne went up to his room for a brief siesta before he started out to present his letters of introduction. The air was filled with a heavenly music. In the next apartment Thibaud, the French violinist, and Moiseiwitsch, the Russian pianist, were practising for their joint concert that evening. Lying on the bed and listening, Norbourne felt very content with Santiago. The first hours augured well for a happy stay. He dropped off to sleep to the accompaniment of Debussy's *La Cathédrale Engloutie*.

Santa Lucia

Late in the afternoon Norbourne went for a drive with a young man named Alberto Fox, a blonde, green-eyed Chilean, who smiled readily.

"But you're English," Norbourne said to him.

"No. Chilean," he insisted, pleasantly. He spoke with an English public school inflection. It was like a Chinese laundryman denying being Chinese, because he lived in Yonkers. "My grandfather was English and he married a Chilean, so my father was half Chilean. My father did the unconventional thing by marrying a school teacher tourist from Bristol."

"Then you are three-fourths English."

"In a sense," he admitted. "But I'm Chilean. I have never been outside Chile."

"But your accent?" Norbourne protested.

"I went to an English school here. All the masters are English and the methods. I remember I used to stuff the seat of my trousers with leaves to take the sting off the canings when I was caught pinching apples. They told me that was done in England."

The streets presented the most thoroughly civilized appearance Norbourne had seen in Latin America. Chile was impressively a white man's country. There wasn't an Indian anywhere, though some of the lower classes had an Indian cast to their features. There wasn't a sign of a Negro or even negroid lips or hair in any of the passers-by.

"No Negroes whatsoever?" Norbourne asked.

"None."

"But there were black slaves?"

"Very few. In the days of slavery the Chileans were too poor to buy them. Gentlemen sometimes kept them as curiosities or for swank, as eighteenth-century English ladies employed little black boys to carry their fans. But the richest Chilean could rarely afford more than three or four. Besides, owning Negro slaves proved unprofitable. The climate didn't suit them. They died off. Consequently our blood is remarkably pure, in that it's all Caucasian, except for the Araucanian in some of the *rotos*."

Everywhere new buildings were going up, department stores, government offices, schools, private dwellings. Santiago certainly gave no evidence of suffering from a depression.

"How are you able to do all this in hard times?" Norbourne asked, indicating the construction work.

"A clever inspiration of the Minister of Finance. All buildings erected in the last two years are guaranteed tax free for ten years. By this means the unemployment situation is relieved, better housing conditions result, and the city's appearance is improved."

Fox was genuinely distressed that Norbourne was staying in Chile so short a time. "To miss Valparaiso and Viña del Mar, which attracts international society folk to its casino—well, that is bad enough," he said. "But to miss the lake district in the south, a combination of Switzerland and Norway with superlative fishing and shooting—that is to be deplored." He told him about the thermal springs with which Chile is lavishly endowed, where one can be cured of asthma, chronic bronchitis, rheumatic aches, skin diseases, digestive disorders, spasms and twitches in spas built at the feet of volcanoes in the midst of gorgeous woodland scenery. Norbourne promised to come back for his rheumatic old age, if not before.

They drove around the Plaza with its ochre-coloured cathedral and ancient arcades of picturesque shops. The planting was lavish with palms and mimosa. This was still Spain, but more energetic and vivacious. Then they drove away from the architecture of Spain into residential sections, which look like bits of Bavaria and English suburban towns.

"Yes, the patio is going out of fashion," said Fox. "And our patriarchs no longer have all their son's families living under the parental roof. One old-fashioned hidalgo has compromised by building a nine-story apartment house and giving a whole floor to each son's family."

Winding back into the Alameda, they crossed one of the iron bridges spanning a canal of the little Mapacho River, which was tearing through the capital with the impetuosity of an Araucanian on the warpath, and arrived at the base of Santa Lucia.

Santa Lucia is a mass of rugged basaltic rock rising precipitously four hundred feet out of the heart of the city, much like the Acropolis at Athens. "It was here in 1540," said Fox, as they left the car and started to climb the twisting paths, "that Valdivia and his hundred and fifty soldiers built the first fort in Chile to protect themselves from the attacks of the Indians. At its feet he founded Santiago, where adventurers built their primitive houses of dried mud bricks and straw. The conquerors of Chile confronted a tough and profitless proposition. There was no advanced civilization as in Peru, no temples with ornaments of gold to loot. And although the Araucanians were poor, unlettered and ignorant of war tactics, they were the hardiest fighters on the entire continent. Valdivia came to the most miserable end of all the heroes. To intimidate the Indians he once sent four hundred Araucanian prisoners home minus their noses and right arms. The Indians paid him in kind when they later captured him in battle. Using sharpened seashells for knives, they cut off his arms, roasted them, and devoured them before his eyes."

Norbourne and Fox went up and down winding stairs cut in the stones. They traversed curving terraces with balustrades, domes, kiosks and pavilions. They made discoveries of basins of blooming water lilies, of sudden rustic bridges, of beds of violets, iris and narcissus blooming around trickling fountains, and of ambushed benches behind fern draperies. "From 1820 to 1872," Fox said, as they paused for a breather, "this hill was used as a graveyard for the destitute, the criminals, the Jews and the Protestants. A philanthropist named Vicuaña MacKenna conceived the idea of transforming it into a park and had the remains of the outcasts conveyed to the public burying ground. Now Santa Lucia is the favourite rendezvous for lovers, season in, season out, day or night."

Wherever they turned, on this level or that, within a few paces they ran into shadowy grottos where rapt couples, as motionless as statues, sat silent, sultry-eyed, in a sort of ecstatic perplexity. On the open terraces, which caught the flashes of the snow's reflection as the flames of the setting sun made the Andes glow like white hot copper, students from the university paced back and forth with book in hand, their brows knitted in ostentatious concentration. Norbourne and Fox exchanged an understanding smile. Like ancient Christian fathers deliberately practising self-control, with temptation to the right of them and to the left, the students sternly kept their eyes away from the grottos and the lovers' nooks. They peered only at the wisdom of the printed pages and the light on the mountain tops.

Norbourne and his companion paused on a balcony hanging out in space and looked down on the city of three-quarters of a million souls—the fourth largest on the continent. At the far end of the town rose the conical Cerro San Cristobal, twice as high as Santa Lucia. The summit, reached by a funicular, was surmounted by an heroic statue of the Virgin.

"A statue of Aphrodite should preside here," Norbourne suggested.

As the winter sun sank lower, a violet haze suffused the ancient lace-like belfries and commonplace modern skyscrapers. The shadows swallowed up the eastern ramparts until there was only one thin line of white flame flickering along the rim of the Cordilleras. Then the purple city began to twinkle, as if stars came out of the ground instead of the sky. Yankee hydro-electric engineers had metamorphosed the cascades of melted snow into illumination.

Club Hipico

A brown-skinned Chilean gentleman of Italian descent and North American manners took Norbourne to the races on Sunday afternoon. He was the local head of an American exporting concern, dynamic, business-like, voluble. In response to Norbourne's question as they passed a big-business Yankee name spelled out on a skyscraper in unlighted bulbs, the gentleman threw up his large hands in a robust Latin gesture. "My God!" he moaned in a deep bass. "The kind of people the Americans used to send down here thirty years ago!"

"As bad as that?"

"The worst of all—all except those damned French." He puckered his thick lips in distaste. Then he smiled, dismissing the past. "But now it's a different story. The United States is sending a high class of business representatives. The Americans are getting more popular and the English are losing their influence." It was what Norbourne had heard in Peru. "The Englishmen who come out to Chile are not the equal of those of previous decades."

"Our business relations are quite cordial?" Norbourne asked the question in the form of a declaration.

"Quite, and improving all the time. In the five year period between 1928 and 1933 Chile bought about as much from the United States as she did from England and Germany combined. And that, mind you, even though since 1932 England has been our best customer."

"Tell me frankly—to what particularly do you attribute whatever dislike Chileans may have for us?"

"It goes back to the '*Baltimore*' incident, in 1891, in the revolution against President Balmaceda. (Harrison was your President.) In a brothel fight at Valparaiso an American sailor was killed by some Chileans. The *Baltimore* forced a sub-officer of one of our ships in the bay to lower the Chilean flag in apology. The commander in chagrin afterwards committed suicide. We nearly went to war with you over that. Chile has never quite forgotten that incident. And as recently as half a dozen years ago in Valparaiso some of your sailors stripped and bathed in a fountain in the plaza and the same gang knocked a girl of good family off the pavement and broke her arm."

"That latter was an accident surely."

"No doubt, but it showed a sort of high-handed contempt. The English and German and Japanese sailors are models of decorum when they go ashore. I must say, however, that during the last three years there has been a marked change in the attitude of your navy. But formerly when the Americans landed there was always likely to be a row."

"Are you prone to judge the United States by its worst examples instead of its best?"

"Very likely. Don't most nations do that? But another thing: With the Yankees owning ninety per cent of the copper output, and virtually all the nitrates, and a large proportion of our public services, well, don't you think it reasonable that we should harbour a modicum of resentment? You know how you yourself would feel if U.S. Steel and Standard Oil were owned, say, by German interests. Of course, we fully realize that we could not have made much use of our resources without your capital and your engineers. The fact that we had to use your money and your skill makes us love you no more. But frankly, our dislike is not deep-rooted. We are really brothers under the skin."

A limousine full of beautiful young ladies with a white-coiffed chaperon passed. The girls were very attractive and looked as if they had a proper sense of their own value, but were a bit bored by having to live up to it. "With all your modern improvements and advanced social laws, you haven't become very modern in your attitude towards women here yet, have you?" Norbourne said.

The gentleman shrugged, twisted his lips speculatively to the side. "We are changing," he said. "I daresay it will work out. Remember, our women didn't begin to wear hats until twenty years ago. When a woman throws off a mantilla and puts on a hat—well, a change comes over her and the boys are quick to notice it."

"You don't trust your girls?"

"We can trust them right enough. It's our sons we don't trust. We remember ourselves," he admitted frankly, and a chuckle rumbled in his throat. "The old way of getting the parents' consent for marriage worked pretty well, though. My son got married last year without my consent and came howling to me to get him divorced."

"But there's no divorce in Chile," protested Norbourne.

"We call it 'annulled,' " the gentleman said significantly, arching his thick brows. "You pay the church and swear to whatever is necessary. We'll have regular divorces soon. Then the courts will get the money."

In the front gardens before the entrance of the Club Hipico, which rose four stories tall, enormous braziers of loose woven iron basket work stood breast-high on filigreed iron legs and glowed with red-hot coals. Like the pious pausing within a cathedral's entrance before the holy water basin, devotees of the track stopped to warm their hands at the brazier fire. The two spots of fire cheered the wintry atmosphere. It was not freezing cold—the thermometer in Santiago never goes to freezing except on the coldest midnights—but it was brisk, like an English late October faintly touched with mist. Just in front of Norbourne and his companion a lady in sables with a corsage of violets made a sort of prolonged curtsey to the outdoor fire. In their turn Norbourne and his host stuck out their palms to the coals. Putting their gloves on again they went through the *pari-mutuel* rooms under the grandstand and out onto the lawn before the tiers of seats.

Norbourne stopped still and gazed. Before him lay the world's most beautiful race course. The satin smooth ribbon of track, the white fences, the oval acres of verdure that looked like a green lake with islands of winter flowers, were backed by the stupendous panorama of the Andes, snow-drenched, sublime. Those thrilling heights were surely the grandstand of the gods. On the vantage point of the mountain tops they had set up their white lacquer pavilions to watch the sport of kings and men.

Norbourne's host nudged him out of his naïve ecstasy with the small end of his field glasses and they moved on. On the marble terrace at the foot of the grandstand other basket braziers glowed with live coals. But these were only knee high. These were for the lower extremities as the ones at the entrance had been for the hands and the face. "At first you warm your hands to handle your betting money more easily, then you warm your cold feet after heavy losses." Smartly dressed women sat in a circle around the braziers like gipsies about a camp fire and pulled up their tight skirts an inch or so, holding their shapely legs to the rosy glow and twisting the Parisian shoes on their small high-arched Spanish feet this way and that.

Instead of sitting, Norbourne and his host circulated among the crowd in the paddock, in the *pari-mutuel* rooms, at the fence. Norbourne was introduced to race-horse owners, diplomats, copper miners, a great number of charming ladies, a radical politician parading about in a spectacular pearl grey Texas Stetson hat. The Chileans of English extraction wore tweeds, the Spanish Chileans wore conventional black coats and striped grey trousers. Norbourne met two Philadelphians who had flown down for the salmon fishing, bringing their equipment with them, rubber boats and all. He met three New Yorkers who had come for the shooting. "No finer shooting or fishing in the world," one maintained. "A party of ten shot 1,300 pigeons in one day, and only twenty minutes from Santiago."

The horses paraded. The throng consulted their programmes, exchanged staccato comments, placed bets. Everyone, everything was full of high spirits. The mountains, the braziers, the flowers perfuming the air, the straining silken-shirted jockeys, the horses, the barmen, the spectators—all took joy in their individual functions. The races themselves were just like other races, the betting no different. The conversation was race track conversation—light, vivacious, desultory, occasionally excited, occasionally professional.

During the intermissions the men alternated between the horses and the ladies. In the café they would decide who paid for the whiskies and sodas by a local game of guessing the number of matches concealed in each other's fists. The ladies in this group were all the wives of the men—four were Chilean, one a Canadian. Only one of the women—the one sitting by Norbourne—had black hair. She had married an American and now lived in New York.

"My wife's family was very doubtful about my taking their daughter to the States," her husband said. "They were particularly afraid of the custard pies. They had seen movies of the pie-throwing era and for ever after judged United States manners accordingly. In their early letters they would sclicitously inquire if she had been struck by any of those pies hurtling through the air."

"Now," the wife added, "they beg me not to jump into those palatial swimming pools with my best dress on as some of the movie stars do."

"The average Chilean has the impression that the Yankee home is merely a passage between one divorce and the other," said a bright-eyed, copper-haired girl with piquant features and fascinating eyebrows that twisted provocatively. "They base their conception on the stories of Hollywood. Amanda Labarca, our foremost feminist, has told them in lectures that there is as much difference between the Hollywood life and that of the average North American family as there is between an artificial flower and a field verbena. But it's hard to refute the evidence of the newspapers and the films."

"Do you know," another girl spoke up, "I think it's extremely interesting that today thousands of South Americans are studying English just to be able to understand the talkies. At first they were indignant at the impudence in sending them English-speaking movies, even though you superscribed Spanish titles. But now they see the advantage—and many use the talkies as an inexpensive and amusing way of improving the English they studied at school."

Norbourne was very much interested in the women of Chile. In spirit and even in appearance they seemed far more akin to London or New York girls than to those of Madrid or Havana. Yet they had a distinction all their own. They held their heads high and they looked one frankly in the eye. Norbourne could not agree with Waldo Frank's judgment of the high-bred Chilean woman as a "fragile bloom that is almost subhuman, having the perfection of the simpler static orders . . ." They have the longest legs and the straightest backs, as well as the most piquant features and the most natural chic of any Latin-American women he saw. As the Chilean man seems less romantic and less sentimental than the run of Latins, Norbourne found the women the least clinging-vine in attitude. But there is a sort of gentle challenge in their approach, nicely moulded chins and a come-hither in their eyes that is very stimulating—a touch of a mountain winter resort about them—sun on snow—that makes a man lift his head. Notwithstanding the scrupulosity of their upbringing, they can talk a man's language better than any other Latin American women. And they have themselves under the smoothest control. If they should stray it would not be because they had been seduced by a man's blandishments.

They all got up and went to place bets. Earlier in the afternoon Norbourne had met a British Chilean who was the owner of Milenko, the English stallion which had won the Cambridgeshire and the Jockey Club stakes. For some reason Milenko had not taken to the atmosphere in Argentina and had refused to function, so he had been sold cheap to Chile, where he liked the atmosphere so well that he had sired twenty-five fine colts at increasing stud fees. Milenko's filly, Mme de Polignac, was running in the last race. "You might risk your money at about 36 to 1," this man had told Norbourne. "I own her. She is better than they suspect."

During the afternoon Norbourne had lost on four other races. And now he had a premonition he was going to win it back on Milenko's dark-horse daughter. The space before the betting counters was so crowded he couldn't worm his way through. People stood with banknotes in hand, thrusting over the shoulders of the front line, begging the officials to take their money. Norbourne all but jumped up and down in his eagerness. But the bell sounded, the remaining tickets were scratched, and he still held his unbet pesos. To the crowd's amazement Mme de Polignac won by a full neck, and Norbourne had lost the equivalent of one hundred and seventy-five American dollars by lingering too long in analysis of Chilean women.

When the last race was over, Norbourne was in no hurry to leave. He hovered close to the fence looking at those white pavilions of the gods. The evening was covering them with silver cloth like the grey dust-sheets attendants spread over the plush theatre chairs when the play is over.

Young Chile

Elliott, who had returned from another flight to Antofagasta, invited Norbourne to tea to meet a cross-section of young Chile. It was to be composed of three friends of his who were planning to ski over the Andes into Argentina. Such a thing had never been attempted before. While waiting for him in the hotel lobby, Norbourne watched other Santiagoans arriving for tea at the Crillon. They were a remarkably charming set to look at, these Chileans, alert, poised, well-groomed. "Cream of the people" was the original meaning of the Indian word "Chile," he had been told. He doubted the derivation, but it served very neatly, he thought.

All the tea tables were taken by the time Elliott arrived, breathless, five minutes late. He had come from a conference where he had been "enjoying a lecture on the influence of relativity on medicine."

"Shall we walk?" he said. "The boys have already gone to secure a table. Chileans have taken so to English afternoon tea that sometimes you can't get a seat. This afternoon we've chosen one of the less fashionable places, frequented mostly by business men, where there is no music, no temptation to flirt with the pretty girls. We can talk better."

"But you're English," Notbourne said to Buchanan, the leader of the enterprise, as he was introduced to three young men seated about a large round table in a corner of the crowded upstairs tea shop.

"No, Chilean. I've never been out of Chile." He smiled broadly, revealing a more perfect set of even white teeth than any Englishman ever possessed. He was a fresh-coloured, muscular young man of medium height. He had a quick, engaging manner, and radiated exuberant health and good humour. The thought flashed through Norbourne's mind: When British men and Chilean women get together the result is indeed remarkably pleasing—he has the well-bred assurance of the British and the spontaneous charm of the Latin.

" His uncle is head of the Buchanan clan in Scotland," Jorge interpolated, "and worth a cool million pounds. John's too proud to be friendly with the old boy, afraid he'll think he's after his money. All he's ever got out of him is a mountain-climbing outfit. He saw John's picture in a London paper with a write-up about his being the champion alpinist in South America and the only Chilean invited to join the twelve Italian climbers Mussolini sent over. John was the first to climb the Cerro Plomo—in 1934. Doubtless you read——"

"Oh, let up," said Buchanan embarrassed. "With all his versatile talents, we think Elliott is best cut out for a publicity agent. He winds up and forgets to turn himself off."

"My tongue started wagging the hour I was born and it's never ceased," Elliott admitted unabashed, and turned to the waiter to order tea. "Let me recommend some palm honey with English muffins."

The second young man was a pale-faced German born in Chile, who had gone back to Germany because of some inheritance. He had got so homesick for Chile that he had recently returned to make his permanent home there and to pursue his profession of scientific agriculture.

The third young man, named Errazuris, was a slender Spanish Chilean, six feet two, with finely chiselled features, melancholy dark eyes, a deep musical voice. He spoke English with a cultured, cosmopolitan accent. His ancestry was Basque on both sides. He would have been known instantly for an aristocrat in Shanghai or Timbuctu. Since the age of five he had lived out of Chile—being educated in Switzerland and spending vacations with his family in Italy and France. He had entered Oxford when the depression called the family home to look after properties. The young man was not particularly pleased at being home. He diverted himself with mountain climbing and skiing. Instead of conversing, he merely smiled politely or answered questions amiably.

"Now that you are at home what are you going to do—besides skiing?" Norbourne asked.

"I hardly know." Errazuris looked troubled. "I hope to become interested in agriculture."

"His people own—how many tens of thousands of acres?" said Jorge briskly.

"I don't really know——" He lit a cigarette. "Too many, I'm sure."

"Why, too many?"

He smiled vaguely and shrugged. The attitude might have signified anything—boredom, distaste for responsibility, the fact that the property was mortgaged, or even a feeling that the bulk of the land should be divided among the peasants. Whatever it indicated, Norbourne felt it signified the end of the gala days of Chile's landed gentry when the agricultural wealth of the country belonged to a few great families, as in eighteenth-century England.

"That's the trouble in Chile," Elliott said, as if following Norbourne's thought, " 'absenteeism.' For years on end many of our aristocrats live in France—draining money out of the country. Some never return at all. This fellow's uncle, a Chilean, who maintains a palace in Buenos Aires and is considered the richest man in Argentina, likewise lives abroad and his palace stays boarded up for years on a stretch."

"You know," Buchanan said, "the peasants do not own land here. They are either tenants or labourers. The people have always been divided into two distinct classes: those who possess wealth and those who do not. The ancestral overlords control the vast wealth which the *rotos* slavishly work to produce. Although forty-two per cent of our people get their living from the land, four-fifths of Chile is owned by less than three thousand people. A property is hardly considered a property unless it has about a hundred thousand acres."

"What are a peon's wages?" Norbourne asked.

"In American money," Elliott answered, "from fifteen to thirty cents a day and some beans or chick-peas. The overseers like to keep the peons in debt so that legally they can't throw up their jobs and go somewhere else. Peruvian estate owners control their Indian workers with coca leaves. We manage ours with alcohol. Some overseers encourage them to drink, sell them liquor from the estate's canteen, and after paying them their wages, they often get it all back the same Saturday evening. But when the *roto* is sober, Monday to Saturday, he makes an unbeatable worker."

"The Chilean *roto* is the most ambitionless man in the world," said the German. "He doesn't even demand a hut. He prefers to sleep out in the open fields under the stars. For all his physical prowess, he lacks initiative and vision."

"But as a philosopher, you must admit, he is invulnerable. By choosing to be content at the bottom of the ladder, fortune can play him no bad tricks."

"It is strange," said the German, "that the Chilean gentry spend as little time as possible in the country. To most of them it is only a retreat for picnics and for horseback and not for a moment to be taken seriously. We Germans could teach the Chileans a lot about their land, the profit and the love to be derived from it."

"I don't doubt it," said Errazuris, as the waiter poured steaming tea into the extra large teacups.

"Though Chile is still aristocratic in principle and feeling, aren't the aristocrats beginning to lose their absolute control?" Norbourne suggested.

"Yes, the middle class is making itself felt politically," Elliott affirmed. "Socially the aristocracy still dominates. It is rather sad in some ways to see the aristocracy breaking up here, as it is all over the world. Many of our fine town houses have been sold. Nearly all of them are mortgaged."

Errazuris raised one eyebrow slightly, half-questioning. "Elliott knows far more about my country than I do," he said.

"But you German and Spanish and English, you all seem so harmonious in national spirit here," Norbourne observed.

"Chile as a melting pot retains its own distinctive flavour," Elliott replied promptly. "Despite the vast extension of territory and the influx of foreign immigration Chile is impressively homogeneous and patriotic." His friends smiled indulgently when he used fine phrases. He had won prizes for oratory at school. "From aristocrat to *roto*, from Chilean-born, flaxen-haired Teuton to swarthy half-blooded Araucanian, we are ardently national in sentiment."

"But Chile needs and wants more fresh blood," Buchanan said. "With a territory as large as Italy and Germany combined, we have a population about half that of London."

"But you are encouraging immigration," Norbourne said to the German, who had spoken little.

"Yes, the *Caja de Colonización* is a state institution for that sole purpose. The government has granted it twenty million pesos for ten years. It provides fenced-in forty-acre farms of arable land, a house and a barn, all ready for occupation at a reasonable cost—ten per cent cash down and it allows thirty-three years for the payment of the remainder. All of it is good land in healthy situations. The climate is enough like Germany to make the immigrants thrive. There are about 30,000 Germans in Chile. In the last decade 10,000 have been attracted to southern Chile. Down there young Indians are now learning German instead of Spanish."

Little pots of palm honey were brought in with the muffins.

Norbourne turned to Buchanan to ask about the details of their forthcoming adventure, skiing over the Cordilleras into Argentina. The leader was confident, refusing to admit the chances against them. The German foresaw all the possible mishaps. Errazuris's attitude was cooly fatalistic. If he was to be killed, he wouldn't have to die later ; if he wasn't killed, his death would be in the future. They were to make the start within a fortnight —on August fourteenth. They would be no less than seven days in the ice and snow, *if* all went well.

Norbourne sat back and contemplated the young adventurers, discussing over tea and buttered muffins a flirtation with death as casually as an assignation with a pretty girl. If they failed, well, they would have had a thrilling time. If they succeeded, well, they would have made history. That was their composite attitude. Norbourne felt the proud sense of security they had in being Chilean—a feeling that admitted certain admirable qualities in others. It was not a boastful pride. It was a fluid, adaptable sense of value, with a relish of humour and without jealousy, bigotry, or a trace of sycophancy. He believed that young North Americans would find these vari-blooded fellows congenial. He admired and wished great happiness for these young Chileans.

Intermission

Norbourne went to Moiseiwitsch's farewell concert at the Teatro Municipal. According to his custom, the pianist played in half shadow, a single diffused light from the top of the stage falling on the keyboard. The audience sat in complete darkness. Moiseiwitsch played as if he were alone, making music for himself out of some private soul compulsion. The audience was impressively dignified, sympathetic. The applause was generous, appreciative, but with no extra Latin exuberance, no shouting claque. In the lighted foyer during the intermission there was little or no gaping at gowns and jewels. The women were well-dressed, assured, very natural, nothing extreme. The Santiagoans went to a concert as intelligent music lovers, not as society mannequins.

Around a white-enamelled petrol-burning radiator in the lobby Norbourne met Winthrop Scott, American Chargé d'Affaires, and his Georgian wife, who was toasting her toes. Both were completely in love with Chile. "An average American can be at home here in two months," he summed it up in a nutshell. "And I don't know another foreign city in the world where that is true. These Chileans are a two-fisted, he-man, pleasure-loving, materialistic people. They win their wars and they shoot square. They love horse races, and they are the best sportsmen in Latin America. They are sharp and clever. Worse hit by the depression than any people in the world, because the bottom dropped out of their nitrate business even before the beginning of the depression, they've staged an amazing come-back."

"Yes," Norbourne said, "tell me how they did it. I see evidences of recovery everywhere."

"The Minister of Finance, Gustavo Ross, is the man who is largely responsible for setting the country back on its feet. He's done a remarkable work. You see, Chile could not wait for a general world trade recovery. She slashed government expenditures and imposed new tax levies on excess profits, volume of business, transfer of property, bachelors. She went in heavily for relief work. Then fortuitously gold came to the country's assistance. The increase in the world's price made it profitable to exploit gold deposits that heretofore could not be worked at a profit. The depreciated value of the *peso* made the work remunerative. The government fostered the enterprise as an unemployment measure. In two years, from 1932 to 1934, the number of pounds produced rose from 2,600 to 16,000. Over 21,000 men were employed in gold recovery at the end of 1934, when the annual output reached seven million dollars in gold. Ross is considered the ablest financier on the continent. You should meet him."

Norbourne wanted very much to meet the Minister of Finance, so the American Embassy arranged an interview.

Interview

Norbourne called on Señor Ross at noon in his office high up in one of the new skyscrapers. He knew little about the financier except that he was a conservative, that he belonged to the aristocracy and that he was supposed to be markedly pro-British. Jewish blood was said to mingle with the Scotch and Spanish in his veins. In a private room they sat at a small desk facing each other.

Señor Ross was a smallish, strongly built, rather handsome man. His black eyes were coolly appraising. His manner, his gesture, his smile were deliberate, energy-conserving, like those of men whose brain must run continually at full power.

They exchanged brief pleasantries, and Norbourne, accepting a cigarette, commented on the impressive vitality of Chile as compared with the other West Coast republics. Then he began to ask questions as they occurred to him.

Norbourne: The first thing that struck me here was the great building activity. Would you tell me about your policy of exempting construction from taxation?

Señor Ross: The law exempting all new buildings from taxation for ten years started before the end of 1935 was passed about two years ago. Its effects have been good for two years, but the law will not be prolonged as the effect for a longer period would prove harmful. The tendency now is to concentrate too much on building activities, and besides, too many workmen left their farms to come to the bigger cities. They must go back to the farms.

Norbourne: I am much impressed with the general order and prosperity in the country. How have you accomplished this, Mr. Minister, in face of the collapse of the nitrate industry which previously supplied such an important part of Chile's revenues?

Señor Ross: It is not correct to say that Chile is prosperous. Actually there is a great deal of poverty in the country, although there is no real unemployment problem. As to the nitrate revenues, we have now discounted them and our budget is balanced entirely without this source. They have been set aside for payment on the foreign bonds.

Norbourne: Chile appears to be about the only country in the world without an unemployment problem. How is this possible?

Señor Ross: In the first place, unemployment was never as serious a problem in Chile as in many other countries. In the peak of the depression, of course, many men were dismissed from the nitrate industries. However, all the men discharged from the nitrate industry have been given occupation in the newly created gold-washing industry. Other unemployed, due to lessened activity in other fields, have been taken up in increased industrial enterprises stimulated by the state since the depression. Vigorously we began to encourage home-manufacturing, scientific agriculture, the wine industries. We have made considerable progress in these fields. We have now some 6,000 manufacturing establishments in the republic.

Norbourne: I hear splendid things of your work everywhere, Mr. Minister—that the present situation is due largely to your continued control and vigilance.

Señor Ross: As to that, I am working every minute. There is not a day that I am not in consultation with Anaconda or Kennecott copper interests and nitrate matters. I must have my finger on the pulse of every activity. Chile today is being run exactly like a big business and I handle the problems of the country as I would a large business. (He emphasized the last remark, and a Yankee-like smile spread over his shrewd dark features.)

Norbourne: How do you feel about Mr. Roosevelt's attitude to South America?

Señor Ross: As far as I can judge I believe he has a broader view and is more sympathetic than any president you have had. The elder Roosevelt, however, was also considered sympathetic to Chile.

Norbourne: Is Communism much of a factor in Chile?

Señor Ross: Communism does not exist in Chile in the doctrinaire sense in which Marxian Communism exists in eastern Europe. It can be said that there is no real Communism, although this name is tagged to any uprising on the part of the discontented groups.

The interview lasted for half an hour. Twice Norbourne offered to go, but the minister courteously waved him to stay.

They talked of Chile's social laws. The Chilean Social Legislation, protecting the labouring class as well as the upper classes, by means of compulsory saving, provides for workers and employees old age pensions, medical attention, insurance against physical disabilities, and ample social service for the lower classes. This legislation the minister believed to be the most modern of its kind in any country today. "Not only public employees are protected by these laws," he said, "but also private employees and journalists as well as labourers, farmers, and domestic servants. Each one of these social groups maintains a separate institution supervised by the government, a kind of savings bank with a certain degree of financial independence. In accordance with the case the State, the municipalities, the employers, and employees proportionately and simultaneously contribute to the formation and maintenance of these security funds."

"But does it all work in practice?" Norbourne emphasized the point.

The minister smiled. "It will work better in time and with improved conditions."

Eventually the interview terminated with a courteous expression of friendship on the Minister's part toward the United States. "Yes, we are sincerely very much indebted to America in Chile," he said simply. "I do not speak primarily of the amount of capital which has been invested, but I speak of services which Americans have rendered us in teaching us to be more modern and how to live more comfortably. You have shown us the light of our own advantages."

When Norbourne reached the door Señor Ross called him back, took him by the arm and led him into another room of his suite to a wide window. With some pride he pointed to the block where an enormous new hotel was being erected. He described the ingenious subterranean parking space that was to be one of the extremely modern features.

"But you already have one of the most pleasant hotels on the continent—the Crillon——"

"We need some larger ones." His dark eyes gleamed with visions of the future.

Woman's Other Place

That evening the Scotts took Norbourne to a cocktail party at the home of Amanda Labarca, Chile's foremost feminist. She was the first woman to occupy a chair in the University of Chile, when in 1922 she was made special professor of psychology. She had a face to inspire sculptors—strong, purposeful features and an expression compassionate, reasonable, and touched with humour. In complexion she is dark, with deep black eyes. Norbourne was introduced to three university professors. But he spent his time talking to the dark hostess and a girl with honey-coloured hair and a distinguished long nose. The girl, unmarried and in her late twenties, was an aristocrat who had become so interested in social work that she had almost lost her reputation of being the most skilled horsewoman in her social set. In love with an intelligent young lawyer of the middle class, she was waiting for a wedding her parents would sanction. Norbourne and Señora Labarca, sitting on either side of the girl on the long divan in an alcove, sipping Peruvian pisco sours, discussed the importance of birth control as a means of remedying world-wide social disorders.

But the girl, who slaved eight hours a day alleviating the distress of destitute mothers, clung to the Roman Catholic attitude. She wept over the sad plight of mothers in the slums, and yet she could not bring herself to favour the dissemination of birth control instruction because of the Church's opposition.

"Her reason and her heart tell her one thing," said Señora Labarca, when the young woman left them to speak to another group; "the pattern of her upbringing tells her another. It is true of so much of Latin America."

She reached for a book on her desk, took a pen, inscribed it, and presented Norbourne with a copy of her latest work, *A Donde Va La Mujer?* It had just been published and was topping the local best-sellers.

Norbourne thanked her properly and turned the book about in his hands. Ivory-coloured silhouettes representing the ages' changes in women's fashions sauntered across the Delft blue background of the jacket. "Where *is* woman going?" he asked.

"I have attempted in this book to ascertain what women can contribute to our country's reconstruction which may be of value. Heretofore, under the old patriarchial system, women's sphere was the four walls of the home. But today, with the new industrialism and the necessity for many women to earn their living, the picture is changed. The problem of the family and the home are the result of economic factors of the whole changing world. They must be settled in town councils, in the parliaments, in cabinet meetings, and even in international conferences. Woman is under a new obligation to take an active interest in political questions."

"What especially can women contribute to the political field?"

Amanda Labarca smiled almost deprecatingly. "May we say first: 'humility' in consideration of our long ignorance? Then—'unselfishness'? Women have accustomed themselves to think of others before themselves, and of the future rather than the mere present. They look to the growing up of their children. Men bring to politics strength and creative passion. Women possess humility and perseverance, silent and gentle obstinacy. It would be splendid for them to fuse into one to save this generation—which is that of our children."

"Your book, then, I take it"—Norbourne had been glancing at the chapter headings—"is a plea for women to get into politics and clean things up—things within woman's province—conditions of the home, the children, the family, marriage laws, divorce, disease."

"I want women above all to prepare to be worthy and ready to vote. Women need to heed this plea for a better home life, because women have suffered more, because they feel the sufferings of children more keenly."

"Incidentally, why is the rate of illegitimacy so high here?"

"Partly because the South American considers promiscuity for the male natural—and partly natural caution on the woman's part."

"Caution!" Norbourne wasn't sure he had heard the word correctly.

"Caution," she repeated with a shrewd smile. "Many a lower class woman is suspicious of marriage. By merely living with a man she can leave him at will if she doesn't want to put up with indignities. The threat keeps many a man straight. Marriage gives her no protection—only duties. We are working to get laws for political and civil rights of women, divorce laws, laws protecting labouring women, children, mothers. We cannot do these things until we have complete suffrage. At present we are permitted to vote only in municipal affairs."

"But your present social laws, your compulsory labour insurance, arbitration, agrarian banks and all of those advanced legislative movements—what of them?" Norbourne protested.

"Alas, they don't work in practice. They grow rusty for one cause or another. The hospitals are inadequate, the housing conditions of the city poor deplorable. There are not enough nurses or doctors. Our death rate from tuberculosis is appalling. We lack sanatoria. We need money for orphan asylums. We need maternity hospitals where medical attention is given free and lessons in hygiene. Our women sit at home and sigh and go on bearing more children and watch them die. Instead of having a few healthy ones, the men believe in having many; they say by the process of natural selection the fittest will live."

"But, really, aren't the children well taken care of? The Chileans appear to me to be an unusually strong and vital people."

"I wish you had time to go even a perfunctory round of social observation with me. Ninety per cent of the school children in the cities are undernourished. Their eyes lack lustre. Many of them have decayed teeth. The record against Chile in regard to infant mortality is unbelievably bad. In 1932, 235 infants out of each thousand died. Compare these figures with those of your own country where only 65 out of a thousand die, and with Argentina just across the Andes, where 111 die, and in Uruguay not quite 100."

"And you attribute this unhappy situation to——?"

Amanda Labarca's dark eyes blazed quietly with accusation. "The men . . . They are too busy with politics, with running the government as a big business."

Adam Was a Cowboy

"The peasants insist that Adam was a cowboy and Eve was a cowgirl," Buchanan explained as he and Norbourne entered a restaurant called *Huaso Adam* to have a typical "lunch of the people." "They speak very affectionately of *Huasa Eva*, Cowgirl Eve."

In one of the dingy, windowless back rooms, five black-browed, fuzzy-haired workmen were sitting about a red tablecloth finishing their meal with hearty smacks and heroic mouth-wipings. "Jesus Christ has done nothing but give the world illusions," one of the men was saying, and paused, scowling at the entrance of the couple. The men were eating with their hats on and they had a strong but not unpleasant smell of toil about them.

"The *roto* is an enemy of water both for internal and external use," said Buchanan as they sat down. "A few years ago an ordinance was passed to wash forcibly the people who wouldn't wash themselves. I saw one woman whose family had been taken in before her, on hearing their shrieks of protest, wring her hands and run up and down the streets yelling, 'They're killing my family!' Three or four of the old people who had never bathed in their lives died from the shock."

The meal started with a *tortilla de erizos*, a Chilean dish, which Buchanan said he relished, but which his family wouldn't allow in the house. A cold, black thing like a wet cannon ball with a thousand vicious prickles was set before Norbourne. The top had been whacked off and the inside was composed of segments of pale pink flesh, resembling cats' tongues, arranged like sections of an orange. They were sea urchins' livers. In the centre of the top a little black crab, about the circumference of half a dollar, stretched his claws.

Norbourne looked at the mess doubtfully, and tried to get the crab on his fork. Buchanan laughed. "I wouldn't eat that," he said. "It might nip your tongue and claw your esophagus as it went down. They are brought to the table alive and kicking to prove the *erizo* is fresh. The crab is a parasite that makes his home in the urchin. The *rotos* eat them, but it requires a special technique. Here, you eat the pink livers. Dip them in this sauce." Buchanan ate with magnificent gusto to encourage the tenderfoot.

Norbourne tried to be a Chilean. He got four of the eight livers down and faintly pretended to like their sea-bottom flavour. Then he managed some of the thick native soup with a crust of grease floating on it. But when his host began to order a dish of the insides of some unfamiliar animal he rebelled and demanded an omelette, "an omelette cooked without grease." The waitress made two trips to the kitchen and returned questioningly. "*Without grease*," Norbourne insisted.

She did not return for an unreasonably long time. "There's been a revolution in the kitchen," Buchanan said, grinning.

But Norbourne got his omelette at last and was so comforted by its international simplicity that he ceased to be chagrined at failing to do as the Romans.

These Charming People

Elliott took Norbourne and Buchanan to tea at the home of a widow who lived in the last house in Santiago before one got into complete country. Norbourne had pictured a grave, sallow dowager in black crêpe. He was greeted by a charming, bird-like little woman with a laugh like the tinkle of champagne glasses touching in a toast. She wore topaz-coloured velvet which went very prettily with her burnished-gold hair. Here was the same piquant nose and chin, the creamy complexion, the slightly mocking and amused eyebrows of other Chilean women.

Her daughters, eighteen- and seventeen-year-olds, came out with their hats on. They too were dressed in velvet dinner dresses —the dark one, in sapphire; the fair one, in turquoise. They were going to a dinner dance with their nineteen-year-old brother, a second-year engineering student, the master of the house. The girls were exceedingly pretty and spoke very little.

The son got out his guitar. Buchanan had brought his mandolin. They played and Elliott sang native songs. During tea the atmosphere was far more lively and unrestrained than Norbourne had ever known in any other Spanish-blooded household. These people possessed so unaffectedly that unconscious faculty of stirring pleasure in others—that quality that is called charm. They gave the stranger a direct pleasurable kind of self-appreciation.

After tea, the widow led Norbourne to a bookcase. On either side hung a small oil landscape. "Which do you like better?" she asked. "They are done by one of our best artists."

Norbourne touched the vivid autumn-coloured one of a boating party on a stream. It had fine tone and feeling. "This is particularly charming," he said.

"That is Chile in autumn." She called her son to lift it off the wall. "I want you to take it home—so that you will not forget Chile too soon."

"But I can't possibly take your painting!" Norbourne protested.

"I can have another painted—you can't," she said, touching a flaming match to the end of a gold sealing wax stick and fixing her calling card on the back of the picture. The butler brought paper and string. Norbourne continued to protest vigorously for several minutes. He called on the others to aid him in pleading the rightness of his refusal. The lady, sweetly ignoring his objections, wrapped up the picture.

At last he said, "All right—I'll accept the painting, if you will keep the frame."

"Where," she demanded mockingly, "could you find in your United States a frame like this?"

"But see the empty space on your wall!" he pleaded. "The companion frame will be lonesome without it." He began untying and unwrapping the package. "I'll bargain with you. I'll hang the picture in my study to remember you by, and you keep the frame to remember me by."

The lady laughed her gay, faintly mocking laugh, and gave in reluctantly. Together they lifted the canvas board from the frame and wrapped it up again.

"I'm really overwhelmed!" he repeated, genuinely touched at her generosity. "I shall be careful not to praise this lovely eighteenth-century cabinet."

He was whisked out into the music room to be introduced to the *cueca*, a native dance done with a pocket handkerchief. It is something no visitor is supposed to miss. The widow sat at the piano; her son played the mandolin; Buchanan and the blonde daughter began the dance. The girl was a bit shy. "Very proud, very proud," Buchanan coached her, as he strutted like a cock, twirling his handkerchief, putting on the airs of a peasant who sets great value on his own worth. There was much bowing and swift changing of step and tempo and fluttering of handkerchiefs. On the man's part it required great agility of leg muscles.

The children urged their mother to dance. The dark daughter played the piano. The little widow and Buchanan danced with spirit and grace and finish, as if they had practised for weeks. The alpinist put all the exuberance of his mountain climbing into his skilful and furious leg work. The lady was properly hesitant, disdainful, coy, until at last after a struggle her femininity was conquered by the male.

"Bravo!" the audience applauded.

The widow laughed and held out her hand to Norbourne. "Now, you must try."

"Señora taught it to the Prince of Wales in twenty minutes," Elliott said.

But Norbourne knew he would only make a fool of himself. Besides it was time for the daughters to leave for their party in the city. So with the exchange of a dozen courtesies, the men got their coats and hats. For wraps the girls wore only smart silver fox scarves. "But your daughters will freeze," Nourbourne protested, "and it's beginning to drizzle."

"Vanity will keep them warm and dry," their brother laughed.

"Oh," the lady said, "would you write in my autograph book?"

"I am flattered." Norbourne bowed.

The dark daughter went to fetch the book from the gilt cabinet. "It's been tucked away ever since we moved from our town house—four years ago." She handed him a book bound in turquoise leather. Bending down over the hall table he tried his fountain pen on an old envelope. He opened the book. The autographs stopped in the middle. He found the last page that had been written on. He stared at it, read it again.

"Really!" he said, glancing up questioningly.

"Yes, he came to our house. That's where he learned the *cueca*."

In a large heavy black scrawl the Prince of Wales had written:

LADY—

I am at your service.

EDWARD P.

"Where is your painting?" the lady called, as they went out of the door.

Norbourne opened wide his topcoat, touching the wrapped board which he had put under his left arm to protect it from the rain. "You see, I have Chile close to my heart," he said.

ROBINSON CRUSOE'S LOBSTERS

Elliott went to the dance with the youngsters and Buchanan dined with Norbourne at the Bahia, a restaurant unsurpassed on the continent. They feasted on the world-famed lobsters, on artichokes and green asparagus, and drank a superior white Mot. Norbourne had never tasted such shellfish. For rich aromatic savour and tenderness it made all the rest of the fresh lobsters he had eaten seem like canned stuff.

The lobsters came from the Island of San Juan Fernandez, 365 miles out in the Pacific west of Valparaiso. It was there that Alexander Selkirk spent his solitary free-will exile between 1704 and 1709. Out of the material of the Scottish seaman's adventures Defoe assured his own immortality by writing his novel *Robinson Crusoe* at the age of sixty.

Buchanan had been there several times on fishing trips. "It's a wild, fascinating sort of place," he said, showing Norbourne some snapshots he had taken. "A tangle of jungles, mountains, and brief, crystal rivers. There's a fine view from the peak where Selkirk set his signal fires when he'd had enough of life in the raw. The cave where he lived is shown to visitors. Once a year a Grace liner includes the island in its winter cruise. Last year on one of the islets we met a shaggy old German who lives alone just like Robinson Crusoe. We found him shooting goats among the ferns."

"Did he have a man Friday to keep him company?"

"In the form of an old gramophone with a series of yodelling records. On the main island there's a little town of three hundred people who live in log cabins and make their living by fishing.

The lobsters are found in the breakers—sometimes a hundred feet deep. I've seen specimens nearly three feet long, weighing over ten pounds each. You know, these lobsters travel like royalty."

"What do you mean?"

"The Pan American Grace Airway has had to put on two lobster specials to fly with them over the Andes to Buenos Aires. A special equipment has also been installed in the passenger planes to keep the creatures alive and comfortable. They fly them as far as Lima and La Paz, and beyond Buenos Aires to Montevideo."

"You mean," said Norbourne, "that in Montevideo, looking out over the Atlantic, I can dine on fresh lobster caught nearly four hundred miles out in the Pacific?"

"Exactly. You'll probably do it. But you couldn't have done such a thing a few years ago."

Honeydew melon followed the aguacate salad.

"I hear tha Chile is emphatically air-minded," Norbourne said, sniffing the melon's cool fragrance.

"Rather. And now with our trans-Andean railroad washed away and no other means of crossing the continent except by plane, we're the biggest boosters imaginable. Until the aeroplane, we were the most isolated country on this side of the world. You know we were the pioneer flyers in South America. We took to the air as naturally as we took to water—we're really the only sailors on the continent and I think we're the most enthusiastic flyers."

"By the way, tell me about Godoy, the first man to fly over the Andes," Norbourne interrupted.

"Well, when they started flying here, of course, it was the ambition of everyone to be the first to cross the Cordilleras. One man after another lost his life until the government forbade the attempt. But in 1918 Godoy, a young Chilean lieutenant, did it in a plane he snaffled from the army. When he landed safely in Mendoza and the news of his successful adventure was telegraphed to Chile, the populace went mad with excitement. But the army chiefs sweated in a dilemma. They didn't know whether to court-martial him for disobedience or take him to their bosom as a national hero."

"They chose the heroic course?"

"Yes. But because the adventure was not subsidized, the heroism was little publicized."

"What's become of your hero?"

"He's living a very private life in the south."

Buchanan dug his fork deep into the melon's delicate green flesh. "Do you know that the honeydews you eat in winter in the United States come from Chile? Incidentally, what do you think of our fruits? Our plums, strawberries, apricots, pears?"

"Without doubt, they are unsurpassed."

"It's the air that has blown over snow that gives them their tang." Buchanan winked appreciatively. "It's the same thing that gives flavour and tang to our women." He took a big bite. "Marvellous, these, aren't they?"

"Superb," Norbourne agreed heartily. "Tell me," he said, looking at Buchanan speculatively, "when you have skied over the Andes, when Everest is conquered and the Brazilian jungle is tamed and industrialized, what then?"

The mountain climber was thoughtful for a second; then he looked up with a grin. "The universe is infinite. There are other planets—man must have his adventure and romance." He finished his melon with relish.

Norbourne had expected some such answer. It was refreshing to sit face to face with this unquenchable zest for adventure, this utter absence of any modern defeatist attitude. Here was the spirit of a Spanish Valdivia that ventured for fun, and the Scots adaptability of a Selkirk. Mason in Peru was certainly right. Norbourne liked the Chileans enormously. They were the most natural, the frankest, the most infectiously optimistic of all Latin Americans he had met. But beneath their charming, care-free, affable exteriors he sensed a something dangerous that commanded discreet respect. The Chilean character may be likened to the nation's principal commodity, nitrate. Everything depends on how you handle it.

INTERLUDE

INTERLUDE

Flight Over the Andes

A telephone's buzzing waked Norbourne. It was the alarum bell to a longed-for adventure. The weather was propitious. The voice said the plane would fly over the Andes that morning. In a moving picture he had once watched aeroplanes sailing through the icy corridors of an Andean pass. As the tips of their wings sometimes seemed to brush the glistening palisades, he had got gooseflesh from a combination of the excitement and beauty. Then and there he had set his heart on experiencing the thrill in the flesh. And now, as he dressed hurriedly and ate the breakfast brought to his room, it seemed that all he had seen and heard in the past thirty-odd days of travel was like the prelude of a love affair, the climax of which would be reached this morning.

Since two planes were flying that day with capacity loads of fourteen passengers each, two buses were used to convey the passengers to the airport. Because of treacherous weather in the mountains, the Tuesday plane's flight had been postponed once and then again on Wednesday. Except where the street lamps cast a glow it was still quite dark. Here and there, out of the darkness, singly and in groups, peasants, muffled to the nose and bearing baskets of blossoms, rushed to secure the best stalls at the open air flower market. Mme Thibaud in the front seat hunched her shoulders and shrunk her face down into the upturned collar of her fur coat. The temperature stood just at freezing point. It was as cold as Santiago ever gets. Moiseiwitsch sat beside her in heavy-eyed silence. He had never flown before, and he was not comfortable in his mind. Besides he was sleepy, for he had been up all night playing cards.

Thibaud was in high spirits. He told Norbourne about Mischa Elman's crossing the Andes when scheduled for a series of performances in Santiago after an engagement in Buenos Aires. It was midwinter and there were, of course, no trains. Nothing would induce Elman to fly. No statistics of safe performances could convince him. So in Mendoza they arranged a mule train to transport him and his luggage over the mountains. The journey was far more hazardous than Hannibal had made by elephant over the Alps. Three mules gave up the ghost en route. After prolonged days of hardship, the battered Elman and what was left of his entourage turned up in Santiago. In the meantime Heifetz had taken a plane in Buenos Aires, flown across the continent and over the Cordilleras in five hours, and received an ovation in the capital.

"In the same number of the *Musical Courier*"—Mme. Thibaud raised her head out of her furs—"appeared a picture of Heifetz jauntily boarding the aeroplane and one of dear Elman uncertainly mounting his ass."

At the airport coffee and biscuit were served, while the pilots checked their papers and the radio operator got the final report from the lookout man on the mountain heights. The activity in the office was expeditious, smoothly expert, exact, confidence-inspiring. A clerk reassured Moiseiwitsch. "Pan American Grace planes have crossed the Andes 1,899 times with only one fatal accident, and that happened in the pioneering days four years ago, and was due to lack of knowledge of weather conditions. But now the weatherman in The Pass keeps the pilot on the ground unless the conditions are completely favourable."

Norbourne looked over the personnel, those who remained on the ground and those who flew. Here, too, they were all youngish. Captain Disher, the pilot of the *Santa Lucia*, the plane Norbourne was to go in, was in his early thirties. Captain Parks, the other pilot, was only twenty-four. "The handsomest man in the service," said Purser Elliott to an inquiring American lady with a twelve-year-old boy. "He's very skilful and married," he added, noting her vague wistfulness as she stared at the dark young man with the amiable, adventurous eyes. Norbourne was delighted to find that by chance Elliott was again to be his steward. He knew he could get lively answers to his questions.

"I'll warn you when we come to the Christ," Elliott said. "It's very interesting. In 1904 at the conclusion of a series of peace pacts and boundary agreements between Argentina and Chile, the symbolic figure was placed on the boundary between the two countries. The statue was shipped 750 miles over the mountains by mule back. It's twenty-six feet tall, and rests on a granite hemisphere five feet high, with the western continents marked in bronze bas-relief. In the unveiling of the monument, the presiding bishop proclaimed, 'Sooner shall these mountains crumble into dust than Argentinians and Chileans break the peace sworn at the feet of Christ the Redeemer.' "

"I want to know about the radio man who lives up there in the mountains."

"Ah, Nemsoff. He's a rare one. A burly young giant. His full name is Gregorio Nemsoff. He's an Argentino born in Russia. You'll see his hut not far from the statue. It is built on Argentinian territory forty feet from Chilean soil. It's two miles from the nearest railway station, which is deserted in winter. This was the first radio station in the Cordilleras of the Andes to communicate with aeroplanes in flight. From February, 1933, until June, 1934, Nemsoff lived entirely alone, sending messages to Santiago and Buenos Aires and keeping in touch with flyers en route. Sometimes at night hungry mountain lions would surround his retreat, attracted by the smell of meat kept in the open air for preservation. Nemsoff says shooting stealthy lions in pitch darkness is not exactly fun. If a plane was scheduled to fly next morning, he would spend half the night clinging perilously to his ropes along the ledges of precipices, noting the direction and intensity of the wind. Excuse me——" Elliott was away in a flash on some routine duty.

Floodlights played on the aerodrome. Like silver dragon flies just alighted on a green pool, the two great Douglases were lined up one behind the other, their twin propellers twirling, their engines making harmonious thunder. The chief mechanic announced to Captain Parks that his plane was ready. After the second bell, the Thibauds and Moiseiwitsch and eleven others followed the captain and assistant pilot up the flight of portable steps. The field manager lowered his red flag. The plane taxied down the field and turned to get into the wind. The white flag was lifted. Skimming the turf lightly, kissing it three farewell kisses, the thunderbird plunged joyously up into the air like a lark scenting the sunrise.

Ten minutes later the *Santa Lucia's* passengers chose their seats. Before and behind Norbourne sat young Doctors of Philosophy, one a lecturer at Colombia University, the other a professor at Copenhagen. They had their laps full of tubes and pumps and charts and diagrams. (Along with eight others from world famous universities, they had been sent by some international scientific organization to study the effect of altitude on human physiology. The others had remained in the mountains of Bolivia.) These gentlemen asked Norbourne to serve as their subject for experiment. He consented on the promise that when they reached The Pass he would not be encumbered with rubber bands on his arms or intelligence tests on his mind.

He settled back in his seat and touched the little oxygen tube dangling out of the blue enamelled woodwork under the window frame. It was rare that any passenger ever needed oxygen, but sometimes one took a sniff just for the fun of it or to prevent a headache. Before he realized it, they were in the air, headed for Aconcagua. With astounding celerity they climbed until they reached an altitude of 15,000 feet. At the scientists' request, Norbourne removed his coat. Outside the weather was zero, but the air-conditioned temperature within was 72°. The professors bound the blood pressure pad about his arm, and pumped, and took the record.

A quarter of an hour after leaving the field, the *Santa Lucia* passed high over the foothills of the Cordilleras. At some exact mechanical demarcation she swerved to the right as naturally as if turning down a hedged country lane. In another minute they had entered the stupendous gap in the mountains known as The Pass. Norbourne demanded to be unstrapped. He walked up the aisle to the front seat on the left, the only one vacant.

The glory of Aconcagua to the left seemed as close as a New York skyscraper seen from the Battery. Norbourne stood transfixed with enchantment. Everywhere was eternal whiteness—the blue-tinctured whiteness of ice and diamonds, an intensely clean whiteness with subtle shadows of aquamarine and sapphire that shifted enchantingly before the vast crystal alcoves. A few thousand feet beneath, the gallery's pavement was the purplish colour of wet violets.

Purser Elliott pointed out peaks and promontories, called them by name, enumerated their respective altitudes. It was as if one applied geography to a mystical vision of Blake. The Indians say that only on the crest of the Andes can one talk with God. This corridor of carved crystal through which they tore like the west wind might have been the approach to heaven's throne. On either side chalky pencils of cathedral spires wrote Andean choruses on the fresh morning's azure slate. And directly in front of them the youthful sun god, hurling gold-feathered darts of light, rose to meet the thunderbird.

Though they could not see the other plane which had taken off just before they did, the captain knew exactly where it was. "When there are two planes in The Pass, the respective radio operators keep in constant touch with each other, giving their exact position by squares on the map of the charted territory." Purser Elliott showed Norbourne on the map the spot where the other plane was at the moment. "Most people have the idea that The Pass is a narrow way," he said. "As you see, it's miles wide."

But to Norbourne it looked like a tunnel. Once he involuntarily tensed all his muscles. "Aren't they going to hit that left bank there?" he cautioned.

Elliott smiled. "It's a good three miles away."

Norbourne looked down on land where no man had set foot, where so small a proportion of the world's people would ever set eye. It was exciting to be breathing in such an age when the most ordinary of mortals had the privilege of acting a part that only a few of the greatest of the ancient seers played in their most extravagant dreams.

Elliott touched his arm and he went back to his seat for a better view of the famous Christ they were approaching. Beneath, like a figurine in ivory, stood a gigantic statue of the Blessed Lord, the right hand raised in benediction, the left clasping a cross that extended high above His head. In the shadow of the lonely Christ stood the diminutive stone hut of Nemsoff. There, companioned only by howling pumas and the shadow of the silent Christ with cyclonic winds thundering out mad symphonies, the young giant lived in Olympian isolation, controlling—with his finger tips and his voice—the trans-continental movements of mail and men.

Disher kindly circled about the statue and the station once again for the passengers' better view. "Whenever possible," Elliott said to Norbourne, as they looked down through the frosty windows, "magazines and bundles of newspapers are thrown from the planes to Gregorio to lighten his monotonous routine. Sometimes we can see him dashing down the mountain side like a wild goat in his eagerness to get them. In the summer he once brought back two women from an Argentine village to cheer his loneliness. But it proved unsatisfactory. The women couldn't adjust themselves to harem ways and fought for his sole affections at the very feet of the Peacemaker. So he got rid of them both, and on good days when no planes were scheduled to fly he would radio that he was signing off to go to the village to get a haircut. The operators in Mendoza and Santiago would smile and call out into the office: 'Nemsoff has gone for a haircut.' Everybody knew what it meant."

"What is that other house?" Norbourne asked, noticing another simple structure alongside the first.

"That's the new meteorological station the Argentinian Government constructed. Gregorio[1] is no longer entirely alone."

Norbourne strained his eyes, hoping to catch a glimpse of that modern messenger of the gods, whose advice pilots in two countries heeded like the word of deity. But nothing stirred except the thunderbird's shadow which passed like a phantom over the invisible boundary out of Chile.

These hanging gardens of crystal, these blue canyons and white promontories were no different in quality from the others. But on the maps they proclaimed allegiance to Argentina.

Norbourne, leaning back, recalled how Melville had believed that the quality of whiteness enhanced beauty in natural objects like japonicas, marble, pearls, because the "quality of whiteness is emblematic of something most worthy of reverence and has for man innumerable beautiful and kindly associations." Here where the landscape was covered with snow whiter than samite, he could feel the supernatural implications Hudson described.

The pilot touched the controls lightly and the thunderbird obeyed his silent commands, as if it were a live and intelligent thing. The great snow-covered peaks and ridges might have been some white monster that had lain there challenging man for generations, as Moby Dick had challenged superstitious seafarers. But now it had been outwitted. The thunderbird flew among its tempting treacheries as serenely as a dragonfly passing over a clump of white plants growing by a meadow brook. The wind was still now. All nature looked hushed, as if it had no ear except for the scientific sounds emitted from the thunderbird's great vocal cords. "Man is normally scientific and loves to get at the bottom of all mysteries, and yet at the same time his older, deeper, primitive, still persistent nature is non-scientific and mystical." Following Hudson's speculations, Norbourne wondered anew at the change wrought by this miraculous mani-

[1]Since the above was written, Gregorio Nemsoff met his death in the civilized streets of Mendoza on vacation, when his automobile skidded over some weeping willow branches that lay across the road.

festation of intelligent life and power, while the primitive in him remained spellbound at the quintessence of whiteness.

"In a few minutes we begin the descent," the purser said. Norbourne would have restrained them if it had been reasonable and in his power. He was loath to return so quickly to the world of pavements, politics, statistics, to bargaining and aimless babble. He would have liked to stay in the air all day flying among those immaculate pinnacles and thrilling precipices.

But the thunderbird knew its business and had no notion of lingering in the region of enchantment longer than was necessary. There was international mail to be delivered; business men to whom time was money to be got to their destinations. The fashionable restaurants of Buenos Aires were impatient for the lobsters from Robinson Crusoe's Island. A lady in Buenos Aires whose ship was about to sail for New York was frantic for fear her set of false teeth made by a Santiago dentist would not arrive in time and she would be condemned to a seventeen days' milk diet and an agony of humiliated vanity.

The thunderbird tore away from the white draperies of The Pass out over a savage undulating plain with tight dry bushes and cactus growing in rocky aridity. Rusty condors flapped wide wings above granite boulders. Below lay Uspallata where San Martin and his liberty-seeking men began their historic climb over a way twice as steep and perilous as the one Napoleon had negotiated in the Alps.

Norbourne took a last look back at the majesty of Aconcagua, now forty miles away. It lay serene against the blue silk of the sky like an exhibition jewel in a show case. Then it vanished from sight like a conjurer's trick, and the thunderbird dropped completely away from the mystery and glory, and sailed out over a "meaningless confusion of piled rocks."

In a state of semi-intoxication Norbourne returned to his seat. The Colombia Ph.D. and the Copenhagen Ph.D. put him to various quick co-ordination tests, made him mark horizontal and vertical lines in white chess-board spaces on specimen paper within an allotted time to test the effect of the altitude on the functioning of his brain.

When he looked out again, they were passing over the dry foothills with their stunted trees and shrubs. Almost immediately they were hovering over the city of Mendoza that reposed like a summerhouse in the midst of illimitable irrigated vineyards, twenty-five hundred feet above the level of the sea. The plane descended slowly so that the ear drums of the passengers would suffer no discomfort. It was a quarter of an hour after they were in sight of Mendoza before the pilot made his imperceptibly smooth landing. The whole trip had consumed only one hour of time. As Norbourne set foot on earth he knew that never again in his life would any hour of travel hold so much.

5

BOGOTA, COLOMBIA. AIR VIEW OF CENTRAL PART OF CITY SHOWING MONSERRATE AND GUADALUPE

6

SHRINE OF THE SACRED HEART AND LA LIBERTAD PARK, RIOBAMBA, ECUADOR

7

INDIAN PLOWING, ECUADOR

8

THE ANDES NEAR THE COAST AS SEEN FROM THE AIR, PERU

9

LIMA, PERU, FROM THE AIR

10

INDIAN, DESCENDANT OF THE INCAS, WITH HIS LLAMAS, AT THE FAMOUS INCA FORTRESS, OVERLOOKING CUZCO, PERU

II

STREET SCENE, CUZCO, PERU, ANCIENT CAPITAL OF THE INCAS

DEMPSEY
TUNNEY
DEMPSEY

12

GRAY, SALMON PINK, AND BLACK LLAMAS DECORATED WITH ROPES MADE FROM THEIR OWN WOOL

13

THE LITTLE CHURCH OF TRAPICE, CATABAMBAS GOLD MINES NEAR CUZCO, PERU

14

AREQUIPA, PERU, AT THE FOOT OF THE VOLCANO EL MISTI

15

CHURCH, AREQUIPA, PERU

V

ARGENTINA

"*We cannot think in terms of material prosperity alone. Our concern should be that prosperity of the spirit out of which all other riches flow.*"

Cordell Hull

ARGENTINA

Glory of Flatness

The people of Mendoza call their town "The Garden of the Andes." From their plazas and promenades they can see the white tips of the Cordilleras. In the late afternoon shadows of the mountains fall across the houses and vineyards. It was winter now, but spring was not far behind. Soon the hillsides for miles around would be strung with millions of rows of fresh-foliaged vines like garments dyed green and hung in the wind to dry. From these irrigated acres of grapes, sufficient wine could be drawn to make Argentina independent of European beverages.

The other plane had landed precisely ten minutes before the *Santa Maria*. The passengers from both planes enjoyed a second or third breakfast in the waiting room. Though no one had had to take oxygen or had felt the slightest ill effect, one or two seemed relieved that a supposedly frightening experience was over. An English playboy, who had never flown before and whose chief claim to significance seemed to be that he had been in a houseparty at Barbara Hutton's, kept stroking his forehead and nose, agreeably surprised, by Jove, that the flight had a happy effect on his sinus trouble. The little boy from New York wanted to do it all over again. Moiseiwitsch had been overcome with sleepiness and had not seen very much. Wide awake now, he said good-bye to his friends and was driven into the town by a delegation of music lovers come to welcome him. That evening he was to give a concert.

A swarthy Don, who had come down to meet Norbourne, favoured Moiseiwitsch and his little black satchel with the searching glance of an amateur detective. "The best patron of aviation was a mystery man who crossed the Andes four times a week—just like a season ticket-holder," he said. "But he had no business. He was imagined to be very rich because at night he would appear at the Casino in immaculate evening clothes, and play first at one table, then at another. Though no one had ever noticed him winning anything extraordinary, at the end of each evening he always cashed in enormous sums. He kept this winning up for months, buying return flights from Santiago to Mendoza regularly. When he ruined our casino they arrested him and got the truth. He had thought out an original way of beating the bank. He would buy a supply of counters at the Casino at Viña del Mar in Chile and fly over the mountains with a satchelful. The Chilean chips were exactly the same in size and texture as those here. But because of the difference in the exchange a hundred peso chip in Chile would be worth four times as much in Argentina."

"I'm sorry I haven't brought some chips with me."

"Now we have our own very, very special kind of chips."

Seeing Norbourne jot down "Mystery Man," the gentleman said, "I'll tell you something that occurred just last week. A local physician's little boy was dying from whooping cough. The father couldn't allay the paroxysms. As a last resort he tried an experiment. He rushed the child to the airport and chartered a plane to fly to Villa Mercedes—two hundred and twenty miles east of here. He and the boy and a nurse went up. When they got high in the air, the paroxysm stopped. They landed in Villa Mercedes, came back here, and made another return trip the same day. The child recovered completely. It was an expensive cure, but the doctor said nothing else could have saved the boy's life."

"Here!" called Norbourne to the effect-of-altitude investigators, "is a case history right to your hand." They brought their coffee cups over to the table and the gentleman repeated his story for them.

Out in front of the airport the passengers began to grow restless. They had been here an hour. The sun was shining brightly. But a fog hung over Buenos Aires, 640 miles away. The fog might have lifted by the time they arrived, but again it might not. Panagra's regard for its passengers' safety would not allow chances to be taken. They could get to Villa Mercedes all right, 220 miles distant, but there were not enough good hotel rooms for twenty-six passengers and six airmen. They would have to wait for more encouraging news from the Buenos Aires station. Since the planes might take off at a moment's notice, the passengers, not daring to leave the airport to drive about Mendoza, resigned themselves to enjoying the sunshine and getting acquainted.

A freight train laden with great casks of wine rumbled out of Mendoza away toward the capital. Another hour passed. "It seems absurd to negotiate the Andes with such ease and to be baffled by a little fog hovering over the flat ground," complained a steel representative from Pittsburgh.

The invaluable Elliott pulled a volume of Pablo Neruda's poetry from his pocket and offered to read some of it aloud to help pass the time. Several of the passengers gathered about, leaning against the white rail that bordered the long walk from the waiting room to the planes. "Neruda, Chile's best young poet, has recently been crowned by the Spanish Academy," Elliott said, speaking in the tones of a lecturer. "For some time he was considered ridiculous, because of his modernism and introspection. However, there is certainly a great play of imagination and a dynamic vividness in his work." With a very English accent, he began to read from a poem called *Death Only*, translating as he read.

There is death in the bones,
like a pure sound,
like a bark without a dog.

I sometimes see
coffins sail
with pale dead, with long-haired women,
with bakers, white-faced as angels,
with pensive girls married to lawyers,
coffins sailing up the vertical river of death.

"Why should girls married to lawyers be especially pensive?" a lawyer from Montevideo interrupted defensively. The others laughed.

To the sonorous death comes
as a shoe without a foot, as a suit without a man,
comes to shout without a mouth, without a tongue,
without throat.

Elliott's high voice rose and fell with Oxford-tinctured inflection. The poem ended:

And there are beds sailing to a port
Where Death waits, dressed as an Admiral.

"It is better to sit here quietly in the sun," Mme Thibaud said, nodding appreciation, "than to face the Admiral in the fog."

The Thibauds got up an *al fresco* game of bridge. Norbourne went to a bench in the sun, opened his brief case, got out a map and a pencil. He had much to learn at first hand about modern Argentina. He knew something of old Argentina, for as a youth he had drunk with W. H. Hudson from that "wild cup of nature" he presented in three incomparable books. He had travelled in creaking ox-carts over the endless pampa with the youthful Darwin on excursions away from the *Beagle*. But what they wrote of the far away and long ago was as different from the contemporary picture of Argentina as up-to-date Tulsa, Oklahoma, differs from the wild cimarron land of 1890. The West Coast republics—Chile, Peru, Colombia, Ecuador—retained so much of their old flavour that a man who had lived there in the nineteenth century would have felt reasonably at home today. But in Argentina except for the purple light that still crept at evening over the vast flat acres, there would be only a lingering essence of what Hudson knew.

Norbourne looked at the map. Whereas nitrous Chile is shaped like a sword, agricultural Argentina is wedge-shaped like a ploughshare, the point towards the South Pole. In the northwest corner bordering Bolivia and Paraguay, the region is swampy, hot and wooded. In the northern torrid region, below Brazil, rosewood, laurel, orangewood, walnut, and quebracho, excellent for tanning, grow in profusion. In the hot, lush section between the Paranz and Uruguay rivers, sugar and cotton are planted in increasing acres. The southern part called Patagonia is cold and arid, something similar in character to the Russian steppes, but excellent for sheep raising. But the grassy, treeless pampa, potent with fertility, spreading fanwise out from Buenos Aires, makes up the principal acreage. There lives the bulk of the population.

It is odd that a country calling itself Argentina should be one without silver mines. The great muddy estuary, La Plata, too, had been so named in the vain hope that the precious metal might be piled up in plate ships like those that sailed from Cartagena and Panama. However, today the country has at last justified her sanguine appellation by becoming the richest and most money-conscious of all the Latin American nations. Argentina's wealth has come not from precious metals; it has come from the fertility of the soil.

The first Spanish settler found no Inca temples to loot, no mines to exploit. The Indians of this vast region were only nomadic tribes, low in civilization's scale. They had no cows, no sheep, no horses. They did not cultivate the soil, but fed mainly on ostriches, gamebirds, armadillos and guanacos. For three centuries the settlers lived with primitive simplicity in mud huts on the Silver River's banks, and left the western and southern sections of the land unexplored and unsettled.

In February, 1516, Juan Diaz de Solís, the discoverer of Brazil, was the first European to reach what is now the Plata River basin. Magellan came in 1520; sailed up the river far enough to convince himself that it was no strait that led to the Far East. Sebastian Cabot came in 1526 and called the estuary La Plata because of some silver trinkets the Indians wore and the tall tales they told him of wealth far up the river into the west. Ten years later Pedro de Mendoza made the first permanent settlement in the Plata region. He founded a town named Santa Maria de Buenos Aires. The City of the Good Airs was composed of mud huts thatched with river reeds and enclosed in a mud wall. After three years of hardship, pestilence, and starvation—so acute that Christians turned cannibals and ate three corpses of their fellows hanged for killing and eating a horse—the city was abandoned and the survivors joined another settlement far up the river at Asunción, the present capital of Paraguay. Before leaving, they destroyed every vestige of construction and took with them "everything but the river and the stars." Forty years later in 1580, Juan de Garay refounded Buenos Aires. In a letter to the king he predicted with assurance that some day the humble settlement would be the most important city in the Indies. Before the end of the nineteenth century his vision had come true.

But during the three centuries of Colonial vice-royalty, Argentina was contemptuously neglected. Mother Spain lavished her affection and interest on her more colourful and profitable colonies in the Pacific. By a happy paradox this last developed and least valued of Spain's colonies was to become in modern times the most solid, rich, and influential of all the Spanish American republics.

The occupation of Argentina was prolonged and laborious. The European population increased slowly. But the descendants of the cattle, horses, and sheep, brought over in the sixteenth century and allowed to range untended and unclaimed, increased by hundreds of thousands until the plains seemed one vast heaving sea of browsing beasts. In the eighteenth century anyone had a right to take as many as 12,000 cattle. If he wanted more he secured a permit from the governor. But cattle were then valuable only for the hides. Hides were the only cargo that Buenos Aires exported.

In the early years of independence, lack of transport, unsatisfactory means of preserving meat, and insufficient labour to cultivate the soil made Argentina an unrewarding country. Only towards the end of the last century did she begin her meteoric rise in the world of trade—after a Frenchman named François Tillier discovered the art of refrigeration. When it was found that fresh beef packed in ice would arrive in Europe in prime condition, all those lowing herds of the plains took on a golden value and men rushed out and laid claims to thousands of head, just as in covered wagon days in the United States pioneers staked out claims to hundreds of acres of uninhabited lands.

Railways made possible the facile transportation of cattle to markets near the ships. The railway and refrigeration were the twin fairy godmothers that made poor Argentina rich. Formerly when cattle were slaughtered for their hides the meat had been left to rot. Now the live cattle were sent by railway to the port, slaughtered hygienically, and preserved by ice.

Windmills began to dot the landscape to protect the animals against drought. An Englishman named Richard Newton had brought to Argentina in 1845 the first barbed wire for fencing. Wire was stretched decisively across the pampas, and what had been communal in ownership became individual.

English cattlemen began bringing over their blooded bulls to improve the Creole stock. Shortly Argentina became one of the most profitable cattle countries in the world. And as great fortunes were being made from beef, the realization came that this grazing land could be turned into one vast farm. Farmers learned that with only the slightest cultivation wheat, maize, oats, and linseed would grow in incredible abundance, that six to ten crops of alfalfa could be cut annually on this soil. In the last decade of the last century Argentina produced little more than one per cent of the world's wheat. Later she became the second wheat-producing country of the world.

Italian and Spanish immigrants began pouring into the country to work the wheat fields. Some who came as share croppers would themselves possess at the end of two years fortunes equal to the richest citizen in their native old-world villages. Though droughts and plagues of locusts often filled them with despair, the good years were so profitable that their pockets bulged with silver. When the news of sudden wealth went back to the old countries, the surging tide of immigration mounted. The flow has not been checked. Nor is it likely to stop soon. Even today there are approximately only nine people to the square mile in Argentina, and experts estimate that 240 to the square mile could be well taken care of.

Argentina is almost entirely a white country. Altogether there are only 300,000 in which there is any strain of Indian blood. The Argentinian colonists pursued the policy of extermination rather than assimilation. As for the pure descendants of the aborigines, only some 25,000 are left. These have been crowded down into the bleaker southern parts of Patagonia almost off into the Straits of Magellan. Seventy-five per cent of the population are of European descent Argentina-born. About twenty-three per cent are foreign born, the bulk being Italian and Spanish. Most of the Italians are from the neighbourhood of Milan in the north, where there is a strain of Teuton in the blood. While the Italians of the south went north to New York, these more hardy Italians of the north embarked south to Buenos Aires.

In 1880 Argentina had little more than 2,000,000 inhabitants. In 1895 there were 4,000,000. Forty years later, in 1935, she had 12,000,000—perhaps the greatest increase in population of any important country in the world. The British community, including those Argentine born of British descent, numbers about 50,000, while in the whole country there are hardly more than 3,000 Americans.

Norbourne was lost in his figures, when a stir among the

passengers brought him back to Mendoza. At last word had come that Buenos Aires weather experts believed the fog would have lifted by the time the aeroplane arrived. Mendoza soon lay far behind; the mountains were gone and so were the nearer hills. Below, stretched interminably to four horizons, spread the most extensive flat pasture on the globe. In summer the pampa would be a green monochrome with wheat fields and grass waving in the wind like a gentle sea. Today in late winter, it was mottled—vast squares of brown ploughed earth, patches of nibbled half-parched grasses. The herds of browsing cattle looked like ticks feasting on a cow's flank.

The roads, the neutral colour of the surrounding fields, were hardly distinguishable from the ploughed land. Monotonously straight, the roads are bordered with lines of barbed wire and telegraph lines, instead of trees or hedges. Since there is no road-building material like rocks or pebbles in all the expanse of pampa, dirt roads mainly serve Argentina's purposes. If they are heavy with sticky prairie mud in wet weather or chalky with deep dust in dry weather, the motorist or the horseback rider puts up with these conditions with whatever grace he chooses.

In the early days the settlers had invented an ingenious chariot for their wives. When a woman wanted to do her shopping at a trading post the husband would seat her on a cowhide laid on the ground behind the horse's heels and tied by leather thongs to his saddle. Leisurely he would drag her to her destination in a splatter of mud or a cloud of dust.

For those who desire today to cross the country by railway, there are luxurious express trains, though the landscape is so featureless that the elaborate observation cars hardly serve any reasonable purpose. Only seven countries in the world exceed Argentina's total of railway mileage. Over the manifold tracks, grain and cattle are ceaselessly being rushed to the elevators and *frigorificos* which will in turn pour them into the insatiable maws of ships which will disgorge in European ports. Except for the line that goes over the Andes, there really was no problem in the construction of Argentina's railways. All the engineers had to do was to lay ties and rails across a surface flat as a billiard table. In some places for stretches 175 miles long there is not an inch of curve.

It was by means of these railways that Great Britain, in the last quarter of the last century, became so closely bound to the progress of Argentina. The Americans entered the picture only when the country began to plough up grazing ranges into fields for corn and wheat. The United States had developed a machine that could plough, harrow, and plant seed all at the same time, and another machine that harvested and threshed with facility and economy. The same sort of farm machinery that was used on the farms of the Mississippi River districts seemed perfectly suited to the needs of the pampas. Europe had nothing to offer in competition. The Italian and Spanish immigrants took to the American mechanical devices, and though reluctant to purchase from the United States anything that she could buy in other markets, Argentina gave in to the demands of her farmers. United States machinery has proved invaluable to the economic well-being of the country.

Norbourne was willing to believe the truth of Bryce's statement: "There is always in this land an amplitude of air and a solemn splendour of the sunset glow to carry the mind away beyond its near surroundings." But from the air he could not feel the spell; he could only feel the loneliness and the monotony. Occasionally the monotony of the flatness would be broken by ranch houses surrounded by shade and fruit trees. The homes of the ranch owners were low bungalows with plenty of guest rooms. Hospitality in these remote places is even more of a boon to hosts than to guests.

At Villa Mercedes the planes landed and the passengers got out for luncheon. While the passengers from the first plane were eating, Norbourne stood outside, in the shade of a chinaberry tree, talking with the little New Yorker. The chinaberry tree was just beginning to put out the first intimation of its buds. He felt he had met an old friend in the chinaberry tree. In the spring his home town was perfumed with the heavy fragrance of its heliotrope-coloured blossoms. "It's a great favourite on the pampas, too," explained the local airport manager, "because it's about the only tree the locusts won't touch. After a plague of them, when the last leaf of everything else is gone, the chinaberry, as green as ever, gives us hope to plant the next year's crop."

"The winds are enemies of the trees too—almost as bad as the locusts," he added, as a blast from the south cracked about them like a whiplash. The little boy turned his face away; Norbourne clutched his hat; the trees stiffened to resist the assault. "When the *pampero*, the harsh, cold wind from the south, blows, the trees look as if they were humanly suffering. The *pampero's* something like your Texas norther."

"That's why Darwin said, 'Trees do not love the pampas.' "

A *gaucho* from some neighbouring cattle ranch rode up on his pony to send a radiogram. As he tethered the beast to the chinaberry tree the breeze blew his snuff-coloured poncho out into heroic folds, but his stiff black hat tied under his outthrust chin with a tight band of elastic did not budge. Over his left thigh hung a brown leather apron, the colour of his sunburnt skin, to protect his trouser leg from the lasso's friction. Huge spurs clanked on the heels of his small booted feet. From his belt dangling over his left thigh hung the long, sheathed knife. The little boy, dressed out of Saks Fifth Avenue, looked at the moviesque costume with envious admiration.

The Englishman who had sent his three trunks around the world said, "I say!"

The *gaucho* disappeared into the telegraph room.

"Not that the *pobre gaucho* is by any means oppressed like the *roto* in Chile," Elliott said. "He has far too much spirit for that. And only in this generation has he really 'gone into service.' "

"Do they farm too, now?" Norbourne asked.

"Oh, no, the *gauchos* have no taste for following a plough or planting seed. The native cowboy descendants of the old wild *gauchos* handle the cattle, while the recent immigrants from Spain and Italy do the agricultural work. Exclusive meat eaters, they are scornful of cultivated vegetation. Oddly, they seem to grow robust and iron-muscled without ever tasting a green vegetable or an orange. *Yerba maté* tea apparently gives them all the vitamins they need."

When the *gaucho* came out they hoped he would tarry, but he mounted his pony in a flashing arc, whirled him about and dashed off, as if uncomfortable before the alien gaze.

For one fleeting instant Norbourne had caught his eye. He saw there the look of a man who is no longer monarch of all he surveys. It was not the right sort of expression for a *gaucho* to have. Once he *was* Argentina, he and what he stood for. Now wheat fields and foreign banks and French culture were just as much Argentina as he. Never again would this type, that had no interest but horses and cattle and treeless space, regain his absolute kingdom. His *gaucho* ancestor had gloried in ruling bellowing herds of cattle by the expert twirl of a lasso or the exactly timed flip of a *boleta*—that leather thong tipped with metal balls and thrown at the animal's ankles. He and his horse had become as close to each other as if they had been demi-natured like centaurs. He idled over the plains, slept in the open, lassoed a wild cow when he was hungry, killed it, sliced off a hunk and left the remains to rot in the sun. He joyed in his own equestrian audacities, his physical prowess, his phenomenal endurance, in the simplicity of his rhythms, his meat and *maté* diet.

And today the descendant of that gipsy of the unfenced pampa, who had recognized no boundaries but the sky and earth and farthest horizons and no other law except the law of force, was hired to great ranch owners who had been shrewd enough to buy the square miles right under the *gaucho's* eyes. Still companioned by three most necessary friends, his horse, his lasso, and his knife, the contemporary *gaucho* has lost the fourth most important of all—that inspired and ruthless independence. Out of all the types of people Norbourne was to meet in this quickly grown nation, the *gaucho* was the only one whose eyes look into the past instead of the future.

Just beyond Villa Mercedes they ran into the fog. Grey drifts blotted out the neutral-coloured earth. Norbourne did not mind. He had seen enough of those monotonous flat acres. He adjusted his chair and lay back in semi-reclining position and took a nap. When he woke up, the thunderbird was hovering over the mist-laden edge of the world's largest city below the equator. Beyond lay the Atlantic. They had crossed the continent.

Cordial Relations

Norbourne stepped out on the soil of Buenos Aires with some foreboding. He knew that Argentinians expected visitors to be humbled by the bigness and richness of their capital. He had heard that they would stand for no adverse criticism, that they had a special dislike for Yankees. His uncertainties were not allayed when in the customs office an Argentinian employed by a United States concern exclaimed in a vicious *sotto voce* hiss, "By God, that Yankee should be made to pay duty on those cameras. The customs officers shouldn't have passed them duty free."

To Norbourne's relief the Argentinian who had come to meet him turned out to be a bland and genial gentleman. Ruddy-skinned, sandy-haired, he bore the name of Alberto Williams. He had been born an Argentinian of British parents, and, like Chileans with similar mixed names, he thought of himself as a loyal son of his father's adopted country and not as an Englishman.

"Argentina has one very concrete reason for her cordiality to England," said Señor Williams, having tea with Norbourne in his room at the Plaza after he had helped get things settled. "The countries are economically complementary. For half a century the United Kingdom has been her leading customer by a large margin. Nine-tenths of Argentina's exports belong to the two general categories of live-stock products and agricultural products. The United States produces within her own borders just about all the beef, pork, mutton, wheat, corn, and oats that she needs. England can't, and Argentina supplies her needs. We want England's hardware and woollen goods. Argentina would have far greater love for the United States if she could sell her more of her products. You see, we buy more from you than from anybody except England, but you rank only sixth or seventh among our customers."

"And the way to a nation's heart is through its commerce," Norbourne added.

"They say Argentina is the only foreign country in which Englishmen have made themselves thoroughly at home. Here they can get all the roast beef they want."

A man with a weary, grating voice telephoned from the office downstairs. He gave an English name, Jackson. Norbourne asked him to come up. To his surprise the stranger entered with a resentful reserve. He was a small man, thin and somewhat worn-looking, about thirty.

"I am a public relations man," he said, "and because of some letters from New York I am here to offer my services in showing you about." Norbourne offered him tea, but he declined. He had had tea, and he couldn't stay long now, but he would call Norbourne tomorrow if he liked.

"I'm relieved to see you," he said, looking Norbourne up and down. "The last American I had to show about was a frightful creature—a woman syndicate writer—an old hag in the face, though I must say she did dress well. But she could ask the most idiotic questions. It's astounding the asinine questions Americans can ask."

Norbourne looked a bit dashed and Señor Williams positively shocked. "Are you English?" Norbourne asked.

"My parents were. I am Argentinian. Some of your Americans have the idea that we're nothing but a lot of feathered Indians." His eyes bulged suddenly with reminiscent resentment. "You pretend to be greatly amazed that we have motor cars and don't ride wild horses into the shops. You think that life here consists of revolutions and tangos. Your writers belittle us every chance they get. The Americans have the most exaggerated opinion of themselves of any people in the world and they don't want to give credit to anyone else. We're a civilized nation with the very latest improvements."

Señor Williams flushed deeply.

"And they can be downright insulting," he went on, sitting on the edge of his chair. "A fortnight ago two oil men I was showing about tried to give me a tip. I was tempted to ram the money down their impudent throats."

Señor Williams was dumbfounded. He rose. Norbourne took three swallows of hot tea before he spoke. "But it's deplorable for you to have to come in contact with such dreadful people. Isn't there any other profession you could get into, where you wouldn't have to see Americans?"

"I must earn my bread," Jackson said with weak defiance.

"You're signally unfortunate. But really you shouldn't judge us all by the specimens you have met." Norbourne paused, and said with casual deliberation, "Suppose, for instance, I should leave Buenos Aires immediately and judge Argentinians entirely by you alone. That wouldn't be quite fair, now would it?"

The fellow shrugged, and admitted the thrust with a sour smile. "All Americans aren't so bad," he admitted reluctantly.

Señor Williams, in getting his hat, knocked a copy of the *Saturday Evening Post* off the table. Jackson picked it up. He looked at the cover and his eyes blazed viciously. "Here's an example," he said, his voice rising shrilly. "Only last month, one of your writers said in a story in this magazine that men appeared in the Jockey Club section of the race course in pyjama coats. It's an outrageous lie."

"But," countered Señor Williams, "men do wear pyjama coats at the races in summer—the lower classes do."

"But they don't wander into the Jockey Club section!"

"The author was merely mistaken."

"He did it deliberately," the other protested vehemently, "just to make us appear savage. By God, the government should bring him back here and castrate him."

The telephone rang. Norbourne answered it in a suppressed rage. It was Mrs. McCutcheon. She had just learned of his arrival and wanted him to dine with her and her husband informally in the grill at nine. "Don't dress," she added. "We're flying to Rio at dawn and our things are packed."

The interruption saved what of the situation there was to be saved. The Yankee-hater looked rather pathetic when Norbourne came back to the table, as if he knew he had made a fool of himself.

After he had gone Señor Williams mumbled a dozen apologies. "I hope you will reserve your opinion of us."

"I know American tourists can be infuriating sometimes. But I'm blessed if this fellow can't outdo them." Norbourne smiled. "I shall need twenty of your most charming citizens to take away the taste of this one."

"I have an invitation for you to visit one of the near-by *estancias* on Saturday. Don Leonardo will help, I hope, to alter your first impression. He's delightful. And his bulls have won more first prizes than those of any other breeder in Argentina."

The McCutcheons' other guests were a young Evanston couple and the seventeen-year-old daughter of an old Spanish family invited especially for seventeen-year-old Jackie McCutcheon. The young woman from Evanston wore black. The Argentine girl wore black lace with a tiny hat of forget-me-nots that matched the colour of her eyes and set off her ethereal expression. All the women who passed through the lobby wore black. In the circular blue parlour where they had cocktails, the only other people there were three sleek, silver-haired old gentlemen in tails, and their three luxuriantly handsome inamoratas dressed in black bouffant taffeta. The black décolleté set off the opulent expanse of pearl-coloured flesh and their great black Italianate eyes. As they sipped innocent-looking pink drinks with studied dignity the diamonds on their fingers and wrists flashed in the blinking eyes of their aging friends like the sunglasses naughty children tease monkeys with.

"Nothing but black in winter is considered chic in Buenos Aires," said Mrs. McCutcheon; "because it's flattering to eyes and complexion."

"I had to get an entirely new trousseau," the girl from Evanston complained. "It's very depressing to look at a woman's wardrobe in Buenos Aires. Rows and rows of garments, and everything, for street and for evening, black, black, black."

In the grill Norbourne sank his teeth into a delicious piece of beefsteak—an inch and a half thick, tender as a mushroom, juicy as a ripe peach. No wonder the *gauchos* grew into such a hardy breed.

"It's incredible—the appetite of Argentine women," the Evanston lady commented. "They eat pounds and pounds of beef and stay as slim as rails. That girl isn't four inches thick in the waist." Norbourne looked down the table at the reed-slender, angel-faced girl stowing away food, while Jackie did the talking.

"How do you like it here?" he asked the Evanston couple during the dessert.

"We're mad about it," the wife said. "There's so much to do here, so much variety. Life seems so much more meaningful, so much gayer—so much more free."

"I doubt the freedom," said the Argentine girl, as her mother arrived to take her home.

The mother had great natural charm and vitality and the air of a woman of the world. "My daughter, in one sense, is an American," she said to Norbourne. "She was born at the Argentine Embassy in Washington. At the time, my husband was in charge of some news-service there; our flat wasn't perfection; and the ambassador kindly invited us to the embassy for the 'accouchement.' In fact he insisted on it in the name of Argentina—" She laughed. "Such a delightfully original invitation that we accepted. That's one of the reasons why we have heart-strings binding us to America."

"You liked the United States, then?" he asked in some surprise.

"Have you ever seen a South American who has actually lived there who didn't?" She smiled warmly.

"I feel more encouraged about the cordial relations between the two nations," Norbourne said, after the mother and daughter had gone. He told them something of his encounter with Jackson.

"That's the way many of them used to feel," Mr. McCutcheon said. "But the attitude is changing. The press is becoming downright friendly and—neighbourly. You will notice they have stopped using the term Yankee, which wasn't meant to flatter us. Moreover, they have stopped resenting our calling ourselves Americans, instead of North Americans. They themselves are beginning to call us Americans now."

"Albeit All Is Fair"

In 1580, Don Juan de Garay of Paraguay with "sixty-six folks of seasoned courage," and four heifers and a bull, founded the present city of Buenos Aires. He aimed, he said, to make a city which men should not be able to destroy—a city which should be the "Gateway of the Earth!" In 1580 he drew his chess-board plans with space for 4,000,000 inhabitants. Not until 1776, however, when the city was made a seat of vice-royalty, did it begin to grow. In 1810, the year of Argentina's declaration of independence, there were sixty thousand people in Buenos Aires. A century later, a million. Then in the last twenty-five years—from 1910 to 1935—its population swelled to two and a half million. If it continued at its present rate of increase, Norbourne reflected, by 1950 it would reach the four million de Garay optimistically planned for.

When at the turn of the century the nation grew rich, the cattlemen and the wheatgrowers invested their quick-got gains in their metropolis, importing from France and Italy architects, gardeners, sculptors, interior decorators as prodigally as another country would import Negro labourers for crop-gathering. Consequently most of the city has been built or rebuilt in the last forty years, and most of it in the grand manner of a caliph who decrees lordly pleasure domes, parks, and plazas with casual gesture.

Nothing, the city fathers said, is impossible to Argentinians. In 1910, three months before the opening of the Centennial celebration, the government decided that the Capitol did not show up luminously enough from the Avenida de Mayo because of crowding business buildings. So, appropriating £5,000,000, it hired an army of wreckers and landscape gardeners. Within ten weeks four blocks of buildings were torn down, trees and flowering shrubs were planted, lawns sodded, a lake excavated, promenades arranged, and a monument unveiled.

The effect of this meteoric growth, however, is somewhat confusing. The architecture is many-blooded like the people and many-epoched: French, Spanish, Moorish, Baroque, Gothic, Georgian. Some quarters are as theatrical as a Riviera setting produced in Hollywood. Of the public buildings none sticks in the mind except the Casa Rosada, the nation's Pink House, where the President lives, and the Cathedral, with its Greek façade and twelve Corinthian columns, which reminds one of the Madeleine. But there are resplendent boulevards, magnificent in conception, and elegantly groomed avenues of French châteaux with pretentious gateways and liveried doormen, which might seem to lead to the Arc de Triomphe were it not for tropical palms and pungent eucalyptus trees.

Buenos Aires evidences superlatively what can be done with an unattractive site. Standing hardly three dozen feet above high water mark on a flat alluvial plain with none of the natural advantages of Santiago, Lima, or Bogotá, it is a tribute to Juan de Garay's extravagant optimism. Although obviously too new, too elaborate and showy, the general effect is neither raw nor harsh. What it lacks is the charm of mellowness.

From his hotel window Norbourne contemplated the piled stone, the lavish planting, and the madding crowd that made Buenos Aires a great world capital. He was not quite happy about it. His first days had left him disconcerted at the bigness, the opulence, the ostentation, the smart newness, the fantastic prices. He found it awkward to adjust himself to the palaces in endless repetitions, streams of motor cars thick as a plague of locusts, queues of business men with Chicago Loop expressions on their handsome Latin faces.

Buenos Aires must be, he thought, the most unfortunate city in the world for the not-well-to-do. He had discovered the cause of Jackson's bitterness in the Renaissance Palazzo on Calle Florida called the Jockey Club. He had been told solemnly that it was the most expensive club in the world to belong to. When he inspected its floors of gloomy rooms hung with expensive French paintings, he was informed half jokingly that they cost "so many thousand steers apiece." He learned the alleged cost of the onyx stairway, and the incredible stakes played for at the card tables. And he gathered from the awesome way in which the attendants crept about and from Jackson's resentful, thwarted look, that to be able to sit down in that heavy atmosphere on a familiar plane of equality with the millionaires was the be-all and end-all of many an Argentinian's ambition. The people of Buenos Aires run the risk of knowing, like Wilde's cynic, the price of everything and the value of nothing.

Down in the street raucous newsboys were hawking the papers of a dozen nationalities in a dozen languages, Norbourne had seen the Greek quarter, the Turkish, Syrian, Hindu, and Yiddish quarters, and the Japanese scattered commercially and strategically in various places. They were still themselves and yet strangely of the Argentine. The national spirit has proved greater than the cliques, the individuals, the varying traditions and prejudices of people from thirty-odd nations. While driving through various quarters of the city, he had exclaimed at intervals, just like every other visitor: "This is Paris; that is Rome; this is Monte Carlo;

that is London." But he knew it was too facile to say, for instance, "Buenos Aires is Paris, Rome, and Chicago shaken together, modernized and speaking the Spanish tongue with a western accent." It is that and much more. Besides the Mediterranean love of beauty and the taste for elegance and sophistication of European capitals, it possesses the distinctive flavour of the pampas. The business audacity of the United States, the solid conservatism and the suburban snobberies of England have joined with Spanish pride, Italian vanity, the *gaucho's* fierce passion for the out-of-doors and blended all the motifs and rhythms into a futuristic symphony, spirited, materialistic, ornate.

Norbourne walked into the bathroom, drew a glass of water from the tap and drank—something he would not have done in any of the West Coast hotels. No city has a better or more up-to-date water supply and sewage system. Indeed, Buenos Aires possesses all the modern amenities and comforts, in full measure, pressed down, running over—first class hotels and shops; first class night clubs, opera, newspapers, race tracks; first class physicians, prostitutes, polo ponies. He thought of the "more than a hundred" parks, plazas, and promenades, the municipal baths, the island beauty spot of Tigre gay with its pennant-strung yachts and boating parties and satin-smooth green lawns, the famous athletic club of Hurlingham, ultra British in appointments and atmosphere. No other materialistic capital offers its people more pleasant diversions to relax them during their diligent pursuit of wealth. Buenos Aires has just about everything—except—except—He doubted if he could ever feel contentment. There ran through his mind the line, "Albeit all is well, there lacketh something still."

Estancia De Luxe

Within forty miles of the capital lies the country seat of Don Leonardo, with twenty-five thousand acres of park and grazing meadows. With one of his sons and a Scottish overseer, the Don met Norbourne and Señor Williams at the gate to save them the two mile drive up the avenue of magnolias leading to his house. Norbourne had pictured this *estanciero* as something like the roaring old *gaucho* chieftain in *The Four Horsemen of the Apocalypse*, who fought and rode and bred sons and cattle with a gusto and audacity that made every man envious who read the book. But out of the parked car hopped a little bandy-legged man with a white Vandyke beard and grey eyes glistening behind gold-rimmed spectacles. He was barely five feet tall. He wore riding breeches and a wide, flapping Burberry raincoat that stopped above the knees. In one hand he carried a gold-headed stick, and in the other a camera. With lively affability he greeted his guests and introduced his quiet-mannered son, Simon, his third child. He had thirteen children in all, not a bad record, but he believed Simon would beat him—"Simon, at twenty-nine, already has six," he chuckled. He gave Simon a flattering poke in the ribs. Although he had only seventeen grandchildren, he hoped by the grace of God and the ways of Nature to live to trot the thirtieth on his knee.

Norbourne and Señor Williams got into the back seat with Don Leonardo, and the overseer took the wheel. They entered an apparently endless pasture. The overseer dashed in and out among the herds as if he had been on horseback. The cattle paid little more attention to the car than they would have to horse and rider. The bulls lifted their thick-necked heads, stared with mild resentment, switched their tails disdainfully. The cows looked up placid-eyed, turned their rumps and went on grazing. They were all magnificent creatures, sleek and heavily padded with meat. The breed was Hereford, roan with white spots.

"They look very gentle—even the bulls," Norbourne commented.

"Ah, yes, they make 'quiet' beef," Don Leonardo said. "We breed, you know, for tender quality of the meat as well as weight. Just as fighting bulls are bred for muscle, speed, and fierceness. I prefer the Herefords above all other cattle, though there are six Shorthorns to every Hereford in the nation and the Aberdeen-Angus has recently been introduced. But Herefords have brought me many championships. I have sold good bulls for £20,000 and £25,000 at auction. These that we are looking at now would fetch £5,000 to £10,000. Soviet Russia is our best customer of registered bulls. Here, Simon, you must take our picture, with the herd for background."

As they posed for photographs, Norbourne wanted to know if they used the surplus milk for butter-making.

"We are going into dairy farming as a by-product and alternative to beef production. And as for Argentine butter! In early summer the grasses are so succulent that we produce butter finer than the most delicately-flavoured product of Normandy."

Norbourne learned many things about cattle. A cow that nibbled in plentiful tender grasses will bear three or four more calves than cows that browse on the tough grass of sandy soil and wear their teeth down so that they cannot get enough food to furnish proper milk. A cow will "keep in" three or four years longer on good soil. "Nature has strange ways of knowing these things," Don Leonardo said, almost reverently. "A pedigreed cow that lived on my best soil had a calf when she was twenty-one years old."

Cows have their notions, and wiles have to be used on them. Last month the mother of a blood calf had died, and they tried to get an ordinary cow to act as wet nurse. The cow refused, so they took her calf, killed it, skinned it, tied the common calf's hide about the breeded calf. When the cow smelt the hide she thought it was her own offspring and let it suck.

"At what ages do a cow and bull get the best calves?" asked Norbourne.

"A young sire and an old cow produce by far the best." He spoke in the manner of an authority. Then noting the expression on Norbourne's face he poked him lightly in the ribs and laughed explosively. "But I do not think that would be good for humans."

They all laughed.

Norbourne whirled about as the old gentleman pointed excitedly behind him. An ostrich that had sprung up out of nowhere went tearing off across the plain. "We could have thousands of them, but we keep only one for curiosity. They eat the partridge eggs. I have several friends with ostrich farms of four and five thousand birds. But we prefer partridges to ostrich plumes. We keep some fields reserved for the partridges, fenced off so that the cattle can't eat the grass. The partridges like long grass in which to——" he hesitated for the right English word—"to condense themselves." A hurt, resentful expression changed his aspect. "In North America you eat many Argentina partridges in your restaurants. The United States won't buy our beef—no, but you take our partridges."

"But we raise almost all the meat we can use," Norbourne said. "We buy our bird seed from you," he added, smiling in mock defence.

"Ah, birdseed—yes," the Don repeated in mingled amusement and indignation. "Birdseed and partridges. You are taking all our partridges. Soon we shall have none. You—you are like the ostriches."

They got in the car and drove over a thousand other acres. The two houses of Don Leonardo's sisters were some miles apart on the estate. Set down before one of the houses with no foreknowledge of what land he was in, Norbourne would have sworn he was in France. The house was a perfect reproduction of a seventeenth-century Touraine château. Finding such an elaborate and uncharacteristic structure on the pampa was like beholding a mirage. Its unreality was intensified when no one appeared. There was no sign of life except the fluttering of disturbed pigeons.

The second sister's house was a palace lifted out of Seville. Here a single ancient servant appeared and showed them in. The patio was done in slabs of black and white marble. Yellow-blossomed vines clambered up the black and white balustrade. It was a charming spot, but it no more belonged to the pampa than the French château.

Norbourne wondered about the ladies of the family and eagerly anticipated meeting them at Don Leonardo's own house. But first they drove for an hour over a park so lovely it might have been in England. The planting had been done with a tree lover's eye. "In Brazil you have to destroy trees, in Argentina you have to plant," Don Leonardo said. He explained that when his grandfather bought this land a century earlier it possessed not a single tree. The thousands of palms and *demaras*, *omus*, eucalyptus, camphor trees, magnolias, mimosas, elms, pines, and English copper beeches had been planted with his grandfather's and father's own hands. They had as great a passion for trees as for cattle. They imported trees from Madeira, from Australia, South Africa, New England. Almost every variety that grows in both the torrid and temperate zone grows in Buenos Aires province.

Norbourne saw the sheep ranges, and prodigious hogs fattening on acorns, and stables worthy of old-time Muscovite princes. He was taken to the tiled swimming pool where the seventeen grandchildren splash on Sundays. "The little boys at one hour and the little girls at another," explained Don Leonardo. "It is not nice for the opposite sexes to mingle too freely." They passed to the church where the families and servants worship regularly and a priest comes out weekly to hear confessions. Don Leonardo walked up to the altar rail and unaffectedly knelt to thank God for his bounty. Watching the old man at prayer Norbourne thought he must be the happiest man in the world with such worthy earthly possessions and with no one to question his benevolent absolute monarchy, not even his Moorish prejudice that rigorously segregated the sexes in infancy.

In the great drawing room where old sherry and *pâté de fois gras* sandwiches were set out to refresh them, Norbourne had the uncanny sensation of being watched from ambush. Once or twice he turned suddenly as if expecting to discover people hidden in the shadows of the heavy antique furniture—perhaps the ladies of the house stealing a glance at the foreigner. Then looking high up along the maroon walls, as if expecting secret windows such as had once made him nervous in an Arab's house in Tunis, he realized it was the bulls' eyes. The fixed glassy orbs of a dozen or more surpassingly regal bulls glared at him from enlargements of photographs. On metal strips hanging from the base of their frames dangled their distinguished epitaphs and memorials, with records and dates of blue ribbon awards, climaxed by championships. Norbourne walked to the wall for a nearer view of the celebrities. This sultanic creature was Turkey, the first Hereford to win the Grand Prize in 1896. Here were Holwer and Lagger and Marvel, and Jubilant that won the championship for the *estancia* four years in succession. This was Fanfare and that Newton Ben; and here were Royal Champion and Lockley's Gleam, who had won in 1933 and 1934. Beside the bulls' heads the oil portraits of proud Aunt Juanita and beauteous Cousin Carmen, and even great-grandfather General Esteban looked oddly unimpressive.

In the dining room a thousand tangible mementos attested the superiority of Don Leonardo's bulls. The great room was as crammed with objects in silver as the hold of a sixteenth-century pirate ship returning from the sack of a city. Urns, pedestals, punch bowls, platters lined the walls in cabinets ten feet high. And some of the gold-lined loving cups were capacious enough to serve as a beast's watering trough. The dining room windows were barred like the Bank of England, and clamorous burglar alarms had been installed. Ten years ago, during the family's absence in the city, a gang of burglars had cleaned out the silver prizes. The trophies Norbourne now gazed on were those of the last decade.

In a sitting room lined with other stately cabinets where reposed the countless gold-stamped blue ribbons, Don Leonardo got out his treasured English Herd Book. Running his agile fingers among the pages he pointed out his commendations. He was the first Argentinian ever to be recognized in the English Herd Book. His bulls had more notations than those of all the other Argentine breeders put together. "I'm sorry you couldn't see my best ones today. They are already in the city for exhibition. The cattle show begins on Tuesday."

Over a second sherry, Norbourne awaited the appearance of the ladies hopefully. "No pictures of cows?" he commented, coldly returning the contemptuous stare of the bull called Jubilant. "No champion cows?"

The old man laughed, bright as a cricket. "The best cows only give milk and have a dozen or so calves in a lifetime. A good bull fathers a thousand cattle."

"I had hoped to meet your mother," Norbourne ventured to Simon in an undertone as they rose to leave.

The gentle Simon looked surprised and somewhat confused. "I dare say she is busy with household affairs."

"A man's world, Argentina," Norbourne thought. "The bull's the thing."

When they went out to the car Don Leonardo's horse, tethered to an *omu* tree and ready for a gallop, whinnied. "I am in the saddle ten hours a day," the old gentleman said, as they went to speak to it. "Not bad for seventy, eh? Come back, and we'll ride over the plain together and you can get better acquainted with the pampa."

"Will you lend me your horse?" Norbourne asked, stroking the slender neck of the fine animal.

"I will lend you one just as good—perhaps better. There are only two things an Argentinian won't lend you—his horse and his wife." He laughed. "But," he made a Spanish gesture with his strong-fingered little hand, "the rest of my *estancia* is at your command."

Danse Macabre

They had luncheon at Swift's Golf Club which was set at the edge of a palm-studded course laid out for the delectation of more than six thousand employees. "The English influence has been responsible for a rapid development in sports," Señor

Williams said. "Individual business concerns, packing houses, and department stores have their private playgrounds for grown-ups in the suburbs—golf links, tennis courts, pools, running tracks. Girls whose mothers rarely touched their silken slippered feet to any soil but that of their own patio play golf and tennis with the enthusiasm of boys. On the golf courses and tennis courts the Argentine women eliminate the 'Mediterranean faults of their figures.' "

After lunch they drove to the freezing works located on a deep water canal. "The meat for which Argentina is unrivalled," said Señor Williams, "is chilled beef, which is superior to frozen beef. Chilled beef is carried to European markets at a temperature only two or three degrees under freezing and arrives in prime condition with all the juice and flavour preserved. The agents of the *frigorificos* buy their cattle and sheep on the *estancias* and ship them by train directly to the yards, where they are slaughtered, dressed, and chilled, and then packed into the insulated ice rooms of the steamers."

As they got out in the spotless, shrub-planted grounds of the enormous structures, Norbourne recalled Darwin's horror at the old open public slaughter places. Then the ground was composed of bones and mud made from blood, and the stench was overpowering. The cattle were lassoed by the horns, dragged by strong horses to the killing spot, where the "matador" cut the hamstrings and, amid their terrific bellowings, stuck them.

The door of the *frigorificos* was opened. A blast of chill air swept out. Attendants slipped white apron coats over Norbourne's and Williams' top coats. Like medical students on their way to an arena to observe an operation white and sanitary, they went down cool corridors through a long room austere as a hospital ward. A troop of señoritas dressed like trained nurses were separating the chitterlings and sweetbreads and tripe, potting meats, canning tongues, making sausage and jelly, and putting up the many varieties of glass-jarred concoctions that liven delicatessen shop windows.

"The by-products of the meat trade are many," said Señor Williams. "Virtually every ounce of the cattle is used, even some of the bones are manufactured into bone articles; others converted into glue. We get animal charcoal for sugar refining, black pigments, poultry food, manure. Hairs, bristles, hoofs, and horns are all conserved, as well as the dried blood and ox-galls."

Swift and Company has had a packing business in South America since 1907. From the year 1893 to 1908 American beef was shipped from the United States to England in substantial quantities. But with the advancing costs of cattle in the United States and increased competition from Argentina, in order to continue on a profitable basis Swift purchased the La Plata plant in Buenos Aires to ship direct from Argentina. The business flourished, and they set up other plants in Rosario, Patagonia, Uruguay, and Brazil.

From the canning room, they went up flights of iron stairs to the third story where the killings took place. They had arrived ten minutes too late for the actual slaughter which was over at two. White-frocked helpers, with water hose and mops, were swabbing up the floors. The last steer had been killed and skinned. But jigging about on an iron-hooked mechanism, which ran with the regularity of an escalator, the carcasses of the last beasts killed were running a butcher-gang gauntlet. Skilled workers performed their individual tasks conversely to men in the assembly plant of an automobile factory. As the whole carcasses passed, they were disassembled, their hearts, livers, kidneys, and internal oddments removed with dexterity and placed in proper trays. At the most expeditious point they were beheaded. And while they went dancing with their hind legs strung up to the ceiling, a trough beneath caught the blood that was to go into nourishing puddings and jellies. Their empty sides were sprayed clean with a water hose. Just before they entered the coldest chambers they were split into two lengthwise halves. Their right halves preceded their left halves through the narrow door.

Norbourne was fascinated by the overtones of the scene's raw naturalism. Nothing is more real than a side of dressed beef, and yet the whole affair was like a macabre fantasy in which the repulsive lost its repellent quality in the strangeness. Butchers flashed their knives and cleaners twirled their water-sprays in a cathedral-like silence, broken only by the mechanical droning of the moving rack.

Last year, Señor Williams told him, Argentina had exported 4,500,000 quarters of chilled beef and 250,000 quarters of frozen beef and 4,000,000 mutton carcasses. The combined Plata River *frigorificos*—those of Swift, Armour, and the British concerns—were equipped to kill and dress 25,000 steers and 60,000 sheep in a day. On this one concrete floor on which he was now standing, in the preceding year 356,741 cattle and 1,079,746 sheep and 317,727 hogs had been struck on the head and slaughtered.

The guide motioned them into the refrigeration room. Norbourne shivered under his top coat as the heavy insulated door closed behind them. He blinked at the uncanny monochrome in coral. The atmosphere was suffused with a rosy glow from electric illumination playing on the coral-coloured flanks of hundreds of vibrating beef-halves, jigging upside down on their iron hooks two feet apart. The cattle danced in a serpentine formation up to white-frocked butchers with extra long knives who slit the halves dextrously to the backbone. They danced away and paused before other butchers who neatly sawed through the last inch of backbone. Attendants heaved the divided halves on to a different set of hooks. And like dancers trooping up one by one before the ballet master for criticism, the quarters paused automatically before a solemn-faced government inspector who put an indelible stamp on the flesh, appraising it according to quality and colour. Then they passed over a section of cable that recorded their weights to the ounce. At last their nakedness was covered in white stockingette, and to complete the dressing for the ocean voyage they were swathed in Hessian cloth. After twenty-four hours' rest on ice, they would be gathered up in great nets and set aboard a ship.

Norbourne and Señor Williams clambered up the plank of a freighter. Brawny, tow-headed Swedes were receiving yesterday's kill from the net lowered by a crane down into the freezing depths of a ship's hold. On their bulging shoulders, they bore the wrapped beef-quarters to their ice-lined chambers, where they would remain until they reached English soil and were roasted in English ovens for the stamina and glory of the British race.

Gateway of the Earth

From the stupendous exhibit of fresh-dressed beef Norbourne was taken to the equally stupendous exhibit of the pre-historic dead in La Plata's museum, ten minutes away. Here is gathered the world's best collection of extinct monsters: elephantine dinoceratans, reptilian dinosaurs seventy feet long, ichthyosaurs, proboscidean dinotheres with downward shooting tusks, and armadillos the size of whales.

As he walked among the reconstructed bones of gigantic creatures more fantastic than De Quincey ever concocted in his opium-soaked brain, he thought of the youthful Darwin who had left England in 1831 with unshaken belief in the creationist point of view. In his six years' sail Darwin saw nothing more impressive than the extinct specimens of Argentina. Shortly after his return to England he set down his conviction of the significance of geographical groupings and the transmutations of species.

On their return to Buenos Aires they passed the district of wretched corrugated-iron hovels where the poorer newly-arrived immigrants camped with the down-and-outs. It was not for lack of interest that Norbourne had not poked his head into shanties. It was limit of time that deterred him. He thought it more profitable to get opinions from local observers and experts than to cull snapshot impressions.

The contrast between the helter-skelter shacks, the dump heap and the magnificent Palermo Park not far away was startling. Palermo's abundant acres were as charming in spots as the Bois de Boulogne and more extravagantly planted and varied. Even though it was not the blooming season for most of the flowers, it was very lovely with the exotic foliage, bridges, lagoons, terraces, and Moorish summer houses built of Andalusian tile. On the willow-lined stream by the Rosary, swans glided among the white gondolas in which men were sculling girls and their chaperons.

In the zoological gardens the animals and the birds had been provided with the kind of settings that would remind them of their native haunts, just as memories of Rome and Seville and London had been utilized in sections of the city to ease the homesickness of foreign-born citizens. In their grottos and jungles the animals looked sleek and contented. Brilliantly plumaged birds preened themselves and sang lustily. Cream-coloured pumas prowled with consummate grace before their rocky caves. On the edge of a green stream dawn-pink flamingoes stood on coral-stick legs, more still than artists' models, while the water gurgled about their feet. A group of gaping immigrants wandered among the arbours and exotic trees with amazed expressions.

"They look," said Norbourne, "as if they had just entered the gates of Paradise."

"What about your proletariat?" he asked Señor Williams. "And your internationalists?"

"Not being an industrial nation we have no great proletarian problem. There is little class-consciousness; little organization of workers. As André Siegfried said, we are a nationalistic, property-owning democracy—a nation of business men and farmers. Men from the middle class and the masses here can work themselves up to high positions just as in the United States. We don't care a hoot about internationalists and revolutions. We've had only one revolution in half a century. That was bloodless and popular with everyone but the incumbent office holders."

Señor Williams's car turned into a road that ran along the city's water front for a dozen miles. Moored schooners, grimy colliers, tankers, and smart new steamers flew flags and pennants of all nations. Grain elevators were spouting wheat into the maws of tramps. Wagons clattered over the cobblestones of the wharves like incessant thunder. Through the ordered conglomeration of stevedores, cranes, hawsers, tow ropes, outgoing bales of wool and stacks of hides, incoming machinery and motor cars, passed the second greatest bulk of the hemisphere's international commerce, and the highest per capita trade of the world's great ports.

Along La Boca, the Old Port, seafarers of all nations eye the pert and tawdry fly-by-nights of all nations that still manage to ply their trade quietly, although the regular brothels have been banished, along with the obscene shows and naked movies, to the suburb called San Francisco. There under policed supervision one could still indulge in the most sensational kind of bawdy free-for-all that formerly made Buenos Aires notorious among sailors. But La Boca was reformed; the savage, sordid waterfront of the glamorous old days had turned respectable. From the cellar saloons in the afternoons now came the troubled, sensual strains of the tango with the added accompaniment of Italian accordians. Immigrants, just emerged from a ship's depths, bearing possessions tied up in table covers, pause on unsteady legs, to listen to the throbbing music. As they cross the cobblestones and step into the baptismal melting pot, they begin to sway to the rhythms of the tango.

Already possessing eleven miles of the world's most modern docks, Buenos Aires is extending them for an unbroken twenty-five miles. "When completed," commented Williams, "the city will be able to put the ships of the universe in her pockets."

"The Gateway of the Earth" de Garay had visioned. "Always the future," Norbourne said. "I hear that when you installed your new electrical plant you insisted not on this year's model but on next year's."

Williams laughed. "What we really wanted was a 1940 model."

Painted Pigeons

Along the Costanera Road, Norbourne suddenly broke off the conversation. He could not believe his eyes. "Look there!" he exclaimed excitedly. A rainbow seemed to be moulting. Hundreds of pastel-coloured birds fluttered in the shaft of late sunlight that fell across the road before them. By their size and movement they seemed to be pigeons, but they were pale green, canary yellow, turquoise, orchid, amethyst, rose. "Is it the effect of the sunset?" He stared at the spectacle before them and at the five o'clock sun. "Stop the car!"

Almost before it halted he jumped out. The pigeons on the grass were as gaily coloured as those fluttering in air. "They're real," he called to Williams, who followed amused.

"They are painted," Williams said.

"Painted pigeons!"

"Yes, they paint them for fiestas and special celebrations. When the President of Brazil paid us a visit they greeted him with thousands of loosed pigeons in Brazil's colours, blue and white. At the Eucharistic Conference they were painted the Pope's colours."

"But doesn't it hurt them?"

"Oh, no, they dip them in a cold dye solution. They don't seem to mind."

Standing on a grassy hillock, people were giving the birds grain from little waxed paper bags. Ragamuffin boys with trays strapped from their shoulders like night club cigarette girls wandered about and accepted contributions in exchange for corn and wheat. Norbourne bought four bags. By the time he had opened the first one a golden-coloured pigeon sat on his wrist and a sky-blue one perched on his shoulder. He spread grain in the palm of his hand. Pigeons every colour of the rainbow settled on his outstretched arm as if it had been a roost and three balanced on his fingers and thumb.

A black-bearded, unkempt man with the rapt expression of a prophet sauntered unsmiling among the people and the birds. Williams introduced Norbourne to him. In a torrent of fierce indignation he began to complain of the lack of adequate support from the government. "My pigeons are the main attraction of the riverside in summer and the municipality keeps me on the payroll as a 'peon' on a peon's salary. The monthly wage amounts to about £40 in American money. They expect me and my mother and my 17,000 pigeons to live on that!"

Because Norbourne was properly sympathetic, Blackbeard showed him his pigeon houses, pointed out twenty different species of birds, fuming furiously all the while about the needed repairs that he could not afford to make. Pigeons that had gone to roost flew out to greet him, hovering lovingly about him so thickly that he looked like a fierce-eyed feathered creature himself. Borrowing some wheat from Norbourne he put a few grains between his lips. Pigeons clinging to his chest picked it out as gently as if they had been kissing him.

"I was so young when I came over from Spain," he said, back in his vine-clad cottage, "I was still hanging to the breasts of my mother." Since the age of eight he had kept pigeons and until he was grown he had received periodic hidings from his mother because he lost wage-earning jobs by stealing time to care for his birds. After many years of vicissitudes trying to earn enough money to support his pigeons, the city had given him this plot near the Costanera and put him on the miserable wage. "If tourists didn't buy the bags of corn and pay generously, my pigeons would perish." Norbourne wondered why so rich a municipality did not prove a more generous patron to this grousing St. Francis whose all consuming hobby had such original publicity value. Painted pigeons seemed as symbolical of the ornate city as champion bulls did of the country at large.

Seeing some sewing lying on the table by a bowl of bananas Norbourne asked, "And does your wife love the pigeons as you do?"

"I have never taken a wife," Blackbeard replied. "I married my pigeons. They are more satisfactory. I'd rather manage seventeen thousand birds than one woman."

Daring

That evening at seven o'clock tea with the doctors from Copenhagen and Columbia, Norbourne met a young Argentino of German descent and an Argentinian girl of Russian-Italian descent. They had each spent a year at Columbia University on government scholarships won in nation-wide competitive examinations. They had come loaded with various invitations for driving, for boating, for dancing, for inspections of schools. Norbourne was courteously included, but as his time was engaged he had to decline. "Then," said the girl, with a dare-devil gleam in her eye, "would you walk down Calle Florida with me—alone, now?"

"I'd love it," Norbourne said, hastily slipping on his top coat before she changed her mind.

"My year in the States has made me bold," she said, as they stepped out into the lively night air. She gathered her furs close up over her mouth in a casual concealing gesture, but the nose veil could not dim the glint in her half-timid, half-defiant eyes. "If any of my friends recognize me I shall be severely criticized if not ostracized."

To make the daring of the adventure more thrilling Norbourne offered her his arm. Tingling with excitement she slipped her arm through his. They walked briskly, breathing in deep refreshing draughts of coolness. She was an athletic girl and could take long strides.

"Why all this nonsense about not being able to walk down the street with a man?" Norbourne said with some impatience. "In ancient Lima it didn't seem so out of place. But in this modern metropolis where you pride yourselves on the last word in up-to-dateness——"

"I know it seems absurd. We are one of the most backward nations in female emancipation. Little Uruguay across the river is far ahead of us. When an Argentinian wants a divorce she has to take the night boat over to Montevideo. We have neither the right of divorce nor the vote."

"Whenever I mention divorce or the position of women, I notice the men always change the subject as quickly as possible."

"Yes. They still like to regard us as personal jewels of great price—or fair game—or cows. Well, it's not going to be so much longer. You see, tonight I am breaking bonds."

They turned into the capital's Rue de la Paix. From four to eight in the evening vehicles are banished from Calle Florida and pedestrians crowd the middle of the street. Some are shoppers, but most are promenaders, sauntering, to see and to be seen. Here the national sport of flirting is indulged in by professionals and novices, with rules kicked into a cocked hat.

Tonight the shopping had almost ended. In some of the fashionable establishments attendants were dimming lights, but elegantly liveried commissionaires still stood before the doors. The street lamps were all lighted. Men and boys paraded with the gleam of fishermen in their eyes, hoping for a catch, but grateful for a nibble. The idea seemed to be to bump into as many girls as possible. They looked at Norbourne and his companion puzzled, suspicious, envious. The men were smartly groomed. Occasionally they would take off their hats and bow whether they knew the girls or not, revealing their world-famous slicked-down fashion in masculine hair dressing. Norbourne had always heard that the Argentino takes his personal appearance more seriously than any man on earth. It seemed that cousins of the late Rudolph Valentino were lurking in all the doorways.

In a short time his companion lost her self-consciousness, relaxed her grip on her furs and began to chat volubly about her year in the States, of the ridiculous ways she had broken through habits of restraint.

They walked on, passing monumental branches of New York

and Boston banks with lighted interiors like their North American counterparts and famous London department stores like Harrods. Here were the familiar French names before shop-fronts, more glittering than their originals on the Rue de la Paix. Jewels, couturières' models, costly furs, objets d'art in lapis lazuli, onyx, gold and platinum, just like Paris. The first spring styles were just being shown. (In New York they were having the August sales.) Electrical devices and modernistic chromium furniture were displayed against rich brocades. Among the de luxe shops a Manchester hardware store set out its solid wares in uncompromising British style. The portico of the Jockey Club was cluttered with ogling youngsters.

Norbourne and the girl were suddenly blocked by a couple of young men who were pretending to flip with their middle finger and thumb the anatomy of two young ladies preceding them.

"A hangover from the old days," his companion confessed. "When my mother was young the men used to pinch the girls' behinds, when they walked down Florida. (She was trying to be as emancipated in her speech as her actions.) In olden times ladies hired little Negresses to walk behind them as protection when they went shopping."

"How do you protect yourselves now?"

She laughed. "We look at their feet. Argentinos have lived in the saddle so much, they have small feet and are sensitive about them. Women are supposed to have large feet because they used to go about the house barefooted. Even today the lower middle class women wear flat bedroom slippers around the house. Now don't look at my feet, please. They are as big as your own New York women's."

She halted at a corner. "Now I must fly back to the corral. It's quite late for me to be out."

Norbourne asked her to dine with him. "Oh, that would be unheard of," she said admonishingly. "That couldn't possibly be explained. I should be utterly compromised. You can't even see me home. A neighbour might see you."

"But what about arriving at home alone at nine o'clock?"

"It's all right since I'm going in the direction of home. If I were seen at nine going away from home, then," she smiled broadly," it would be as you say, the very hell to pay."

Norbourne raised his hand to call a cab. "Oh, no——" She stopped him. "It isn't proper to go in a taxi. I must take a public bus—this one coming—it stops at my corner."

She breathed deeply and stretched out her arms exultantly and laughed as the bus bore down on them. "I've done it." She lifted her chin high. "Look!" At the end of the street above the glitter of the electric lights the Southern Cross hung aslant the Argentine night sky. The spiritual serenity glowing from the arrangement of platinum stars did not seem to accord with the modern city any more than its Moorish treatment of women.

"Thank you for the walk," the girl said. "You think I'm crazy, I know. But I've done it! I feel as Lady Astor must have felt the first day she took her seat in Parliament." She entered the bus with a kind of odd satisfaction.

"If walking down a street with a man can mean so much to an Argentine girl——" Norbourne stood there speculating.

"Hey," said an American voice behind him. "What are you up to? Come and have dinner with me at the American Club."

It was the pilot who had flown him over the Andes.

French View

After dinner Norbourne met a French aviator. They talked in the lounge over a Benedictine. He was not typically French in physiognomy or physique. He was a strong-bodied, full-lipped, honest-eyed man, dark as a Portuguese, and equable in manner.

"You may have noticed," he was saying, "that money and the price of beef are the favourite subjects of conversation."

They had been discussing a duel that had recently taken place between a minister of state and a senator, following an altercation in the senate chamber when a senator was shot and killed during session in an argument over the price of beef.

"The value set on money here is unfortunate. In Santiago, they take pride in old families—in Buenos Aires in the number of leagues of camp one owns, or the head of cattle, or the financial rating in gold pesos. Except in a few exclusive Spanish colonial families social distinction is something to be bought for a price. They are tremendously money-conscious in Argentina, but it's different from our French bourgeois penuriousness. They are ostentatious in their spending of money and forgo essentials to buy frivolities.

"From a Frenchman's point of view the young man here is glaringly 'unfinished,'" he went on quietly. "His flirtations on Florida Street are the most juvenile exhibitions. And as they say, it doesn't take a few days to learn how and when to kiss a woman's hand; it takes generations." He took up his liqueur glass.

"What do you really think of Buenos Aires?"

Norbourne hesitated. "It lacks originality, of course. But on the whole, the city's rather magnificent."

The Frenchman shrugged. "It may be magnificent, but it's not picturesque. Have you ever seen a lovely photograph of the place? No. The favourite tourist office photograph is a scene of Avenida Alvear crowded so thick with motor cars that you can't see the pavement. Incidentally this one country owns about 60 per cent of all the automobiles on the continent—95 per cent of them of American manufacture As Jorge Blanco said, in pointing out the increasing influence of the United States, almost all the films the Argentinos see and hear are Hollywood productions, they play American talking-machine records, wear ready-made American clothes, shave with American safety razors, drink American cocktails, commit their murders and suicides with Yankee firearms. They proclaim their love of England and France in reiterated bombast, but they are getting more Americanized every day—somewhat against their will, but doing it, nevertheless."

"But they still don't like us?"

"Because you both have many of the same defects," he replied promptly. "A country naturally likes to forget its own defects by contemplating another country's imperfections. They have known you principally through your salesmen, your movies, your jazz, and your dollar diplomacy. They see in the bragging, cocksure, money-getting type of Yankee a blurred image of themselves. That makes them sore. And when the Americano refuses to be sufficiently impressed at Argentina's progress it fills them with fury. They used to keep a special supply of chips on their shoulders for the Yankee to knock off. But the attitude is changing. England's influence is slackening, and the United States and Argentina are going to tie up in very friendly relations. And I'll tell you why you two nations are going to get together. In a sense, as world civilization goes, both nations are kids. Argentina and the United States are each something like precocious, ambitious children, unsuppressible, and occasionally bad-mannered. But for all their petty quarrelling, kids really understand each other and get along better playing together than with grown-ups."

"Europe is grown-ups; we are kids. Is that it?"

"Yes. Europe is old people—and tired, disillusioned, full of suspicion and hate. You are both young, full of vigour, with maturity to look forward to."

"That's very interesting," Norbourne said. "Perhaps you're right. Certainly the most impressive thing about this nation to me is its unquenchable spirit. You feel it in the pulsing life of the streets. Chile is energetic too, but the vitality here is different in quality from that of Santiago."

"Ah, but Santiago touches both the past and the present in its approach to the future. Buenos Aires leaps to the present and lives in the tomorrow. Argentina regards her future almost as a heritage. She says her future has a quoted value on the stock exchange. Make all the money possible and spend it, for there's much more to be made—that's the slogan. Buenos Aires is not content to be the largest city south of the equator, and the second largest Latin city in the world. Its present goal is to pass Paris. Its people expect it eventually to pass London and New York. Manhattan, they say, can only grow vertically. Buenos Aires can spread out into thousands of leagues of pampa."

"Well, the city bears her growing pains happily, I must say," said Norbourne. "As a municipality, Buenos Aires is cleaner, healthier, better-policed, far more law-abiding, and less politically corrupt than Chicago. And in civic planning, with its playgrounds, parks, boulevards—even the out-of-door statuary and monuments—it is far and away ahead of New York."

The Frenchman turned to bow to a white-haired gentleman taking a seat alone by a window. "That's the famous Eduardo Bradley. The first man ever to cross the Andes by air."

"I thought the Chilean Godoy was the first."

"By aeroplane, yes. But there's the man who crossed two years before Godoy—by balloon. He's a friend of mine. Would you like to meet him? He's now a local executive in Pan-Air."

They went over to the table where the gentleman was drinking port. Señor Bradley was pink-complexioned with ice-blue eyes. He spoke quietly and was as modest in manner as an aging draper's assistant in Bond Street. "On one side I am descended from an American who came to Argentina in 1818," he said. "My father was a relative of President Grover Cleveland." Norbourne had to lean quite close to hear him. He asked about his balloon flight.

"I made my first ascent in a free balloon in 1909," Señor Bradley said with a hesitant, slightly Spanish accent. "After several years of practising this sport, during which I obtained all balloon records in the country, I decided to study the possibility of crossing the Andes in a balloon. The flight has to be made from west to east on account of the winds above 5,000 metres, known as 'contralisios' which come from the western quarter. So I started from Santiago. After three or four unsuccessful attempts, at last on June 24, 1916, I was able to effect what at that time was the chief aspiration of any person interested in aviation. It was midwinter and the Cordillera was completely snow-covered. My ballast ran out in the middle of the Cordillera and I had to throw everything possible overboard to make it lighter, as a descent in that region meant death. Fortunately the wind was strong and I soon arrived in the valley of Uspallata where there was no snow, and I was able to descend on the slopes of one of the hills. I was the first person to cross the Andes by air and that was very important to me." He spoke as softly as a modest little boy telling about winning the boarding school medal for diligence and deportment. Like all air heroes he was astonishingly modest.

"And do you fly now?"

"Not at the controls. In the Bennett Cup Balloon races in the United States in 1929, I broke my knee in three places and injured my spine. So now I let the other fellow do the work and I relax." He settled back in his chair to finish his port. "I made another record too," he added, "a much less exciting one than the Andes crossing, but still a record. I was the first passenger from South America to arrive by aeroplane in the United States."

When they stood on the pavement waiting for taxis Norbourne asked the Frenchman, "Why did you come over here?"

"For two reasons. First, the same reason they all come for—money. Second, the opportunity to fly. The aviator's profession was overcrowded in France after the war. I came here and flew mail planes in those reckless days when the sentimental slogan was, 'The mail must go through!'—I have had many chances to go into other work. But," he made a gesture of surrender, "aviation is like drugs—once you fly you can't stop."

"But you don't like Buenos Aires."

"Oh, yes, for all my frank criticism, I am very happy here. I think you will find the intellectual liberals of the upper-class feel just as I do. I enjoy being part of the experiment. I wouldn't enjoy living in France in these uncertain days."

New Concepts

The array of night clubs in Buenos Aires is as diverse and dazzling as the formidable lists printed in the *New Yorker*. After his dinner party at the Plaza, Mr. Swift chose one called The Charleston to take his guests to. The walls had been metamorphosed into old-fashioned façades of the South Carolina port. The Argentine lady he put Norbourne next to was lovely—slim, white-throated, delicate-featured, with soft dark hair. Mr. Swift said she was not only beautiful but clever.

"Oh, but you are missing the real soul of Argentina not to have stayed a night on the pampas," she was saying in a modulated voice that was gently ecstatic. "The effect of the purple light that suffuses everything at evening is unlike anything else in the world."

"I have read about it," said Norbourne.

"Even Hudson couldn't describe it. You can't ever quite get its essence. It is incomprehensible. You can't really see it and can't hear it—you can only feel it. You won't know what we are like unless you experience that purple light on the pampas. There is something moving and uplifting about it, and yet something profoundly sad." The look in her dark violet eyes seemed to bring the pampas close.

"You don't mind foreigners commenting on strains of melancholy in your national character?"

"But why? It's so obviously there. Perhaps it's the nostalgia for the lands of our ancestors still embedded in us."

"What are you?"

"A little Spanish, more Italian, and part English."

"What do you feel you are, inside you?—Italian?" There was a delicate moulding of brow and a gentle harmony of feature and fragrance of disposition about her such as he had felt only in women that matured under Italian skies. But he guessed wrong.

She smiled and confessed forthrightly. "I feel as English as roast beef."

The orchestra was playing a tango, slow, pulsing, tender, melancholy.

"I had never realized before how sad the tango is. It positively weeps."

"But, of course. It's like your Negro 'blues,' with a difference. The tango is the swan song of the *gaucho*, of romance and guitars, of chivalry on the purple plains."

Norbourne knew that the tango evolved just at the turn of the century at the death of the old order and birth of the modern nation. In it the Mediterranean and the pampas met and fused. Paris added sophistication to the primitive music and made it fashionable at *thés dansants* just before the World War. But the tango remained communal and ubiquitous. It belonged equally to the upper class, the bourgeoisie, the slums, the brothel. It was played here, there, and everywhere; morning, noon, or night.

"Listen, hear how memory-haunted and plaintive the music is? One dances it to relieve the heart of regret and longing."

"Where our women relieve the heart in nerve sanatoria, you Argentinians dance the tango," Norbourne suggested.

"Our lives are much less complicated," she said, smiling.

"I think security must be the most prized possession of the Latin-American woman."

"I'm afraid it is. And it isn't admirable. We are beginning to learn another side. Did you see the *Standard* this morning—the front page article about the lepers?"

As a matter of fact Norbourne had read the article with considerable astonishment. An unfortunate leper had presented himself the day before voluntarily to the police and begged to be locked up because he was unable to obtain a bed in any of the hospitals. Señora Blaquier, president of the Patronato de Leprosos, declared there were "1,000 lepers in the capital and 15,000 in the country"—that only a small part of them receive the necessary medical attention.

"But is it true, or is it yellow journalism?"

"I know it is true. Because I help Señora Blaquier in her work." Norbourne was still more amazed. "Visitors see only our wealth and show. They don't notice that lepers walk up and down Florida Street."

"What?"

"Yes. I assure you it is true. Some have no homes whatever to go to. They sleep in alleyways. It is a shameful state of affairs." Her eyes blazed with indignation.

"But surely they are segregated," he insisted.

"The law to segregate and care for lepers has been in existence for over eight years, but no definite efforts have been made to enforce it. Our organization has only three hundred hospital beds available. I am doing what I can. Well, perhaps not all, but I work four hours a day, making garments, collecting books, interviewing government officials. Please don't think it's just a society fad. We are deeply in earnest."

"Do you come in contact with the lepers?"

"My husband won't let me go into the leper hospital. I'm not afraid, but he forbids it. We have to be careful on account of our daughter."

"You have a daughter?"

"As large as myself. She can wear my clothes. She's fourteen." Norbourne looked incredulous. "I was married at seventeen," she added.

It was still incredible. She did not look even twenty-five. What was it besides the even-temper of their days, the temperance, their enhancing Latin modesty, that kept the women of Argentina so young and fresh and desirable? Paul Morand, charmed at their delighted astonishment when one proposed to talk to them alone over a cup of tea, had used the word "adorable" to characterize them.

The intimate, insidious throbbing of the violins began to excite Norbourne. "I should like to dance this tango with you," he said, "but I have never learned properly."

"It's very simple. You simply walk to music. The attitude of the features is the most important. The music tells you how to move."

They got up and went to the dance floor. "You must promise to be tolerant and patient with me," he said, looking down at her. Her eyes were more lovely, he thought, because of the new concepts just beginning to trouble her sheltered inheritance. He put his arm about her. Her body was as fragile and resilient as a flower stem. Morand had used the perfect word—"adorable."

"Peace Must Be Our Passion"

"Do you agree that the feeling of confidence and friendliness in South American countries towards the United States is stronger than at any other time in our history?" Norbourne asked this formal question of Ambassador Weddell, during the cocktails before luncheon at the embassy.

"As far as I can judge," the Ambassador replied. "There is no doubt about the change since President Roosevelt came into office and more especially since Secretary Hull's visit. And not alone in official, but in general circles. In Argentina, certainly, there is belief in the essential singleness of our motives. The repeal of the Platt Amendment, the withdrawal of Marines from Haiti, the assertion of our good neighbour policy—all these things have had their very positive effect. Besides, the personalities of the President and the Secretary of State have impressed themselves on these people. They are considered *hombres simpaticos* and that, as you know, means a vast deal in Latin American countries." It was just what Mrs. Bates had said in Arequipa.

The Ambassador turned to greet some other guests. Norbourne walked over to a window with one of Argentina's under-secretaries.

"The South American public has taken to heart Roosevelt's good neighbour policy," said the gentleman, continuing the thread of conversation. "But what they admire even more is his social idealism. That has touched the masses. They don't like the ways of Russia—Communism is no grave menace here at all. They abhor Hitler and Mussolini, even if they themselves have dictators. They believe that Roosevelt aims at some sort of reasonable state socialism or collectivism that will eliminate 'entrenched greed' and elevate the economic standards of the deserving under-dog. And that is precisely what the majority want and are working for down here. So they look to Roosevelt as a sort of spiritual leader. Imagine. It is incredible—such a total change of attitude to the Yankee."

At luncheon a Supreme Court Judge sat at Norbourne's right. He was remarkably young for such a post and turned out to be the brother of the lady who had been invited to the Argentine embassy for her accouchement. His wit and charm transcended his force and disciplined intelligence. While the rest of the guests drank vintage wine, the Judge and Norbourne partook of a special Virginia rye whisky aged in charred wood which the Ambassador had had sent down from his native state. "I'm sure," the Judge said, savouring the liquor, "it was whisky like this that Thomas Jefferson drank to stimulate his great logic."

When he asked Norbourne what he had enjoyed most in Argentina, he seemed pleasantly surprised to learn that it was his morning at Don Leonardo's *estancia.*

The gentleman at Norbourne's left had just returned from the capital of Paraguay. "I had never been to Asunción before," he said. "It's as different from Buenos Aires as Bagdad is from Paris—a pleasantly old-fashioned place, built in the Spanish-Moorish style with red-tiled roofs and patios and a profusion of sunshine and orange blossoms. Its peaceful appearance belies the fierce, bulldog tenacity of its people. They are a mixture of Spanish and Guarani Indian for the most part. The Paraguayans have always been stout fighters. I think they wouldn't mind fighting Bolivians until the last man of them was dead. One officer laughingly said to me, 'We are incurably romantic about ourselves. We love to get decimated. We are obsessed with the idea that the world is watching the Indian on a moth-eaten horse!'

"Paraguay is like—like—" he paused for the comparison he wanted, "a gamecock that would attack an ostrich. You doubtless remember when that one little country—they have altogether only about 800,000 population now—went to war with Argentina, Brazil and Uruguay all at the same time. It began in '65, just when your Civil War ended, and lasted four years. Lopez, the Dictator, fell in love with a French-born Irishwoman, named Eloisa Lynch. She wanted to be an Empress, like Josephine and Eugenie. She inspired the dictator until four-fifths of the male population were killed. There were only 30,000 men left to re-establish the race."

"And," interpolated the Judge, "that abnormal shortage of males caused the ladies of Paraguay to throw decorum to the winds. Wealthy widows would go down to the docks at Asunción and lure sailors off their ships, take them before the priest, and make them lords of great *estancias*. So many ships lost their crews that for several years ocean tramps had to stop going up to Paraguay. They would anchor down the river and send the goods up by small boats. When you see an Irish red-head among them today, you know the reason."

"Have they ever decided what the Chaco War's about?" Norbourne asked, turning back to the gentleman on the left.

"It was just a misguided scramble between two people who think they're right. The Bolivians are prisoners of their own propaganda."

"Who gained anything from the war?"

"The big United States motor corporations which sold the tanks."

Norbourne acknowledged the dig. "The League of Nations failed completely in its efforts?"

"Completely," the Judge said. "The fight would be going on yet if the Argentinian and Chilean Ministers of Foreign Affairs and United States special representatives had not got together and helped to patch up a peace. The negotiations to end these hostilities may set up a new policy in international law. By the new precedent, Pan-American settlements of territorial problems are to be based on justice. There shall be no more victors or vanquished."

"This is the first time South American republics have really wanted our help in these matters."

"Yes, because for the first time an American president has taken them into his confidence, and won their confidence. Now we have great hope for the Inter-American Peace Conference which is being planned. If it works, we may have compulsory arbitration for all American disputes by a Pan American Court of Justice. And it must work because the nations of the other hemisphere are looking at us."

"By binding the republics of the three Americas together you think we can keep free from European and Asiatic entanglements?"

"Yes, I do, if we present a solid front and they know that we won't join their dog fights in any capacity—why, it might even act as a deterrent to their starting something. We have a fine role written for us if we only have the grace to play it properly. Cordell Hull struck the keynote in his first speech on South American soil when he said, 'Peace must be our passion.' "

The sun was warming enough for the coffee to be served in the embassy garden where the first peach blossoms were just opening. Norbourne sat on one of the marble seats with an economist.

"When the census director calculated in 1931 that Argentina was the richest country in the world per capita," the economist said in reply to his question, "he forgot that public services, railways, street cars, telephone lines, and about half of the capital invested in commerce and industry belonged to foreigners, largely to the English. A recent estimate places the total foreign capital invested in Argentina at about £4,000,000,000. Of this, £2,750,000,000 stands to Great Britain's account, £425,000,000 to that of France and some £350,000,000 to the United States."

"How do you feel in general about the influence of American capital?"

The economist smiled with a superior pooh-poohing expression. "European nations continually try to frighten us South Americans with the bogey-man of American capital. Even England does it —England, which has eight times as much invested in Argentina as the United States has. Why should we be afraid? England hasn't absorbed us. We have used England to our advantage. Why should we fear American financial domination any more than English? As Labriola said, 'We are not going to be swept away by the torrent of Yankee gold—and we aren't going to be dictated to by Europe, to be used as a rampart against the Yankee conquest as the Europeans wish us to.' We expect to develop our own independent form of western civilization and we are going to do it with our own destiny in view and not Europe's. We use English and American money to develop economic wealth and to help us discover ourselves. The Argentinians have no apprehension of being absorbed by Anglo-Saxons. Our cultures are too different. Argentinians can't stomach Yankee Puritanism. And there is this peculiar difference in our money-making attitude: the Americans make it for the sake of making it, we make it to enjoy spending it." He took a cigar from the box the footman was passing and held it to the flame of the lighter. "What absorbing there is to be done here, we are going to do. Just as all kinds and classes of immigrants resign themselves to becoming Argentinians, so American interests here must eventually resign themselves to merging with the spirit of Argentina. Why should we be apprehensive?"

"Why, indeed? What about your proposed industrial expansion?"

"Ah, that's another matter. As you doubtless know, because of the lack of coal and iron to develop manufacturing industries, we import seventy-five per cent of our manufactured products. But even so we have made considerable improvement in our industries. In the last two decades manufacturing plants have increased six or seven hundred per cent. Two million of our five million employed are hired out to industry. At present our manufacturing industries are based largely on local raw materials like meat packing, wine-making, flour milling, sugar refining, boot-making, baking, and brewing. We are making rapid strides in cotton industry. During the coming season the cotton acreage in the northern subtropical area will be increased twenty-five or thirty per cent. Some 800,000 acres will be devoted to cotton cultivation. The state plans to aid cotton planters, to stimulate colonization, to furnish seed and encourage scientific methods. We already have some eighty odd cotton gins and 330 cotton mills. Economically Argentina is in its childhood. The exploitation of natural wealth has just begun." They both rose. It was time to go.

"Well," Norbourne said, recalling something Mr. Stark Young had written about the southern United States, "I hope Argentina won't be stampeded out of her own character by the noise, force and glittering narrowness of industrialism."

The economist smiled shrewdly.

"Please don't think," Norbourne hastily reassured him, "that I say this in dread of the United States losing her market here in machinery and automobiles. I say so sincerely because I think Argentina would be a less attractive place to live in if you reduce cattle breeding and wheat growing in order to set up deafening boiler factories and smelly paper mills. Why should Argentina enter into industrial competition with old-established industrial nations, when she can sell her field products for machinery and textiles and vehicles, and profit handsomely on the trade? In any event the great material destiny of your nation is assured so long as the world's stomach requires substantial food—instead of synthetic pellets made in chemical laboratories." Norbourne had underscored the word "material."

"I gather," said the economist, "you do wonder somewhat about Argentina's spiritual growth and future state of grace?"

"Heaven knows I'm not trying to suggest a superiority in those respects on the part of my nation. In fact, I was hinting that you might profit by the example of those things for which you most severely criticize us. Perhaps I am trying to say that I think Argentina's spiritual salvation lies in her loyalty to the out-of-doors."

"Frankly, I do too," the economist admitted.

Escutcheon

The next noon, before he flew to Montevideo, Norbourne stopped in at the Palermo cattle show which was to open on the following day. Three-fourths of the entries were already installed. He passed before the supersleek, silken, overnourished bulls lying on beds of straw soft as roses. They were magnificent creatures. Tomorrow the cream of Argentinian society would come to bow in homage before these golden calves. It was the climax of the winter season. As he watched the insufferably smug expressions on the beasts' dumb faces he thought of the lepers devoid of a night's lodging.

On the Costanera Road, hordes of painted pigeons fluttered like feathered rain, gilding the artificial lily that was Buenos Aires. Bulls and painted pigeons—these are the symbols which should be enamelled on the city's resplendent escutcheon. Bulls and painted pigeons—and ladies adorable.

IV

URUGUAY

"*The* Banda Oriental *itself has vanished and has become the model republic of Uruguay, the virtuous child of the South American family.*"

William McFee

URUGUAY

Lusty Violet

The hundred and twenty-five miles' flight over the bilious waters of La Plata to Uruguay's capital was dull and without interest. Like flyspecks on green-brown glass, river craft dotted the broad surface. Some of those boats came from far up beyond Asunción in troubled Paraguay. Some of that unlovely water rolling along to join the ocean began as trickles in the heart of the Brazilian forests, born of rain that had filtered through exotic leaves and dripped on to fecund soil where no man has yet set foot. Out of the very core of savagery sprang this water that made possible the finest harbour and the largest capital on the continent. From a tenuous spidery beginning, one river had merged with another and another, until the climatic Plata was so swollen with bigness that it was said to be as broad as it was long.

In the Sikorsky S-38, seats had been arranged three abreast without an aisle. Norbourne sat wedged in between a priest from Chile and the actor manager of an English company which had just presented a repertory of Shaw plays to Buenos Aires. The players were now booked for a season in Montevideo and the rest of the troupe were taking the night boat over. They had had an excellent season in Buenos Aires, the actor said; the British colony had supported them royally and the Argentinians had elected to make them the vogue. The next evening they were opening in *Pygmalion*, the comedy Shaw had written for Mrs. Patrick Campbell. They were to play in Montevideo's leading theatre, the Teatro Solís, named in honour of that indefatigable Portuguese navigator who had discovered Uruguay in 1515. On his return in 1517, de Solís had been killed by Charrúas Indians and his remains had gone to fertilize this land he took for Portugal.

It was not de Solís who had given Montevideo its name, however, but Magellan. In 1518 when the later explorer, searching for a southern passage to India, had arrived there one rosy dawn, his lookout called from the poop deck in old Portuguese, "*Monte vide eu!*" "I see a mountain!" Magellan had so named the place. The mountain is merely a *cerro*, or hill, rising abruptly from the flat surface like a tall conical sixteenth century hat lying on the floor. For hundreds of miles along the Atlantic seaboard it is the only eminence. For centuries it has stood out as a loved landmark to sailors fed up with the sight of too much sea. In 1762, when seven colonizing families from Buenos Aires arrived on Christmas Eve, they took up their abode around the natural fortress of the *cerro* and retained the baptismal name Magellan gave the place. As numerous writers have commented, the citizens of Montevideo have lived up to the sonorous name. Their energy, pluck, and valour have been admired throughout the world. In character they are reputed to be sturdy, honest, and upstanding like the lone granite hill that rises above them, a rallying point and an inspiration.

No ground has been more bitterly fought over than this *Banda Oriental*, or East Bank, as the territory is still often called. After the freedom of Brazil and Argentina from the mother countries, each turned to bind Uruguay to herself. Time and again they fought. At last in 1828 England intervened on the grounds that the conflict was playing havoc with her South American shipping. Because neither Argentina nor Brazil would yield the territory to the other, Uruguay's independence was granted. Thus sprang into being the smallest republic on the continent.

In area, with its 72,000 square miles, Uruguay approximates the six New England states. But there is virtually no waste land. Her vast undulating plains, with woodlands only along the river banks, give her a higher percentage of arable land than any country in the world, and the black soil, opulent in potash, produces grasses more nourishing than those of Argentina. Rarely troubled by droughts or floods, with a generous rainfall evenly distributed throughout the year, the land is also blessed with a temperate and invigorating climate. The temperature never goes below 35° in winter; frost is a rare curiosity; and the summer heat is moderated by refreshing salt breezes from the Atlantic.

When the *Banda Oriental* became a nation it took for its name the Indian appellation of its western river. "Uruguay" means "The River of Birds." In early days the woods and fields about the stream were a birds' paradise. Flamingoes and black-necked swans traced their picturesque careers between the iris-bordered banks and the azure sky in the free profusion of the first days of creation before man.

"Look, behold! My God, how beautiful!" The priest had clasped his hands together in happy excitement as the amphibian taxied along the aerodrome. "They have all come to meet me. They are my relatives—that crowd." His eyes glistened with tears as he pointed down to a long line of people three or four deep standing a little removed from the stragglers and officials. "I have not been home for fifteen years. This morning I flew over the Andes from Chile. I shall not know them all. Many were not even born when I went away."

The priest was a thin, ascetic-looking man with benevolent black eyes heavily shadowed, but now lit with unrestrained emotion. Norbourne had been introduced to him at the Buenos Aires airport. He bore one of the greatest names of South America, San Martín. He came from the family of the hero.

The three-deep line of relatives moved forward slowly in silence to meet him—middle-age people, old, young, children, who were more awed by the aeroplane than the occasion. It was a nice-looking group, Norbourne thought. Each one hesitated to rush forward to receive the first embrace. The priest stood still too choked with emotion to speak. Then he stretched his arms out wide as if to encircle them all at once. A lovely grave young woman advanced ahead of the others. She and the priest buried their faces in each other's shoulders. The ice broken, the crowd surged about him.

Norbourne was met by an American business man to whom he had a letter of introduction. The man had not lived in the States for sixteen years. In the Falkland Islands he had married an English girl and now he spoke with a British accent and was dressed in the best conservative Bond Street taste. He saw Uruguay through three pairs of eyes: those of an American, an Englishman, and a native.

They drove off in his Chrysler. There were still two hours before dark in which to see the capital of this country that Koebel spoke of as "a violet by a mossy stone half hidden from the eye," because among nations it was the most neglected by European visitors. Opera singers stop at the capital in season and Scandinavian whalers yearly make Montevideo the anchorage of their Antarctic-venturing flotillas. Now the English Players were to present a Shavian repertory. But since Bryce in 1911, most foreign interpreters—Frank, Eshmid, Guedalla, Morand, Siegfried—had passed over the one Latin republic among the twenty perhaps most worthy of emulation.

No foreigner who has ever lived there has failed to speak or write of it with affection and admiration. Even when the youthful Darwin paused at Montevideo in 1831 on his famous *Beagle* expedition, when the place was slowly recovering from a devastating war, he recognized the inhabitants for "a much finer set than at Rio de Janeiro." He commented on the men's "handsome expressive faces and their athletic figures." Norbourne, in his one first glimpse of Uruguayans at the airport, was struck by their vigour, good looks, and seeming good nature—an honest, hearty quality, for which the best word seemed "wholesome," which in no sense meant "smug" or "bland." The people reflected the climate's stimulation in their strong supple bodies and their sanguine countenances. Even these city people had the breath of the out-of-doors stamped upon them.

Although one-third of the entire population of two million live in the seaport capital, Uruguay is largely one expansive pastoral scene. Sheep browse right up to the city's borders. "Wool is Uruguay's greatest source of income," said Norbourne's host as they drove past a flock of these nibbling sheep. "Less than ten per cent of the land is in cultivation. You might say meat is the bread of life to Uruguay. The country is given over almost entirely to pasturage. The *gauchos* do not like to plough, and the *estanciero* takes the easier way of raising cattle by letting them take care of themselves. As a rule he doesn't even bother to fatten his cattle with oats. A few of the more progressive ranch owners import blooded stock from England and Argentina to improve their herds, but most of them just let nature take its course. God sends enough grass, so why plant oats? Some day, of course, cattle breeding will be managed on a far more scientific and profitable scale than it is now.

"The great agricultural development is yet to come too. Our agricultural exports amount to only about £4,000,000 a year, compared to £60,000,000 animal products. The export of oil seeds is significant—we export about 50,000 tons of linseed annually. We raise just about enough wheat for ourselves. Some day we may be one great granary. But we are in no rush. Uruguayans are not hell-bent on amassing quick fortunes like their cousins across the Plata. They are a strange mixture of progress and old-fashioned attachments—if that makes any sense to you. But you'll see what I mean after you've been here a day or two." Norbourne noticed that he said "we" and "they" interchangeably with ease.

The car had swung into one of the residential park sections almost entirely hidden behind thick planting. Bougainvillea cascaded over walls and flat house roofs in violet and magenta profusion. Peach trees were twigged with buds and the air scented with orange blossoms.

"Uruguay boasts four million peach trees—and a million and a half orange trees. When we learn better how to control the orange blight, citrus culture will become an important industry.

We have the soil and the climate to become another Florida or California."

They turned into the Prado, world famous for its eight hundred varieties of roses, which gives Montevideo its nickname, "The City of Roses." Except for freak specimens here and there, the roses were not yet in bloom.

"You should be here to see us and smell us at Christmas time. The effect is almost overpowering. By moonlight this park is incredibly lovely, both with the perfume and the blossoms. You never saw such roses, so red."

> "*I sometimes think that never blows so red*
> *The Rose as where some buried Cæsar bled,*"

Norbourne quoted, remembering that from 1810 to 1826 no country ever saw more continuous and bloody fighting. When their great patriot Artigas was decisively defeated by the Brazilians in the last battle of Tacuarembó in 1820, he fled the field with some three hundred men, leaving behind eight hundred dead and only fifteen wounded.

"They fought with hand to hand fury in those days," said his host. "That's where they get the fiery quality that lives just under their amiable exteriors. They are complacent and audacious at the same time—very sure of themselves and yet impulsively ready to try experiments. Scratch even a settled, prosperous Montevidean and you'll find a vagabond whose heart is still in the country."

The Uruguayans, who love the open more than any Spanish Americans, have brought as many gardens as possible into their capital. Even Buenos Aires has not given so high a percentage of its area to parks, plazas, and promenades. There is a gracious spaciousness and roominess about the suburbs. Even the more modest streets of the town are much wider than in other Latin cities. There is little need of alley-way thoroughfares to trap the summer shade and Montevideo spreads open to catch the breeze from the sea.

"I like this spaciousness," Norbourne said, settling back at ease.

"The city fathers won't permit real estate dealers and property holders to profit at the expense of crowding," the Anglo-Uruguayan-American explained. "In 1916 an ordinance went into effect that within the city limits no building could be erected within thirteen feet of the front boundary line of the streets. It makes the construction of artistic fences of iron grille-work or wood obligatory, even for vacant lots—for no wire netting is permitted. Outside the city's radius one has to leave at least a thirty-two-foot space on all sides. Suburban neighbours have never less than sixty-four feet of breathing space between their houses. They can turn this into gardens or playgrounds for the health of their children."

"A blessed law!" Norbourne said. "Why don't all the nations go to school to Uruguay?" He thought of his charming old town in the South damaged irremediably by greedy real estate dealers slicing old estates into fifty-foot lots where silly people put up houses so close together that they can hear each other's potatoes frying.

"It's too bad, though, they don't carry their civic vigilance here one step further."

"How is that?"

"The only blight on the landscape is this bastard type of domestic architecture in these recent houses."

The older houses with the enhancing patina were obviously Mauro-Spanish in type; the newer ones were derived from the baser period of Italian and French Renaissance; and the spanking new ones were 1930 extreme modernistic or a fancy kind of pseudo-Spanish California bungalow.

"Why couldn't they follow—Venice, say? In Venice a house-owner can't even paint his window-shutters a new colour unless the council approves."

"Not a bad idea," the townsman said, shifting gears at a street crossing where a hill began to climb.

It was a relief after the flatness of Buenos Aires to find that Montevideo was built on a group of rocky knolls and a low promontory that thrust itself out between the ocean and the estuary. The busiest quarter was set on a rocky peninsula where the streets were born in the sea, lived for ten blocks, and then died in the river. Along the mainland on La Plata's side lay the harbour and docks; to the east along the ocean lay the silver chaplet of half-moon beaches which has made Montevideo the continent's most popular bathing resort.

Norbourne always liked to get his direction straight in a new place. The south side of the city, he saw, faced the yellow river. The east looked upon the blue-green ocean. The north and west sides stretched into the life-giving pampa with the purplish hillocks from which Uruguay is called The Purple Land.

"Up to the last quarter of the last century," Norbourne's friend said, as they drove along the Rambla President Wilson, "Montevideo was by all odds the most important port south of Rio. Now Buenos Aires has far outdistanced her. Yet even today 5,000 ships enter our port annually. What it lost in shipping prestige, it has gained as a bathing resort."

Montevideo is the only summer resort capital in South America. Its season is December to April. Then wealthy Brazilians, Argentinians and Chileans join well-to-do Uruguayans and take their summer villas-by-the-sea, lounge on the white sands, sip iced drinks in their painted cabañas, and at night crowd the gaming tables of the Casino. The profits go to the municipal treasury for city improvements and charitable works. "We find it," commented Norbourne's host, "a most palatable way of taxing the rich for the poor's benefit."

The closed villas along the sea usurped the flashing colours of a tropical garden. The houses were painted heliotrope, poinsettia, pansy purple, myrtle, hibiscus red, and morning-glory blue. They looked more attractive from a distance than on closer view. Yet, tenantless, they bloomed like summer and enlivened the winter beaches. The sands, freshly windswept, were immaculate and invitingly touched with the soap bubble tints of late afternoon.

"In its city hotels Montevideo is conspicuously lacking in smartness," the Uruguayan-American admitted, "but the beach hotels—they are all closed now as you see—are so sumptuous they are run at a loss to attract visitors to the Casino. Montevideo has little night life in winter. At this season the Montevideans take the boat over to Buenos Aires for their excitements. Many fly back and forth. In the summer, when Argentine families live on the beaches here, the husbands journey to and fro by aeroplane. Like New Yorkers whose families live in the Berkshires, the husbands come for the week-ends. Speaking of husbands," he said with a grin, as he slowed down to make a complete turn, "the Uruguayan is less severe and less jealous than other Latins. Still, don't get caught in a married man's house! Even if you have only called to take tea, it is risky. If the husband should shoot you, he will be vindicated on the grounds that you had no business whatsoever being there."

When they had started back, they stopped short to wonder and admire. The setting sun, playing upon the distant city towers, the near beaches and the surf, drenched them with the colours of crème de menthe, absinthe, and aquamarine. In an operatic set of *Otello* in Dresden once Norbourne had seen an amazing apple green sunset. He had thought it too fantastic to be possible. Three weeks later as he stood on a terrace of the Pincio Gardens in Rome looking to the west, the dome of St. Peter's was suffused in an unearthly pale green light and behind it the sunset was as luminously green as a firefly at first dark. Here in Montevideo he saw his second actual green sunset. He and his host remained on the beach road for some time, watching. The heavens rippled like green silk gauze blown up from the horizon. Then as a note changes in a colour-organ, the green turned gradually to soft gold, like an apple ripening, and Montevideo became mellow with golden light.

"That is the difference between Buenos Aires and your city," Norbourne said as they started back. "The magnificent Buenos Aires has not mellowed."

Though Montevideo waxed in population and prosperity—increasing from 70,000 in 1876 to 700,000 in 1936—it has remained somewhat like an old Southern town, like Savannah, Georgia, magnified many times. And while it hastened to be the first to acquire the civilized amenities in the matter of sanitation, hospitals, schools, public transportation, park improvements, in the city proper it has kept much of its old-fashioned character. The material prosperity of the city has not affected its equanimity. While it hums with activity, it seems complacent and restful.

"Even your church bells ring calmly," Norbourne said, listening to their soft music when they were in the city again. It was strikingly different from the frenzy and fury of those on the West Coast.

"You saw the fuss they made over the priest at the aerodrome. Well, it wasn't because he was a cleric, but because he was a relative and a San Martín. The church has less power in Uruguay than in any other Latin republic; hence—I hope I won't offend you—the progress. Perhaps you've noticed that the more power that remains to the church the more backward the civilization. There is no state religion here. The majority of the people are Roman Catholics. But we receive no Papal Nuncio, and we are not represented at the Vatican. Religious processions are taboo. All beliefs are free. But religion is not permitted to stick its nose in politics."

"Politics are very simple here, aren't they?"

"Very simple, yet fierce. One is a *Blanco* or a *Colorado*—a conservative or an advanced liberal. A man is one thing or the other: White or Red, but staunchly, intensely whatever he is. He generally inherits his political faith. There are no independents. Voting is compulsory. Men are fined for not voting. The new constitution of 1934 provides for compulsory universal suffrage. The Reds have brought about the beneficial social legislation. The term Red, of course, has nothing to do with Communism. There is no Communistic bent among the masses."

"They are too well off," said Norbourne.

"Yes," said his host. "However, the incumbent Soviet Legation has been giving them false notions. Last night I went to a dinner at the Soviet Minister's. It was very elaborate. I never saw so many solid gold candlesticks or such imposing livery. Champagne, of course—and that meant champagne for the servants as well as guests—it's part of their creed. And what's more, champagne had to be served to all the waiting chauffeurs in the courtyard. No tit-bits for the privileged alone. Tit-bits for man too, whenever master has them. How the Russians afford it, I can't see—with their folk at home fortunate to munch raw cucumbers and gobble sour bread. My chauffeur was tremendously impressed—not unnaturally."

"He got the idea that Communism meant champagne for the under-classes. Just what it was calculated to do."

"No doubt. But I don't think we shall be troubled with Communism here, or Fascism either. We have too strong a safeguard."

"Your advanced social legislation?"

"Just that. The best safeguard a nation can have."

The Queen

They drove up to the leading hotel in one of the plazas. The gentleman said good-bye to Norbourne. He had to take the night boat over to Buenos Aires for business conferences and would be gone several days. But he would send his chauffeur for Norbourne at seven in the morning to take him out to the cattle market where some cattle buyers would take him with them about their business.

The hotel was an old-fashioned hostelry with no ground floor lounge, and the lobby no larger than a bathroom at one of Buenos Aires' elegant hostelries. A large lift wheezed to the fourth floor. Norbourne was shown into a room on an inner court. (All the better rooms were occupied.) The bellboy opened the double doors and drew back the long écru linen portières. It was like stepping into a novel laid in the early 1900's. The acme of outlandish bad taste, nevertheless the room had a strange harmony, reminiscent of a highly respectable house in the red-light district of a small American city. The walls were papered in purplish red, the ceiling so high that the transom seemed like a skylight. The baseboard was of sky-blue glazed tile. In the corner by the dressing-table stood a spittoon wreathed in pink roses. Gracing the entrance were looped écru curtains twelve feet long and so heavily embroidered they must have taken months of application to produce. The vast bedstead, piled high with mattresses and embroidered bolster slip, was of glittering brass, ornately fashioned. It looked like a bed of sin if ever a bed did. It was such a funny room Norbourne sat down and had a hearty laugh. The bellboy looked pleasantly bewildered at the North American's good humour and handed him a folded copy of *The Sun*, Montevideo's newspaper printed in English.

Wondering what would be of foremost interest to English newspapers in Uruguay, Norbourne shook open the sheet and looked at column one, front page. "Queen Mary Has Gone To Stay At Sandringham Before Leaving For Balmoral."

It was quite comforting. For all its parade of progress Uruguay had not wrenched itself too violently from its allegiance to the past as both his hotel room and the local interest in Queen Mary showed. It had not let modernity turn its head.

He took off his coat, flopped down on the great bouncing bed. He stared at the ceiling up where the top of the next storey might have been. How nice that Queen Mary was going to have a little visit at Sandringham before proceeding to the Scottish hills! How nice that some people in far-off Uruguay were interested. It made the world such a cosy little place.

"Perfect Republic"

Lying there on the voluminous bed Norbourne let his thoughts drift from the Queen's vacation to the "perfect republic" as W. H. Hudson called Uruguay as far back as 1885. The gallant little nation had been its own guinea pig. Since 1877 when it made elementary education compulsory and free, Uruguay has carried the bright banner of democratic liberalism at the front of the procession of Latin-American nations. The advanced educational methods of Uruguay—it even furnishes the tools of learning: text books, paper, and pencils—have helped to make its government uncommonly progressive. Whereas the largest item in the budget of most Latin American governments goes to maintain the army, in Uruguay it goes to public instruction.

Uruguay has been the experimental station, the self-set-up laboratory of social legislations among the nations of this continent just as in another sense Sweden has been in Europe. It was the first country in South America to divorce the Church from the State; to legalize divorce between husband and wife; to give the vote to women; to abolish capital punishment (its crime record is very low); to establish a minimum wage law, an eight-hour working day, and old-age pensions. In 1929 a law was passed decreeing that pensions to their employees must be granted by limited liability companies. Since 1913 a sum of 200,000 gold pesos has been appropriated annually for free seeds for farmers. A system of old-age pensions has been in operation for eighteen years. In 1927 the government passed an inflexible bank-inspection law; and in that same year took control of the telegraph, telephone, and postal services. In the welfare of its people the Board of Health spends 12,000,000 pesos annually. It is now working towards free medical care for its entire population.

As Uruguay is still the only country on the hemisphere where an adult is fined for failing to vote, so it was the first to grant legal status to illegitimate children. After all, Norbourne's friend had explained, Uruguay believes that no nation is better than its bottom stratum. That is the chief difference between it and the United States. Until the last few years, the United States has concentrated its major efforts on strengthening the position of its privileged few and letting the under-privileged root out their own haphazard salvation. Uruguay, knowing that the upper stratum can take care of itself, has sought to build up the self-respect of its lowest ranks. She has respect for herself because she has given self-respect to her lowliest citizen.

In many of the most debated New Deal policies, Uruguay has preceded the United States. It put through certain liberal ideas a decade before the United States dared to suggest them. Norbourne wondered if President Roosevelt had not got some of his inspiration and his courage to experiment from Uruguay. Consciously or coincidentally he had certainly followed the southern republic in instituting innovations, giving them a trial, and retaining those which proved good and serviceable, while discarding or modifying the less useful.

But in numerous manifestations Uruguay is still far in advance of the United States, and those who cry out against the "ruinous un-American ways" of President Roosevelt have only to regard the splendid state of Uruguay's politic and economic health and the esteem in which this courageous little country is held by the world at large. Norbourne's host had been most revealing when he had said the Uruguayans look with amazement upon the strongly organized opposition to President Roosevelt's new social legislation. To them it is like a naughty display of tantrums by the spoiled little boy who wants every toy in the shop for himself.

No Smut

In the midst of Norbourne's ruminations, Captain Parks, who had piloted him over the Plata, telephoned to suggest dinner together. He knew a German place where they had Wurzburger and incomparable sauerkraut. The place looked like one of the barroom restaurants hanging over from the gay nineties that one sees on the East Twenties in New York today. For his first meal in Montevideo Norbourne had intended to eat lobster from the Pacific while he sniffed Atlantic breezes. But instead he, too, ordered sauerkraut and frankfurters and Wurzburger. They had the large restaurant almost entirely to themselves.

In a far corner there were two women who were just finishing their dinner. Parks rose and bowed like a Latin to them when they went our. "Argentinians," he said. They were upper-class women, very smartly but conservatively dressed. "One of them is here getting a divorce, the other is her sister. Montevideo, you know, is sometimes called 'The Reno of South America.' "

"That must be pretty hard luck on it."

"Not as bad as it sounds. There's one special thing in which the culture of the United States is far behind that of Uruguay—the Press. Here the Press and speech are free, but any airing of dirty personal linen in public is frowned at severely. Divorce cases are ignored in the newspapers as unworthy of attention. The most notice they ever get is a line or two in the back pages. They are private affairs between the contracting parties and the judge."

"No public trials, no reporters, no sob sisters, no pruriency?"

"Not a speck of smut."

"Uruguay sounds too admirable. There must be some fly in the ointment."

"Well," Parks said, "I suppose it is the locust. In unpredictable years they come from the north in cloud-like swarms. They strip the vegetable gardens and the orchards, and clean off the weeds as well as the grass. Once when my wife and I were going by rail into the interior to a house party our train was delayed for ten hours—blocked by locusts. They were piled up on the track a foot deep. At noon it grew as dark as twilight. You never saw such a sight—and such a mess as the train made crawling through them. And when we got to the *estancia* the place looked like a plucked fowl. Only the chinaberries were left green."

Tablada Colon

A polar wind sent chilling gusts sweeping down the city's street and through the hotel's opening doors, as Norbourne came out of the lift. A tall fellow in a blue béret and thick reefer jacket was standing at the desk asking for someone. This was the chauffeur he had been told would come for him. He was a good-looking square-jawed man, muscular, tightly knit. He opened the door to the back seat of the car with the manner of one who liked doing a service to his fellows. Norbourne declined the back seat and got in front.

"It is not tender," the chauffeur said in a low soft voice, commenting on the brisk wind that was blowing, "but it enlivens the blood." He smiled appreciatively, just as if the wind was blowing solely for the sake of their constitution. His grey eyes were frank, honest, naïvely gentle. There was a quality about him that suggested he had never suffered an indignity in his life.

They passed the Anglican church and turned down a quiet side street. "Here is where the French and Polish women used to offer themselves," he said, "and the sailors would spread diseases. But that's all done away with now. It was too hard a life on the girls, even though most of them were working to send money to their parents in Europe."

"Where did the girls go?"

"Away. I don't know. Perhaps back to Europe. Or to the cemetery. Or to Rio."

"Are you married?"

"Not yet." The man smiled. "I am not quite forty. I still have some wild oats to sow. I have lived in the city only ten years. I come from the country." He continued smiling placidly like a self-contained youth with his life and fun before him.

"Women are not all alike, as people say," the man went on evenly. "They are as different in temperament as horses. On the *estancia* it used to be my job to break in colts. I was very skilful. I knew when to be rough and when to be soothing." Without continuing the analogy, he turned a corner and slowed down to a snail's pace. Though the street was entirely clear, they crept along as if they had joined a funeral procession. Norbourne looked interrogatively at the man, at the accelerator, at the empty street. The chauffeur's expression was bland. In silence, they proceeded for one block and then for another in slow motion. Norbourne got fidgety. "Why?" he blurted out at length.

"*Los ninos*," the chauffeur said, with a bland smile.

"But I don't see any children."

"Soon they will be coming to school."

It was only seven something in the morning and *los ninos* were doubtless just waking in their beds. But the law said they must be fully protected and the man obeyed the law to the letter.

"If we were to go fast and the police saw us, we should spend a week in jail. The jails are clean and very nice and never crowded, but—I do not think we would enjoy their hospitality, even so."

Out of the *los ninos* zone, he increased speed. After a moment he said, thoughtfully, "I am not sure the law is altogether right. It teaches the children to be stupid. In the country the peasant children learn to get out of the way of wild cattle and drunken *gauchos* by themselves. There they learn quicker to be men."

He gave a dignified cordial greeting to the driver of a bus, which passed them carrying workmen into the city. The bus driver was another handsome square-jawed fellow not unlike himself. "That was my brother," the chauffeur said with modest pride. "He runs two buses. A man here can own two buses, but he has to drive one himself. There are no concessions to big companies as in your country where you let one man run everything. Everyone is given a fair chance here to make money for himself. Our President, Dr. Terra, is a very fine man and full of courage. Of course, everybody does not like him. When the President of Brazil was here on a visit, a bad man shot President Terra—shot him in the shoulder at the races. The President went to the hospital, had the bullet pulled out, and went back to the Palace. An hour later he got up, dressed himself and went to the dinner for Señor Vargas. And what do you think he gave him for a present?" He paused to give emphasis to his surprise. "The bullet the doctors had cut out of his shoulder. He had it mounted on silver. He made a joke of it. He has the courage and wit of a *gaucho*."

They had reached the outskirts of the city where the pavement stopped. The dirt road that wound up the long low hill to the market on the heights was punctuated thickly with different herds of mud-yellow cattle on their last mile to the death houses of the packing companies. They were sold and slaughtered the same day. Stumbling, panting and distraught, they trotted or ran, sometimes bellowing like half-witted women being chased by hallucinations. The car swerved out of their way again and again. With each herd were two or three *gauchos* enveloped in wind-blown *ponchos* that fluttered like great wings behind them. On their heads they wore Basque bérets. With set expressions on their strong faces and eyes flamingly intent on the business of keeping their herds intact and separated from the others they looked like creatures from another planet.

The *Tablada Colon*, or Colombus Cattle Market, was mainly a bare terrain that looked like a series of vari-sized terra-cotta bowls lying face downward. There was not a tree, not a bush, not a sprig of grass—just a merging of raw hillocks, without one fence post or one strand of wire. The *gauchos* themselves with their lightning swift horses were the fences. With their dashes and whirls and their intangible circumferences they made the corrals and shifted them about over the hills at the buyers' convenience. In the midst of the knolls one large building had been constructed as an office for the exchange of money and signatures, and for a café and lounge. Alongside it were a parking place for automobiles and a shed for the feeding of the cowboys' and buyers' mounts.

Norbourne was sorry when the chauffeur said good-bye and turned him over to one of the assistant buyers. He liked the Uruguayan's harmonious personality, his utter absence of sycophancy, his engaging courtesy.

The assistant buyer, Mr. Morse, a cordial-mannered American, borrowed a horse for Norbourne from a peon and lent him his short whip. Norbourne had not known that he would have to ride, and his long trousers and Harris tweed top coat seemed conspicuously unhorseman-like. The pony himself snorted disdainfully as he threw his leg over the saddle. Out of the courtyard the *pampero* yanked at his broad-brimmed hat, but he jammed it down over his eyes, and gave the pony an authoritative rebuke with the whip. Off Mr. Morse and he galloped over the terra-cotta hills to inspect a herd of cattle just arriving. His top coat flared like a *poncho*. In a few moments, he had forgotten his self-consciousness of unsuitable riding clothes. Despite the small dust scraped up by cloven hooves, the atmosphere had a kind of absolute purity of early morning like that of the Scottish moors in September. Norbourne breathed deep of the chill air blown from the south and felt exhilarated.

The cattle did not impress him. They were not to be compared with the superb creatures on Don Leonardo's plantation, and of course they brought a commensurately lower price. The buying was the simplest sort of transaction. The buyers rode a couple of times around the herd, which the *gauchos* managed to keep remarkably still during inspection, and then made an offer to the owner who stood by on horseback. He refused and set another price. The buyer declined in his turn and offered a compromise. The owner generally accepted the compromise. The cattle were then driven off to a wooden floor-scales where hundreds could be weighed *en masse*.

As Norbourne and his companion proceeded across seven hills to watch the weighing, a rebellious steer broke loose from the herd. With tail hoisted he tore by Norbourne as if he had been stung by a legion of horseflies. Norbourne pulled up short as a rush of wind almost blew him from his pony. A cowboy with *poncho* flying like the flaming wings of an avenging angel streaked past, outran the frenzied steer, whirled his horse in a flashing arc, blocked the beast's way and turned him back. At the same time other steers, infected by the rebellious one, shot off from the compact herd in haphazard directions like shooting stars. The four *gaucho* drivers of the herd all sprang into action, as quick as firemen descending a greased pole. With astounding virtuosity they charged, stopped short, circled, whirled, making fascinating patterns of direction with an alacrity that was thrilling to watch. When peace reigned again the look on their faces was that calm, but elated, self-satisfaction matadors have when they have conquered their bull.

The colours of the fringed *ponchos* were a complete surprise to Norbourne. They were all pastel. He would have expected either bold, vivid colours: crimsons or purples; or sober colours like navy blue, brown and black. But these steel-muscled, iron-jawed men affected ethereal, fairy-like colours. Their *ponchos* were whitish pink, flesh, primrose, champagne, soft lilac, wood ashes, absinthe-in-water, and the palest virginal blue. They were not rough blankets, but woven of the finest cashmere-like wool.

"They are expensive too," said Mr. Morse. "Good ones cost thirty or forty dollars. The *gaucho* takes great pride in his *poncho*. You see their horses are well covered with oxhide to protect their clothing from the animal's sweat. Even in the back country the *gaucho* is not averse from making a respectable appearance. You notice these chaps all wear the flowing neckerchief? To go without one would be like your leaving off your collar and tie when you wear a dinner jacket."

"Are they ever troubled with cattle ticks here?" Norbourne wanted to know. Cattle to him was always associated with dipping to kill ticks—a ceremony at which he had assisted with great gusto in his boyhood.

"They used to be terrible—a vicious kind, called *garrapatas* that sucked so much blood cattle died of anæmia and fever. Before they learned to dip them, the only help was the *chingolos*. They were a kind of sparrow that lived on the cattles' backs and and got their dinner by digging the ticks out of their burrows in the hide. When the cattle were driven to market it used to look as if the beasts had sprouted feathers. Their backs and flanks were covered with fluttering birds. Now they dip them, and *chingolos* seem to have gone with the wind."

"I don't see any mares," Norbourne said.

"A *gaucho* would as soon be caught pushing a perambulator as riding a mare. Uruguayans have mingled scorn and respect for their female animals. Mares are treated like harem ladies. They are never made to plough or chase wild cattle or draw heavy wagons. Their feminine flanks never feel the goad of *nazarinas*. They spend their lives plucking at clover and frolicking with their colts in the green pastures. When they are in the mood they receive the periodic visits of their sires. It's a soft life, a Uruguayan mare's."

"What are *nazarinas?*"

"Those vicious spurs. Like a crown of thorns. The cowboys made up the name *nazarinas*—like a crown. Suggests Christ's suffering."

"Uruguay's greatest improvement in the last decade has been in roads," he went on after a moment. "But in many parts of the land there is nothing like a regular road. In winter there is a rutted track across yellow pampa clay. The drivers love nothing better than to get bogged. To extricate a stuck waggon from a quagmire gives them the thrill of their life. With wild horses snorting and the lashes of long whips cracking and men yelling, it's more exciting than a Roman chariot race."

They turned back towards the office house. Norbourne's pony, obviously glad to be shed of him, cast him a look of suppressed scorn for his patronizing pat of thanks on the neck, and whinnied at his peon master as if saying, "How could you turn me over to this alien amateur?" Norbourne shook out his legs. Although he had not been in the saddle for some five years there was no stiffness in his joints. The Uruguayan air was both stimulant and liniment.

In the big barnlike café, the atmosphere smelt heartily of leather, tobacco, ammonia, masculinity. About heavy wooden tables Uruguayan ranch owners and buyers for Armour, Swift, and British firms met and talked cattle, while cowboys talked horses. All the men kept their hats on. The cowboys almost invariably wore the béret. Their *bombachas*, balloon-like trousers, much like plus-four golf trousers, were tucked into wrinkled calfskin boots. To their ankles were attached the large spurs, vicious looking as a game-cock's, but rounded like a crown of thorns. Norbourne took a closer look at their soft silk neckcloths. They too were all in delicate colours: white, orchid, rose.

Gauchos sat about on benches sucking their maté through silver quills out of hand-painted earthenware pots which they always carried with them. Others sat at wooden tables and drank tiny cups of black coffee. Out of skin pouches still others took swigs of caña—a rum made from fermented cane juice. A café boy was carrying about a pot of boiling water. He would pour it into gourds into which men had stuffed yerba maté leaves. A row of young bucks lined the bar, talked louder than the others and drank bar drinks. The strong male flavour of the café suggested a Wild West saloon in early days, but the place was much less rowdy, and devoid of females. Most of the men at the tables, even when there were three or four together, had an attitude of sitting by themselves. In a corner a herdsman sat twanging his guitar, oblivious and indifferent to the presence of others.

At the next table, facing Norbourne, sat the handsomest man he had seen in South America. He was a *gaucho*, apparently approaching fifty. In other costume he might have passed for a British admiral, a Russian opera singer, or a Wall Street banker. The stiff, curly hair that stuck out from under his black béret was iron grey. His face was a little stronger, his complexion a little more fresh-coloured than the other cowboys'. The bony structure of his face was formed to model for male anatomy or physiognomy—determined jaw, chiselled mouth and well-defined strong nose, a noble brow. His blue-grey eyes were widely spaced, full and deep-set. Their expression was friendly, assured, apprais-ing, and slightly amused. With a shapely hand he stirred a tiny cup of black coffee. Before him on the table lay his silver-handled whip. With him sat a compact, resilient stripling that might have been his son. The younger man's *poncho* was white and fringed. It could have served his mother as her best tablecloth. He wore a white broadcloth béret and a wide black silk scarf about his flat middle like a pirate. He was eating thick slices of cold meat. The *gauchos* looked Norbourne over casually and then dismissed him. He was far more curious about them than they about him. Norbourne knew the reputation of Uruguayan men for the best physiques on the continent. The proof was manifest in the cowboys all about him. It backed up his pet notion that climate makes the man.

The ink-black coffee came in small cups. One of the ranch owners, a dark, thin-faced, youngish Spaniard, pulled out a small packet of cigarettes. "Would you like to try a *Jacu?* They are a Brazilian cigarette. The *gauchos* all smoke them. We call them *cigarillo economico*, because they are the cheapest we can buy."

Norbourne took a *Jacu* and asked if the *gauchos* were exclusive beef eaters.

"Meat eaters—but it's mainly mutton," said the sharp-faced young Spanish *estanciero*. "Beef in Argentina—mutton in Uruguay. A peon's family is allowed fifty to a hundred sheep a year for his table—according to the number of his children. Mutton and yerba maté are the country diet, but *gauchos* eat four and a half pounds of meat a day."

"Maté is fine for the nervous system," said one of the Americans. "It contains a mucilaginous substance that is soothing to the throat, and it aids the digestion. It is nourishing and gives endurance."

"Sounds like our American cigarette ads," Norbourne said. "I wish I could see some maté growing."

"It doesn't do well so far south as this. We import it from Paraguay and Brazil. It looks like an orange tree growing, though it is larger and its leaves not so stiff. Belongs to the ilex family. The leaves and branches are dried over fires and crushed with flails made from tree roots. Then it is sacked and sent to the *estancia* for a second crushing and packing."

"Maté is really the name of the container from which the infusion is sucked," Mr. Morse interposed. "But you can drink it from a cup like regular tea. I've often thought it might become a vogue in the States if advertised as something fashionable and a nerve tonic."

"They tried it a few years ago, but it didn't catch on," Norbourne said. "Look at that!" he added in a low voice to the man on his left. He couldn't believe it.

Leaning against a door jamb stood a black *gaucho*. With gold-rimmed spectacles, greying hair and dignified mien, he looked like a coloured professor from Tuskegee College. His poncho was sober grey, and instead of a béret he wore an Argentine stiff-brimmed patent leather hat tied under his chin. He was as incongruous as the hotel room.

"These niggers drift down from Brazil," said one of the American buyers. "There are not many of them. Just an odd family here and there. He probably brought some cattle down from near the Brazilian border."

An *estanciero* on the other side of the table was telling a scoffing buyer about a remarkable species of Uruguayan bird. "It drills holes in solid granite to build its nest."

"Makes the woodpecker seem an amateur, eh?"

"But it's true," the *estanciero* affirmed, "and the bird is no bigger than a robin. Come and see for yourself. I live only 200 kilometres from here. If I'm lying, señor, I'll give you my *estancia*."

Norbourne wondered about the English ranch owners. He knew that a quarter of a century ago some of the ranches contained over half a million acres where the *estancieros* maintained private polo grounds and golf links in remote districts fifty or more miles from a railway on roads impassable most of the winter. He had friends who had visited there in the gala days of the British *estancias* where dozens of house-party guests rode to hounds and shot pheasants imported from Scotland. Some of those ranch owners were once remittance men, ne'er-do-wells, whose sight their correct English families could no longer abide. The open spaces, healthful airs, and inviting saddles of Uruguay proved to be fine sanatoria. Toughened in fibre by nature's ways, they learned to suck the steaming maté through a *bombilla* from a gourd and lost their alcoholic cravings.

"Do any of the British still hold their vast estates?" he asked.

"A few," one of the men answered. "But increasing taxation and increased land values made it convenient for them to sell off most of their holdings. Some returned to Europe. Some remained on the smaller properties. Almost all the big estates have been divided. Hundreds now own land once owned by one, and work for themselves instead of a landlord."

An oldish *gaucho* came up and plucked the ranch owner courteously by the sleeve. The gentleman got up and they went and sat on a bench together. The *gaucho* began explaining his business. They leaned their heads closer together very naturally. Norbourne saw something warming in the intimacy and understanding of the scene between servant and employer. He thought of how Hudson had been moved in describing many similar scenes of seven decades earlier. "Here," he wrote, "the lord of many leagues of land and unnumbered herds sits down to talk with the hired shepherd and no class or caste difference divides them, no consciousness of their widely different positions chills the warm cement of sympathy between two human hearts."

Business Lunch

Pleasant and homelike and progressive as Montevideo was, there was really little of interest to be seen that could not be managed in two or three days. There were no ruined temples, no feathered mummies, no treasure-troves, no coca-chewing Indians. Existing pleasantly among the furniture and saddles and homely courtesies of yesterday, Uruguayans relished today but kept alert to tomorrow. Like Argentina, Uruguay is exclusively a white man's country. (They are the only two in Latin America.) Its stock is predominantly Spanish: largely the industrious, honest Basques with the physique and vigour that came from the Pyrenees. Half the people are of Spanish descent. Almost thirty per cent are Italian; five per cent are French. The other fifteen are English, German, Swiss, Argentinian, Brazilian and American. The

British community of Montevideo numbers about a thousand, as in Lima.

Norbourne went to the weekly luncheon of the business men's club with Mr. Meyer, the English editor of *The Sun*. The editor had been praising the sterling qualities of the Uruguayan character.

"Are the British and the Americans liked by the Uruguayans?"

"Personally, as individuals, yes. I believe the American and English colonies are more friendly with the Uruguayans than they are with any other Latin American people. England likes to think that Uruguay has a natural affinity for the British," said Mr. Meyer. A shrewd smile lit up his heavy, intelligent face. "But the truth is, the Uruguayan lumps together the nephews of John Bull and Uncle Sam and dubs them all *Los Ingleses*. English journalists on brief visits here write fervently of Uruguay's love of Great Britain and all things British. The truth is that the Uruguayan's ideals and sympathies are mainly French. His social ethics and customs are Spanish. His sartorial ambitions are Italian—he dresses like Milan, not London. In the University schools of law, medicine, and architecture, French text books are used. And so far from discovering any affinity for things British, my greatest triumph has been to obtain a grudging admission that the English customs and rules of social and sex life might suit *Los Ingleses*, but certainly they were not suitable to the Uruguayan temperament."

"What if an Englishman takes a Uruguayan wife?" Norbourne asked.

"The husband adopts the social customs of Uruguay. He may still keep in touch with his fellow countrymen at Blanqueada or round the Club billiard table, he may still give financial support to British institutions—but socially he is really as much lost to the British community as though he had never formed part of it.

"Don't let the journalists fool you. Uruguay hasn't been influenced by the British. Only in one respect have the Uruguayans followed English ideals." He made a b-b-bur-r! sound simulating cold as they entered the Alhambra where the luncheon was to be held. "They never have their houses properly warmed."

In the bare-looking private dining-room the walls were hung with the Stars and Stripes and Uruguay's Golden Sun. The other guests of the luncheon club were the Bermudian father-in-law of the National City Bank's brisk manager; a young German who had risen in a few years to a responsible position in a Uruguayan firm; the manager-star of the English Players; and Dr. Monroe of Princeton, who had been invited on a speaking tour by the South American universities. In the course of an excellent address in which he pointed out to business the folly of intervention, Dr. Monroe made this statement: "It would have been cheaper for the United States to buy up every United States business in Nicaragua than to maintain marines. Where there has been intervention the value of investments protected has been less than the cost of intervention."

Norbourne was called on to speak. In the minute or two he was on his feet he said he was in full accord with all that Dr. Monroe had said. Then he paid Montevideo the compliment of calling it "the contenting city." He commented on its temperate and well-ordered prosperity. He said he believed that the real well-being and prosperity of a nation could be measured only by the sympathy that existed between its top and bottom. He said he believed Montevideo was the only city in Latin America besides Santiago de Chile in which a North American might find himself quickly at home.

"I am glad," he wound up, "that Uruguay has neither a sacerdotal nor a hypocritical aversion to changing its constitution, whenever it may mean the greater good for the greater number. A half a century ago W. H. Hudson revealed the very heart of Uruguay when he wrote: 'The unwritten constitution mightier than the written one is in the heart of every Uruguayan to make him always a republican and free with a freedom it would be hard to match anywhere on the globe.'

"May 'the virtuous child of the South American republics' as

William McFee called you, continue to lead the onward march of health and progress. May Uruguay's impulsive and courageous idealism and sound common sense become more of an inspiration to the other republics that hesitate with reaction."

There was applause. Norbourne grinned, sat down, and fell to his dessert. He was surprised to find how really enthusiastic he did feel about Uruguay.

Grievances

After luncheon, Norbourne, feeling that of all the people there he would learn more in a brief time from the wide-awake, honest-faced young German, engaged him in conversation.

"Do you like it here?" he asked as they moved away from the others.

"Yes, very much. I'll tell you why, particularly. Frankness becomes very easy in Uruguay. It's this: in Germany anybody is as efficient, hardworking, and clever as I am. Here I am exceptional —even though Uruguay is the most progressive country in Latin America." He paused to see whether Norbourne was critical or sympathetic. Then he confessed further: "I have two small sons, twins. I shall send them to Germany to be educated, so that they will come back and know things and impress people more easily with their extra knowledge."

He drove Norbourne back to his hotel a roundabout way so that they could talk. "From 1926 to 1930," he said, explaining the business situation, "Uruguay bought almost twice as much from the United States as from the United Kingdom, and three times more than from Germany. Not because she was partial to the United States, which ranks only fifth or sixth among her customers, but simply because the United States had at convenient prices what she wanted. Now Uruguay has adopted a 'trade-with-those-who-trade-with-us' slogan, and arranged an elaborate quota system. It's an infernal nuisance and works like this: importers are allowed to purchase no more than the total amount the United

States has bought the preceding year from Uruguay. For instance, after Uruguayan purchases have equalled those of the United States, our importers, or even private citizens, have to buy in other markets. A beauty shop won't be permitted to purchase, say, Elizabeth Arden cosmetics, because the quota is filled. It is forced to buy French or German cosmetics. The same sort of thing happened to me. I needed certain drawing materials from the United States. I wasn't allowed to get them there. I had either to wait a year or buy them elsewhere. A sculptor here wanted a ton of Belgian clay. He couldn't get it direct from Belgium. He had to buy it through a country where the quota wasn't filled. Now a man has to get a permit to order a fountain pen from the States. It's a damned nuisance, but a national self-protection. The United States' high tariff barriers put on in the time of Coolidge and Hoover made the Uruguayans see red. We hadn't much confidence in American business's fair play anyhow. For after the war, when foreign markets were depleted, we were forced to buy from the States, and they sent us inferior goods and charged outlandish prices and made us pay cash, because they could. They sent us cargoes of rotten lumber for which we had paid in advance. No, frankly, we had no call to love the United States, until the visit of Cordell Hull changed this attitude.

"And now with the reciprocity treaties and a fifty per cent reduction of your tariff on canned meats and wool, a healthy flow of trade is commencing. Now you are buying our stuff and we are going to buy your automobiles and lumber and all sorts of manufactured products. Good times are coming back to all of us."

INTERLUDE

INTERLUDE

Montevideo Conference

Norbourne had followed the progress of the epoch-making Montevideo Conference through the newspapers, the magazines, and especially through the reports of that brilliant and clear-brained Latin American authority, Hubert Herring, who attended as a commentator. In every capital in South America he had heard of its successful outcome and of the resultant friendship it had produced between the United States and Latin America.

Pan-American Conferences have been held between Latin America and the United States seven times since 1889. Originated to promote friendly relations between the republics and to stimulate mutual trade, they had become, however, mere figures of speech. The fine sentiments expressed had had few concrete results. The United States, while spouting sentiments as full of noble bombast as the Latins, had continued her pernicious "dollar diplomacy."

Norbourne had heard in every republic he had visited of examples of United States ruthlessness and unfairness. "They hated our guts" was the favourite expression Americans used in summing up the relationship. It was not unnatural that the Spanish American countries should have little love for the United States. Many of the former political appointee diplomats had succeeded by their arrogance, ill-information and sometimes bad manners, in making enemies instead of friends. "Yankee imperialism," "the big stick," "manifest destiny," and "intervention" were threats under which Latin American pride and dignity continually chafed. There was a loose tendency among certain business men to regard the Latin republics as scum. Short-sighted manufacturers often spoke of expecting "to dump their surplus on South America." Railway officials once proposed "to send their out-of-date railway equipment to some of those dago republics."

So when the conference was called to meet in Montevideo, few expected anything but the former empty rhetoric. Part of the Latin American Press was writing the usual sceptical editorials on the farce of pretended "friendship."

When the Secretary of State arrived quietly in Montevideo in December, 1933, the summer atmosphere was gloomy and apathetic. As a direct slight to the United States, Argentina had determined not to send any delegates whatsoever. The Argentinians were going to remain contemptuously aloof across the River Plata and criticize every move the United States made. Secretary Hull's job in demonstrating the realities of President Roosevelt's good neighbour policy was double: first to overcome the hate and fear inspired by other administrations, and second, to build on its ruins a new understanding and friendship.

Straightway on his arrival Secretary Hull called on President Terra. He made it very clear that he had no business in view except to be helpful. He explained that he had left affairs in Washington with considerable sacrifice and that if nothing constructive was to take place, he was considering returning home at once.

In the next two days Mr. Hull busied himself paying friendly calls on every delegation, after ascertaining in what hotels or legations or private homes they were staying. After he had left his apartments, his aide would telephone the delegation about to be visited to say that the United States Secretary of State was on his way to call. Often there was a tremendous scurry and flurry to prepare to receive the distinguished visitor. If the delegates were in the cellar or garret, Mr. Hull sought them out and paid his visit, making it clear to each that he had no business in view except to make friends and be helpful when he could. By his straightforwardness and charm Mr. Hull won the liking and admiration of all the foreign representatives he had called upon. "Ah, at last," they said, "here is an American statesman who is really *simpático*." President Terra, impressed by Mr. Hull's sincerity, and realizing that it would be something of a reflection to have the conference break up in failure in his capital, began to bestir himself to make it a success.

Argentina across the river, with its caustic editorials partially prepared, was apprised by the Uruguayan President of the unprecedented doings in Montevideo. Dr. Saavedra Lamas, Argentina's Minister of Worship and Foreign Affairs, whom many considered the strongest enemy of the United States, and the nominal leader in bitter critical attacks on us, decided that after all he and an Argentine delegation would attend the conference. So they packed up their bags, together with their curiosity and doubts, and took the night boat over to Montevideo. Before the Foreign Minister was well settled in his hotel Cordell Hull called. After a chilly greeting, Dr. Saavedra began to thaw. The cabinet ministers talked for two hours and found themselves in accord. Mr. Hull was most sympathetic to a peace pact of which Dr. Saavedra was the proud author. At the end of the two hours' visit, the Argentinian and the American were friends. In a few days they were as "thick" as cousins.

Mr. Hull urged President Terra and the Conference to "leave off the superfluous dinners, and work." And they did. Having begun in a fog of futility, the Conference settled down to a programme of real team work, and the twenty-one republics for the first time in history took up their joint labour in the spirit of unity and co-operation. The United States delegation did not try to muzzle certain gentlemen who rose to attack and berate the United States on the intervention question. It listened unruffled, knowing, in view of the recorded evidence of Roosevelt's proclamation, that the United States had finished with interventions in Latin America, the orators were wasting their gilded stings. And when Saavedra Lamas rose and defended the United States for two eloquent hours, the great turn was made.

At the Conference the United States hoped for several things: a beginning in economic co-operation for the furtherance of trade; an end to war in the Chaco; a strengthening of North American relations with all Latin American peoples, especially with Argentina. Mr. Hull urged the construction of the Pan-American Highway and dwelt on the effect of this highway in creating cordial relations, racial understanding and good neighbourliness, and in the unlocking of economic wealth now inaccessible. These aims set the pace and determined the course of the Conference.

Beyond everything else, Mr. Hull emphasized the idea that "prosperity of the spirit" out of which all other riches flow should be the chief concern. "Peace must be our passion," he said, repeating a line from his Rio speech. "Its cost cannot be too great in the light of the frightful cost of war. We know now that it is madness for international strife to inflict famine and despair upon whole populations. So we must take stock of all our blessings in this favoured part of the world—all our cultural, political, social, and material assets—and bring them to bear, by united efforts, to help right a topsy-turvy civilization. By being the best of neighbours, let us offer the finest possible example for a jaded and disillusioned world."

The achievements of the Montevideo Conference were such as to mark the beginning of a new epoch in this hemisphere. At the adjournment of the Conference, a complete revolution of feeling had taken place among the nations of the Americas, and an unwonted attitude of friendliness, of understanding, and of trust in the motives and purposes of each other had resulted. By his inspired diplomacy and the sympathetic charm of his personality, Cordell Hull had won the confidence of a continent, Central America, and the island republics of the Caribbean. President Roosevelt made good all Mr. Hull's implied promises and assurances with such tangible acts as the abrogation of the Platt Amendment, the withdrawal of marines from Haiti, and the launching of the reciprocity trade treaties.

In June, 1934, President Roosevelt signed an Act of Congress authorizing the Chief Executive to enter into reciprocal commercial agreement with other governments for the purpose of promoting international commerce. The Trade Agreements Act brought into being a tariff-bargaining machinery designed to restore our foreign commerce as an essential step in the progress toward national and world economic recovery.

Within two years, reciprocity trade agreements were concluded with five Latin American nations (Cuba, Brazil, Colombia, Haiti, and Honduras), four European nations, and Canada. Instead of the disastrous consequences prophesied by ultra-high tariff advocates, there has been a steady, healthy increase in trade with each of the countries which signed the agreements. For example, take Cuba: During the first fourteen months of the new relations with that republic, trade improved almost seventy-five per cent. Compare the figures on four items sold to Cuba for the years ending 1933 and 1935: In 1933, only 440 passenger cars were imported; while in 1935, 3,159 passenger cars were imported. In 1933, only 463 American trucks were sold to Cuba; while in 1935, 2,177 American trucks were sold. American radio manufacturers exported a total of 2,820 radio sets to Havana in 1933, compared with 26,473 sets in 1935. For every American incandescent electric lamp bulb imported into Cuba in 1933 more than five were imported in 1935.

Total trade with countries with which agreements were in force twelve months showed an increase of 36.7% from 1934 to 1935, while trade with other countries showed an increase of only 134%. For the four months ending April, 1936, the increase over the four months ending April, 1935, was 20.5% as against 11.1%.

The reciprocity trade treaties have definitely stimulated business. But, even more important than the improved business is the friendship and the feeling of mutual benefit. Regardless of the large or small material values accruing immediately from the reciprocity trade treaties, the psychological effect in producing more cordial feelings is incalculably advantageous.

16

CHILE NITRATE PLANT FROM THE AIR

18

SKIING IN THE ANDES ABOVE SANTIAGO DE CHILE

19
SNOW IN THE ANDES

20

FALLS OF THE IGUAZÚ, FLORIANO FALLS

21

ARGENTINA, GRAPE PICKING IN A TYPICAL VINEYARD

22

BEACH SCENE, MONTEVIDEO, URUGUAY

23

THUNDERBIRD ROUNDING SUGAR LOAF, RIO DE JANEIRO

24
RIO DE JANEIRO

25
RIO, AT NIGHT

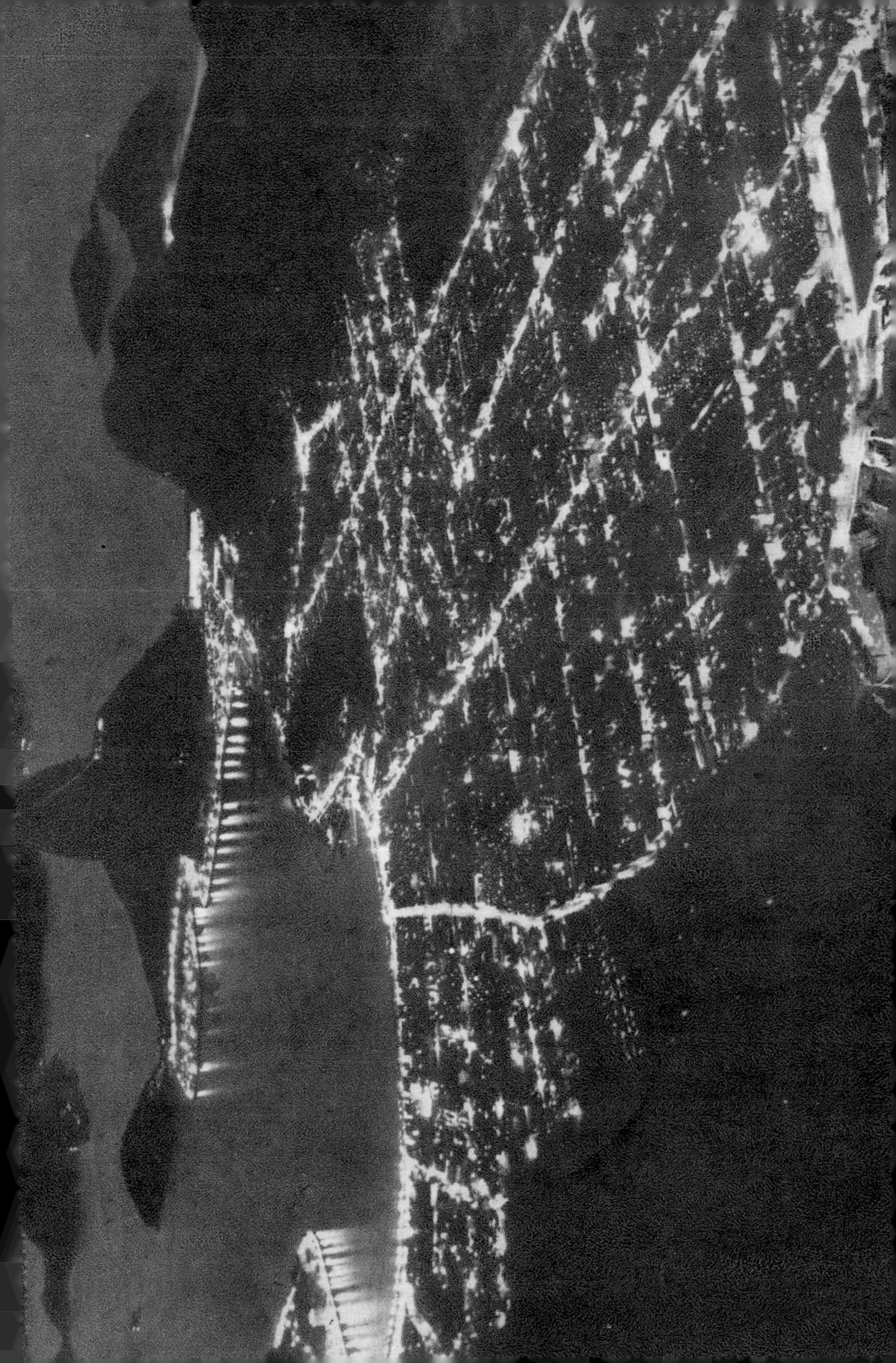

26

WATERFRONT, BAHIA, BRAZIL

27

THUNDERBIRD AND SAILING VESSEL

VII

BRAZIL

"*All the wealth-of earth, beneath or above loam, crowds the promise of Brazil.*"

Waldo Frank

BRAZIL

Superlatives

Northward from Uruguay to Brazil there was no unfertile land. The seaplane flew over what is called "the lagoon country," where Uruguay merges into Brazil so imperceptibly that one cannot tell the difference. Cattle grazed on succulent grasses to the edges of the lagoons and beach sand. Hudson had been deeply concerned lest future progress might hang like a yoke on the Uruguayan herdsmen. But Norbourne had seen that the cowboy wore progress not like a yoke, but like a silken neckerchief about his throat to be laid aside at will. The free wild flavour of the *gaucho* still pervaded Montevideo and gave the city its distinctive atmosphere. Progress of the most advanced sort had come to Uruguay, but the scarlet and white verbenas called "margaritas" continue to scatter their wild petals on the plains. The flamingoes and the black-necked swans that Hudson loved still breed about the blue lakes. And in western rocks where the topaz and the amethyst are mined for commerce, the azure air-flowers cling, tenacious and serene, like forget-me-nots enamelled on a peasant's brooch.

The colour became more intense. Palms were growing wild. Occasional parasol pines raised their tight green shade against the heat of the sun. The Commodore swept down on Rio Grande at the entrance of Lagôa dos Patos. The city ranks fifth among Brazil's ports and is her chief cattle market. The painted roof signs on Swift's enormous *frigorifico* were in Portuguese. The signs on the breweries, the jute mills, the cotton mills, were in Portuguese. At the airport the people were all talking Portuguese.

That Brazil should speak Portuguese while the other Latin American nations of the mainland speak Spanish is due to the treaty of Tordesillas of 1494, by which Spain and Portugal virtually divided the undiscovered world between them. The agreement gave Portugal the right to all lands east of a meridional line drawn from pole to pole 370 leagues west of the Cape Verde Islands. Thus the great bulge of Brazil came within the limit of Portugal's share.

In 1500 when a Portuguese named Pedro Alvares Cabral, on his way to India around the Cape of Good Hope, got out of his course and touched the Brazil coast at Porto Seguro, he took the country in the name of Portugal. He sent one of his ships back to Lisbon to proclaim the discovery and on it a cargo of reddish dyewood, very like a rich Arabian wood much prized in architectural decoration. The Portuguese name for this wood was "brasil." So the country was called the land of red-dyewood.

The supreme fact in Brazil's history is that the territory was settled by Portuguese. Its population, estimated to-day at 45,000,000, is not only the largest of any nation on the southern continent, but greater than that of all the combined Spanish-speaking South American nations.

Norbourne was staggered when he considered the immensity and the opulence of Brazil. Larger than the United States by another Texas, the country is twice as large as India and three-fourths as large as Europe. Sixty-five Englands could be set down in the same area without overcrowding. From north to south its extreme length is 2,700 miles. It is almost as wide, 2,690 miles. Its seaboard, prodigally endowed with harbours and scenic beauty, extends 4,000 miles from the Uruguayan border to the edge of French Guiana—a considerably greater distance than that between New York and Liverpool—twice the distance from the tip end of Florida to Portland, Maine. The great pouter pigeon breast of Brazil pushes so far out into the Atlantic that its extremity is 2,600 miles east of New York. From New York to Rio by steamer or by plane one covers almost 7,000 miles—about the distance from New York to Japan as the crow flies. Containing almost half the territory of the entire continent, Brazil's boundaries touch upon those of every South American nation except Chile and Ecuador.

In all the books Norbourne had read on Brazil superlatives were strewn through the pages, and temperate men in conversation assumed an unwonted eloquence when speaking of the country. Its river system is the greatest in the world, with 30,070 miles of explored navigable rivers and regular service of vessels plying up and down 17,000 of those miles. It supplies over sixty per cent of the world's coffee, and is the world's foremost producer of cacao and yerba maté. Once it led in tobacco exports and sugar. Before the development of rubber plantations in the Malay States and the Straits Settlements, it was overwhelmingly the greatest rubber-producing country.

Six million tons of corn, the leading cereal crop, are produced annually. In export of nuts Brazil leads the world. More than 30,000 tons of Brazil nuts, or nigger-toes, are exported annually; 9,000,000 bunches of bananas, 87,000,000 pineapples. Yet only some four per cent of Brazil's 2,000,000,000 acres are in cultivation. The mineral deposits of Minas Geraes are fabulous in extent. According to conservative estimates they contain over 12,000,000,000 tons of high grade ores.

Lists of Brazil's outgoing cargoes sound like a romancer's version of a mythical kingdom's trade. Diamonds, silk and monkey-fur. Isinglass and arrowroot. Chromium and frozen beef. Gold, coal, and manganese. Asbestos, oil and iron. Digitalis, ipecacuanha, butterflies, and orchids. Black diamonds and rose diamonds, opals and cat's-eyes, garnets and chrysoberyls, and beryls of green, blue and pale gold. Diamonds harder and more brilliant than those of Kimberley are mined. One stone found at Patos on the Areado River weighed over 2,000 carats and was valued at $800,000. Well over a thousand varieties of orchids have been identified and thirty thousand species of butterflies.

Norbourne knew it would be hard to restrain superlatives about this land of coffee and spice and orchids and diamonds. And restraint would be misleading. Here lay the greatest undeveloped possibilities for productive wealth to be found on this globe. And here were the greatest contrasts. On the coast live the sophisticated upper-class city dwellers, who spend half their time in Europe, speak five or six languages and live in imperial splendour, bothering as little about the aboriginal Indians who live in primeval savagery in the jungle as the savages do about them.

Everything Norbourne had read or heard attested that life in Brazil is multiform, profuse, opulent. God, the Brazilian says, fashioned their land in his most lavish mood. They go further. God himself, they affirm, is a Brazilian.

Good-bye to Winter

After Rio Grande the coast line is jagged with variety. Little peninsulas stick their fingers and sometimes whole arms out into the sea. The shadows of gleaming white lighthouses shimmer in the blue-green water. Gardens of green vegetables crowd the tiny river basins dotted with white cottages. For five minutes the aeroplane took to sea, for the next ten minutes, green land lay beneath. But it was the coast line that was capricious, not the seaplane. At length, rounding a point and entering an estuary sprinkled with islands, the thunderbird circled about the hilly city of Porto Alegre. In that unsung happy harbour live as many people as in Peru's fabulous Lima. The port lies exactly as far below the equator as New Orleans is above.

The sun was just at the point of setting when the thunderbird dipped and skimmed along the surface of the river. Three youths in pale green trunks were sporting among water-lily plants. Swimming trunks at sunset meant that winter was definitely left behind. As the passengers walked up the long-railed wooden walkway that ran out from the quay to meet them, the soft breath of the tropics blew gently from the north. The bathers pushed their way through the lily plants, took off rubber caps and shook their blond heads. Their skin was fair, their bodies Nordic. A million Germans live in the southernmost Brazilian state of which Porto Alegre is capital.

Up the hilly paved streets, where trams were frequent and motor cars many, the passengers were driven to Mr. Schmidt's hotel. It was all very clean and orderly, with Germans drinking *schnapps* in the bar. Norbourne had little desire to explore the town. It was a new place, a city of business and industry. Well-lit, efficient, progressive, laid out in an attractive setting, it was stamped with German comfort.

German Wedge

The three fertile southern states of Brazil, lying on an elevated plateau, are excellent for cereal and fruit growing. They are ideally suited to permanent habitations for the white man. Most of the territory south of Rio de Janeiro is comparatively recent in settlement. The pasture lands of this temperate zone were ignored by adventurers. Harry Franck has seen maps printed as late as 1865 marking the southern provinces as "unknown and inhabited only by Indians." But the map was slightly exaggerated. For the Germans had begun to come in. The Emperor of Brazil had the sagacity to encourage sturdy husbandmen from Germany and Switzerland to prepare the wilderness for civilization. He was generous and allotted each adult male immigrant 175 acres. The exodus from Germany to the promised land caused the Kaiser to forbid immigration after 1859. But thirteen colonies had been established there before Germany halted her emigrants. The Germans have given tone and substance to the district, and they have kept their own ways and customs. Germans whose grandfathers came to Brazil even before 1859 still look upon themselves as Germans, not Brazilians. In many southern towns to-day the inhabitants speak German instead of Portuguese. Some second and third generation Germans in Porto Alegre do not even yet speak Portuguese. Teachers in the schools are German pastors.

In 1896 Germany removed the ban prohibiting emigration to Brazil. In the meantime the Italians had rushed in. The Italians took to the high lands and planted corn, coffee, and the vine. The Germans preferred the low, and in the river bottoms raised green vegetables and hogs.

Before the war the Germans got control of the dried beef industry and established a German monopoly, working with German commercial interests in Europe. Many people are of the opinion that the Kaiser had planned to use the pan-handle of southern Brazil as the wedge to German domination, if Germany had won the war.

Flying Up to Rio

From Porto Alegre to Rio de Janeiro the trip by air is not to be compared with that by steamer; for by steamer, like the sailor in the ditty, one sees the sea and nothing else. The larger ships do not call at those delightful fairy tale towns of Florianopolis and Paranaguá. Together with Santos these towns are like little Rios. Unfolding in three successive stages in increasing beauty, they prepare the north-bound flier for the climax. Florianopolis, the capital of the state of Santa Catharina, stood embowered in palms and flowers on Santa Catharina Island. The water of the ocean was tropical blue again, rich as indigo. The vegetation was joyous. It was the first heady abundance of green Norbourne had seen since Ecuador. But here it was disciplined, with no hint of suffocation. The air was femininely soft. On the hillsides the houses shimmered in the morning light, and the long bridge that connects the island with the mainland joined beauty with beauty.

Slender-winged frigate birds gliding through the lucent air, full of curiosity about the resting thunderbird, made smears of shadows on the rippling turquoise bay. For all the shipping that might pass, for all the barter and trade, Florianopolis was definitely within the territory of lotos-eaters.

A hundred and forty-four miles beyond, up a coast as full of curves and surprises and delights as a woman's body, the lovely Paranaguá lay in a lagoon-like harbour. Secure in colonial heritage and opulent natural beauty, she casually exports beverages—yerba maté and coffee—to the far ends of the great world, and is content to admire her own image in the mirror at her feet.

The contrast between the sturdy masculinity of Montevideo and the feminine allure of Brazilian coast towns was as marked as the sharp division between the rank Ecuadorian jungle and the desert of Peru.

Coffee Pot

At Santos a meandering river and an amphitheatre of soft green mountains join with the foaming sea and bizarre promontories to make a picturesque setting for the world's foremost coffee market. Until forty years ago, however, Santos was a notorious hot-bed of yellow fever. Bryce recounts how once, during a vicious siege of the plague, forty-three British ships lay idle in the river, their crews all dead or dying. Now, since Dr. Oswaldo Cruz practised General Gorgas's sanitation methods in Brazil, the town has bloomed with health as well as abundant beauty.

For a stretch of three miles, freighters, bow to stern, waited their turn to suckle their fill of the perpetual flow of coffee that comes from the aromatic *fazendas* beyond São Paulo up on the high plateau. The docks can accommodate fifty freighters at a time. In total exports Santos surpasses even the great Rio. Once loin-clothed singing Negroes helped in the feeding, bore the coffee bags on their shoulders from the railway station to the ships. Then stouter and more dependable Portuguese superseded the blacks. And now machinery has wrested the jobs from the Portuguese. Bags are dropped from trucks into manholes in the street, where a system of mechanical belts receives them and bears them underground to the ships' holds.

A short walk from the docks on the Rua Quinze de Novembro, an insignificant crooked little street, stands the exchange which handles some sixty per cent of the world's coffee business. During the hot middle hours of the day into which the business men from São Paulo crowd their span of work, the place is something like a Black Hole of Calcutta turned into bedlam. But in the midst of hurly-burly under the palm trees, with mechanical belts hustling thousands of coffee bags into the freighters' depths and ticker tape clicking tensely, there is still something that touches the average man more than his acquisitive materialism. The hard way of life of the business man with the ideals of Wall Street and The Loop is tempered by sensuous rhythms. The important work transacted, half the brokers and plantation owners shake from their boots the money-changing dust they have themselves stirred up, and take the train for São Paulo, almost three thousand feet above among the peaked hills. The other half go to the residential hotels built on the superb beaches and throw off commercial emotions in the splash of the sounding surf. Climate will ever bind the ambitious of Brazil within certain limits. No matter how boldly they desire to hack out their own destinies, climate will be an agent of divinity to help shape their ends.

São Paulo

The most spectacular and costly of railroads climbs abrupt slopes to São Paulo. It is patronized chiefly by directors and brokers who travel daily from their highland villas to the port, and passes through breath-taking scenery sprinkled with waterfalls and festooned with orchids that look like birds and studded with birds that look like orchids.

São Paulo, rising with the peaks of the narrow hills, seems to have sprung up since the turn of the century. But the up-to-date city will celebrate its four hundredth anniversary in 1953. A Jesuit missionary founded the place. The first Portuguese settlers took Indian wives and reared their dusky broods in semi-savage ways. The people grew into an aggressive race, explored for gold, raided other settlers in far-off districts. The spirit of the first Paulistas has descended to the fourteenth and fifteenth generations. In a large measure the Paulistas dictate the policies of the state. Theirs is the most independent as well as the richest of Brazilian states.

In 1875, São Paulo was no more than a country town with gardens full of humming birds which the Brazilians call "kiss-flowers." To-day, spreading over fourteen square miles in area with a population of a million, São Paulo is the third city of South America. Everything is brand new. Skyscrapers glitter in the sun. The streets are choked with fine motor cars. Everything is "the latest," well-organized, well-managed—the tram service, the street lighting, the water supply, all of the best. Its cinemas, cabarets, orchid gardens, opera, and municipal market are all briskly patronized. Its sudden growth has been more meteoric than that of Argentina's capital. In spirit it is more akin to Buenos Aires and Chicago than to Rio. Of all South American cities it is the most North American in flavour. The commercial and industrial houses are largely conducted and controlled by foreigners: Italians, Portuguese, Germans, British, and Americans. The upper-class Brazilians own most of the plantations, and give their talents over to politics or spend half the year abroad, where their wives are outfitted by the couturières and jewellers of the Rue de la Paix.

The rich red soil of São Paulo State and the three adjacent states is sometimes six to nine feet deep. And on this earth is grown Brazil's chief commodity for foreign sale. Coffee constitutes more than seventy per cent of the country's total exports. Years before the United States experimented in crop restriction, the Federal Government restricted the export by a quota system apportioned to each state. Overproduction plunged the Defence Scheme into difficulties, and by 1934 a whole year's crop was in storage. In 1934 with a crop estimated at nearly 30,000,000 bags, the government had to buy 11,000,000 bags of "sacrifice" coffee.

The only place of historic interest in São Paulo is the Ypiranga Museum, a palace of white marble, built five miles from the city's centre on the site where the twenty-two-year-old heir to the throne of Portugal uttered the cry of independence in 1822. Not far from the museum is the aerodrome where brokers too pressed to wait for a train, take a plane and drop on to Santos, as quick as a falcon making a strike.

At Santos a young lawyer of Rio, who had been educated at Harvard, boarded the seaplane and sat on the lounge seat by Norbourne. He had no luggage except his brief case and a copy of Proust's *Du côté de chez Swann*—"for relaxation," he said. He had gone down by train to sit up all night working on the land title of a coffee plantation owned by an American.

"A *fazenda* is feudal in atmosphere," he explained, since Norbourne had not had time to visit a plantation. "Some are old fashioned, some modern, but all feudal. The proprietor's house is a manor, often elaborately furnished. The overseers live near the lines of workmen's cottages. The cottages are backed by garden allotments. The commissary—where the workers must buy their supplies and clothes—is supplemented by a church and a school. Some larger *fazendas* provide a cinema, restaurant, and a hospital. A generation may be born and die without ever leaving the place. A single labourer is assigned to tend two thousand trees, or six acres under cultivation. The coffee land is weeded six times a year. Life is not bad for the workmen on an old place. But it's pretty nasty clearing jungle and laying out new plantations in the broiling sun. The Italian peasants seem to be the only men who can stand it. You'd never get a Negro to do it.

"Incidentally," he added, as he stretched out and prepared for a nap after his sleepless night, "let me give you one word of advice: be careful how and with whom you discuss Negroes here. We have a saying in Brazil—the Negroes themselves started it, I believe—'Never inquire too intimately into a man's family tree, for it's apt to lead you back into the kitchen.' Get the point? Of course it's a libel. But there's a germ of truth in it that gives it a sting. However, the aspect of Brazilian sociology that strikes all foreigners most forcibly is the absence of race conflict and prejudice. You're bound to notice it. And you will notice, too, that complexions grow darker as you go north.

"But," he smiled, "have no fear. You won't have to take a 'high yaller' in to dinner. Sixty per cent of us are still pure white."

The Ultimate

The seaplane raced with time to reach Brazil's glittering capital at sunset. Norbourne had misgivings. All his life he had been told that the sight of the harbour was the ultimate in worldly beauty. In many parts of both hemispheres he had looked upon beauty raw and beauty wrought to strange perfection by man's imagination and ingenuity. He had seen the Sahara's relentless desert dunes waving under a waning moon. He had gazed upon Palermo in a still platinum dawn when the semi-circular mountains, the city towers, the smacks and junks of fishermen spreading sardine nets in the bay all seemed created from pure silver. At sunset in Taormina he had seen, through almond branches in full flower, Mt. Etna's snow-clad cone turn to a mountain pile of diamonds. Only a fortnight previously, flying over the hump of the midwinter Andes, he had said that no half-hour of travel could surpass it. He got up and walked toward the cockpit and gazed through the window between the shoulders of pilot and co-pilot. The thunderbird throbbed steadily, devouring distance with magical celerity.

Faintly, as if breaking through gossamer, the wavering southern silhouette of the Twin Brothers, forty miles distant, began to solidify. The declining sun sent out shafts of flattering light. To the east the unstable Atlantic stretched like a continent of variegated jade. Far to the west, suffused in dusty rose colour, great mountains, as if to keep the sun company, turned their stupendous backs on the capital and stalked off towards the Brazilian jungle. Beyond the Twin Brothers, where a golf course wound hazardously about the slope, the jagged peak called the Hunchback rose two thousand feet straight out of a residential district. On its summit the heroic Christ turned to white gold under the sun's last alchemic flare.

As the thunderbird approached its nest, Guanabara Bay gleamed like a lake of quicksilver. Its seventy humped islands became violet-coloured sea-monsters, gathered for some mythological assembly. The famous Sugar Loaf mountain reared precipitously out of the sea, a wandering polar iceberg changed to porphyry by tropical air. Now, looking directly down upon the city spreading over seventy square miles, Norbourne saw that its plan possessed little of the formal chessboard geometry of other Latin municipalities. Its sugar-white beaches, its rocky points and spurs rushed unrestrained into various inlets and bays, and made capricious outlines of new moons, butterflies, and orchids. Mountains smothered in tropical luxuriance tumbled about the heart of the city, terminated shopping streets, stepped boldly off into the ocean. Orange-coloured crags formed the back terraces of gardens. Rainbow-tinted villas perched on precipices like eagles' eyries. Double rows of royal palms paraded for miles on end up avenues, their feathery crowns half a hundred feet above the red roofs of dwellings. The licorice and cream-coloured pavements, formed of small rounded stones set in whirling patterns, were fairy tale confections laid out to allure children. Such fantastic harmonies of mountain and sea, of fashionable bathing resorts and jungle wilderness, of French baroque architecture and ships flying flags of all nations, were as unreal as dreams that lie in opium pellets. It was beyond credibility. Rio, like Xanadu, was a fabulous city created in a romancer's imagination.

As the thunderbird tilted a wing and swooped towards its resting place Norbourne came back and sat down again in the lounge. He looked out of the window. Against the north-western sky just above Petropolis, where the Emperor had had his summer residence, the distant Organ Mountains raised their granite pipes towards the salmon-streaked heavens. "The Fingers of God" dominated the landscape for thirty miles around. The sculptured digits uplifted in eternal benediction over the Deity's own climax of creation.

"You see," said the lawyer, "why we say, 'God is a Brazilian.' "

That evening after dinner Norbourne had coffee and Cointreau on the marble terrace of the Hotel Gloria, set solidly in rock above the palm-bordered esplanade called Avenida Beira Mar, the most beautiful drive in all the world. The city wore the illumination of the evening like jewels. The incandescence of a million electric globes, perfectly spaced, outlined crescent shore-drives, straight avenues, parks, the near and far hills. Southern stars pricked dazzling patterns of unfamiliar constellations in the sky's rich blue silk. Through the hotel's French windows came eighteenth-century melody played by a string quintet ranged about a spindle-legged piano. People in evening clothes strolled about, talked, laughed, whispered, lighted cigarettes, sipped liqueurs, drank in the view at the balustrade. Drawn on its invisible string towards the heavens, the electric-lit aerial car floated leisurely to the dizzy top of Sugar Loaf like a gigantic firefly from the jungle. Then as if by a conjurer's command, an enormous oblique globe of liquid gold rose from the blue-black horizon. The moon, two days past its full perfection, flecked the purplish islands with gold dust. A broadsword of quivering light slashed the bay in two and blunted its point on the rocks beneath the seawall.

Guests on the terraces paused in their movement, murmured, or were silent. For the initiated a familiar ritual had lost none of its sublimity. To the stranger the magic of moonlight held new meanings. Rio was as unbelievable by night as by day, and more mysteriously beautiful. For once the word "breath-taking" could be judiciously applied to scenery. But Norbourne knew no extravagant words could ever explain the place to one who had not beheld it. This glamour of strangeness had to be savoured to be even half believed.

By Daylight

When Norbourne awoke at dawn he still felt as if Rio was a place he had dreamed. He reached for his dressing-gown and looked out of the window. There lay the incredible harbour right enough. But the glamour of strangeness had not ended with sunset and moonlight. Framed by the balcony window was the monochrome of mercury-coloured bay. The grotesque islands, streaked with tarnished silver, were watching a boat race practice. Slashing blades of a hundred oars engraved the burnished breastplate of the bay. From afar came the barked orders of the Brazilian coxes, like whispers of the island monsters breaking their own enchantment.

Norbourne drew the blinds, went back to bed, and awoke three hours later to intense bird song. A fleet of bird cages had been strung across the adjoining balcony and a chorus of canaries were straining their throats with ecstasy over the winter sunshine. Down on the Avenida Beira Mar the stream of whizzing automobiles was punctuated haphazardly by bronzed men in swimming trunks crossing the street on their way to Flamengo Beach. Norbourne telephoned for sliced orange, coffee and brioche, and breakfasted in his pyjamas in a rectangle of his room warmed by sunlight.

He put on a white linen suit for the first time since he left Yucatan and drove to the Botanical Gardens, the most extensive and beautiful in all the world. They contained more than six thousand varieties of exotic shrubs and flowering plants, which in their exuberance lost control of themselves and climbed half way up the precipitous mountain that screened the gardens on two sides. Two long avenues of polished royal palms intersected each other and divided the acres into four great sections like a pie. Norbourne spent the whole morning wandering in areas perfumed by nature, enlivened by babbling brooks, bridges, and beguiling paths through fern and bamboo. And along the paths Brazilians were already at the game of love-making.

At luncheon back at the Hotel Gloria he met a gold-wigged lady, who looked barely thirty under her nose veil, but who was said to be past sixty. While feeding some strange breed of small white dog, smartly barbered and scented, she recounted an odd tragedy of her life. On her honeymoon in Tunis her French bridegroom lost her at cards to a sheik. She created a terrific uproar by refusing to be collected. When the sheik came for her she fled in disguise and left her bridegroom disgraced by his inability to settle his debt of honour.

In a corner sat Gigli, who had finished his season in Argentina and was to sing *Manon* that evening in the Opera House with its great staircase copied from the Paris Opera. At the table next him a mulatto family from the provinces lunched with urbane aplomb. The huge diamonds on the mother's wrists and her protruding white teeth flashed in unison as she raised her fork. Her son, who without his family might have passed for complete white, forgot to eat, he was so busy ogling a blonde American girl who ogled him back a bit uncertainly.

After luncheon Norbourne presented a letter which had been given him by friends in Santiago to an American and his Brazilian wife, Mr. and Mrs. James Hastings. Hastings came from California and his work took him to most of the capitals of South America. His wife, who was a blue stocking and an ardent patriot, belonged to the old Empire aristocracy, but was intensely liberal in politics.

The day was auspicious, for the Hastings and Norbourne liked each other. Hastings called his wife, Magda. She was a beautiful woman, with skin white as milk, eyes and hair black as a Nuit de Noël bottle. While their home was being redecorated they were staying at the Gloria. They asked Norbourne to dine with them that evening. But they sat talking then and there until four o'clock. They talked mostly world politics, and Norbourne was amazed at the woman's scope of interest and the gentle assurance of her convictions. Here was the mythical *femme de monde* one read so much about, inoffensively sophisticated, completely feminine, without a trace of hardness, poised and vivacious, charmingly simple and simply charming. He asked her to give him the history of Rio in a nutshell and she did so without halting, vividly.

That the city of Rio de Janeiro should have been named River of January was due to a mistake of the explorer de Solís, who took the harbour to be a river's mouth when he dropped anchor there on a hot New Year's Day in 1516.

Notwithstanding the superb harbour facilities, Rio progressed haltingly and did not become the capital until 1763. The year 1727 might be said to be the birthday of Brazil's life, for it was in that year diamonds were discovered and the first coffee plants set out. For many years gold miners in Minas Geraes had used uncut diamonds as gaming counters. A missionary priest, who had learned what diamonds were in India, coming upon the scene, took off bagfuls of the gems which the inhabitants freely gave him as souvenirs. When he made his discovery known in Portugal, the Crown appropriated the mines. From 1730 to the discovery of diamond mines in South Africa, Brazil was the world's principal source of the gems. The little settlement of Rio de Janeiro lying conveniently on the route of the diamond mines assumed so much importance that the seat of government was removed there from Bahia.

Sudden glory was thrust upon Rio in 1808 by a left-handed gesture of Napoleon when he reached out to grasp Portugal. Leaving an empty shell of victory in Lisbon for the conquering Corsican, King John VI departed with his valuables, his regal trappings, and "four hundred of Portugal's noblest families." Some fifteen thousand persons in all, including lesser government officials and poorer relations of the nobility, crowded the eight battleships and forty merchant vessels, which were convoyed across the Atlantic under the protection of Great Britain. In this new colonial capital King John set up an old-world court overnight. Under the title of "King of Portugal, Brazil and Algarve," he built palaces, imported royal palm trees, laid out gardens, gave unrestricted freedom to agricultural and manufacturing industries of the country, invited the merchant ships of the world to come and trade. Prosperity abounded. As the opulent earth yielded quantities of diamonds, timber, gold, sugar, coffee, and chocolate, foundations of great fortunes were laid. Magnificence and munificence became commonplaces in the gala doings of society.

In 1821, the situation in Europe having cleared, the King returned to the mother country, leaving his popular twenty-year-old son as regent. When Portugal became irksomely oppressive to her prize colony the following year, the young prince uttered the cry of freedom at Ypiranga and threw off the Portuguese domination. For his revolutionary sentiments, the people proclaimed him Emperor Pedro I. At the very time neighbouring Spanish American colonies were setting up republics, Brazil chose to be an empire. Nine years later the monarch abdicated quietly in favour of his six-year-old son, who subsequently became Emperor Pedro II. He held his throne until November 15, 1889. This reign of over half a century—comparable in length with that of the Great Louis and the English queens, Elizabeth and Victoria—was one of the most benevolent, shrewd, and peaceful in history. The Empire fell at last because the abolition of Negro slavery in 1888 ruined the great planters. Brazil's behaviour in both her social and governmental upheavals was remarkable. The exile of the royal family and the freeing of the blacks were accomplished without the loss of a drop of blood.

"The Empire fell because it was too democratic," Mrs. Hastings said. "The Republic fell in 1932 because it was too imperialistic. While the politicians in power spread crime and error, the boys and girls of my generation who fought for liberal ideals had no time to be young. They had little leisure to love happily and laugh gaily. They were centuries old. But we won with Vargas in 1932, and the real patriots, those who love Brazil and not their own pocketbooks foremost, trust him and would defend his purposes to the end. Incidentally, the United States has no better friend in South America than Vargas."

Marry a Boxer!

Norbourne had been waiting in the reception room five minutes when Mrs. Hastings came down. She apologized, saying her husband was still with his trainer. She and her husband had a trainer every evening before dinner to put them through exercises, she explained. Most of their friends had trainers. Would Norbourne be interested in seeing the trainer's work? She telephoned to ask her husband if she might bring Norbourne up.

Up they went to the Hastings' suite. The husband, drenched with sweat, was just ready for his shower. The trainer was a dark brown Brazilian. He was hardly four feet six. His shoulders were so developed that he seemed as broad as he was tall. The first thing Norbourne knew, he had taken off his coat, waistcoat, and tie, and was bent back over a dressing table seat with his feet hooked under a chest of drawers and his hair grovelling in the rug. He got so interested in learning how to preserve youth and vigour by various contortions that they didn't go down to dinner until after nine.

"Why do you have the man at this odd time of day?" Norbourne asked Hastings when his wife went up to her room for something she had forgotten.

"He works as a bank clerk from two to six."

"A bank clerk!"

The husband laughed. "Magda got the job for him. She has a relation who is a bank manager. She felt sorry for the masseur because he didn't make enough money to get married. So she persuaded her relative to make him a banker. The relation could refuse her nothing. Brazilians are like that. They are tender-hearted and they love to be accommodating. We have some Brazilian friends who have just got their trainer a job as inspector of high schools. When he went out on his first inspection he entered a high school for the first time! It's a strange place, this Brazil."

Magda had brought down some sweet oranges for Norbourne's dessert. "Even to this day a part of Brazil has never ceased to be nostalgic for Empire," she said, beginning to peel an orange in some special Brazilian way. "My great-grandmother, now ninety-four years old, was a reigning beauty of those glamorous days. When she said good-bye to the Emperor and Empress she went home, put on mourning, and refused to go out for thirty-two years. She has emerged from the seclusion of her home only once since the Empire fell."

"Tell him about her," Hastings said.

"Please," Norbourne urged.

She told briefly the story of her great-grandmother.

In 1922 the old lady put on her bonnet and went to the harbour to receive the bodies of the dead Emperor and Empress brought back for burial. She hobbled behind the royal biers to the cathedral, along with other members of that fading circle who appear like wraiths at funerals in their own exclusive set and like wraiths scatter and vanish immediately afterwards, either to musty riches or to musty poverty. They do not appear again until they answer the bidding of the next embossed funeral invitation. To-day Magda's grandmother, whose tropical beauty and wit had been admired by three courts of Europe, reigns reminiscently in her shadowy drawing room. Her grandchildren and great-grandchildren come dutifully to kiss her hand once a week. When they speak of the dubious new outside world, she is only faintly interested. But her filmed eyes grow younger by half a century, and her regally coiffed head lifts with imperious interest when they report optimistically on the vague movement to bring back to the throne the dead Emperor's grandson, the Duc d'Orléans y Braganza.

When Magda told her great-grandmother that she was going to marry an American, the old lady was shocked beyond measure. "Marry a boxer!" she indignantly protested.

"She thought all Americans were prize-fighters," Magda explained. "She had never met an American in her life—that was to the best of her recollection—perhaps at some obscure European court sixty years before. But she knew all Americans were boxers nowadays. She had got the idea firmly fixed in her mind at the time of the Dempsey-Tunney fight when her great-grandsons chattered about the championship. She refused to meet the bridegroom or go to the wedding. At last curiosity got the better of her and she asked to see the American. She received James alone. When the family crept in after the prolonged interview to hear her opinion, my grandmother's eyes were atwinkle. Smiling like a shy girl she confessed, 'My dear, if I could do it all over again, I believe I might marry an American myself.' "

All for Love

After dinner the Hastings and Norbourne drove about in their roadster admiring this and that while they talked random talk. The people in Rio never tire of riding the street cars on moonlit nights just to see for the thousandth odd time the beauty of their city. The open trams were crowded, but no one was standing up, for that is against the law and Rio is law-abiding. Couples locked in embrace sat on benches beneath the palms and the moon shadows.

"But despite enthusiasm for English soccer and American baseball," said James, "love-making remains the national sport, and is ubiquitous—as you see. Courtships among the proletariat are carried on *al fresco* on the esplanades."

"Courtships in upper circles are often conducted in the grand manner," said Magda. "Brazilians like to play-act while they love. A few years ago a wealthy young friend of ours asked his lady love what he should do to make her accept his hand. 'Within a year and a day,' she replied, 'present me with an Arab kingdom.' The jester proved prophet. Within a year and a day the suitor brought the lady with her chaperon to an unfamiliar Moorish gate in a familiar street. Turbaned servants, salaaming like Arabian Nights' eunuchs, ushered her into a scene of Araby. His extensive property had been transformed into an Eastern palace garden. Brazilian trees had been uprooted for trees imported from Arabia. Red and azure pavilions glittered with lacquer, arabesques, and opals. Jewelled lamps swung from silver chains, thrust daggers of light into Persian rugs, oriental silks, and billowy damask cushions. The air was scented with sandalwood, attar of roses, Arabian fruits and sweetmeats. The lady gazed enchanted, like Madeleine on St. Agnes's Eve."

"And I'll bet she didn't marry him in the end!" Norbourne said.

Magda looked at him in surprise. "No, she didn't. Why did you think that?"

"Because," said her husband, "when a man has nothing more to do in life than such tomfoolery, a woman really hasn't much respect for him."

"Oh, you Americans!" she said wearily. After a pause, she added, "You laugh at us Latins because we dream our lives."

Wild Monkey for Tea

The fantastic Arab garden was no more amazing than an everyday Brazilian one to which Norbourne was taken next day for tea. Behind the century-old house set on a miniature plaza that suggested a corner of Blois, the garden was laid out in five terraces. The topmost one ended abruptly in a sheer mountain side, which dropped ropes of twisting lianas down on to the turf like elongated snakes stooping to drink at a grass-green pool. Victoria Regina water-lilies hid the nakedness of a real pool by spreading their petals to a circumference of twenty feet. Yellow orchids glistened on trellises. Magenta bougainvillea clambered riotously over gates and summer houses. While the guests were having tea and whiskies and soda about a long table, a black monkey shot down the precipice along a tortuous vine on to a swaying bamboo branch. He hopped to a pawpaw tree above the table where the company sat staring with curious delight. With impertinent aplomb the little beast plucked the choicest fruit, broke it open, dug his fist deep into the apricot-coloured meat, smacked his lips with relish, and spit one of the slimy seeds at a young Argentinian. Then he vaulted through the air to drink at a holy water basin of marble set into the wall. When he had drunk his fill he shot, like Jack of the Beanstalk, up his rope-vine stairway to his home in the mountain.

The host took Norbourne and the Argentinian over to examine the holy water basin. He had rescued it from a ruined church and set it up as a wall fountain, trusting that lady guests would not remark that a pranking sculptor had metamorphosed some of the decorative eucalyptus leaves into unmistakable phalli.

In the house the host showed his foreign guests inherited antiques, cabinets and inlaid chests brought back by Portuguese grandees from the Orient three centuries ago, tables of Brazilian ebony turned by the Emperor's cabinet-maker. It was the finest furniture Norbourne had seen on the Continent. In glass cases set into the wall were family jewels. Besides necklaces and bracelets, one drawer held a collection of thimbles used by the daughters of the house for six generations; gold thimbles rimmed with diamonds and some of carved coco-nut with chased silver bands. There were collections of daggers and golden spurs; others of sunshades and fans with sticks of amber and pearl and gauze sprinkled with diamond dust.

The house was a museum, but there was nothing musty about the atmosphere. It was modern in comfort, and the host himself, a tall handsome fellow ready to talk on a hundred subjects, belonged to the present and not to the past. His name was Rudolfo, but his friends called him Rudy, for despite his wavy black hair, he looked as English as Anthony Eden.

"Destiny gave him everything," said a Brazilian lady, speaking of him affectionately. "The stars were all in good aspect at his birth. He has brains, good looks, a noble family background, fortune, a sense of humour, and best of all, a good heart."

"You have Latin blood in you?" the host said to Norbourne with assurance as the party broke up.

"No, I'm afraid not. As far back beyond America as I can trace, it's all pure English on both sides. But I've always suspected some Latin illegitimacy crept in somewhere, for I feel entirely at home with Latins. And you?"

"Mongrel," he said heartily. "Complete mongrel. Portuguese, Spanish, French, Scotch, and Welsh—and a sixteenth part of Indian."

Norbourne turned to the Brazilian lady. "Instead of the stars, maybe it's merely the triumph of amalgamation."

Tropical Boulevard

Norbourne sat at a little café table one afternoon with a young Rumanian drinking coffee. The Rumanian had become a naturalized Brazilian and was very knowledgeable in the ways of his adopted country. Though whisky and soda is the favourite drink of foreigners and is always offered to guests, coffee, which has furnished the means for Brazilian prosperity and culture, is overwhelmingly the national beverage. Punctually and patriotically at ten and three-thirty, shopkeepers, clerks, labourers, and professional men stop work for a little cup of coffee. American business concerns, who have had to make friends with the native custom, have found it more economical to serve coffee free to their employees within doors rather than have them lose the time in going out. Ten little cups of coffee cost about ten cents. The Brazilians take it as it is served in the *souks* of Tunis, very strong and very sweet.

The crowded pavement cafés of the long triple-tree-lined Rio Branco made the luxurious avenue look like the Paris Boulevards, removed to flowering tropics. On their way home from work, the wage-earners were elbowing cordially with the half of Rio that does not toil: chaperoned ladies emerging from smart shops, idle sons of plantation owners, college students, tourists in white linen. Paris dictates the styles of women's dress, just as Paris is the world centre of art and thought to the Brazilians. Educated Rio speaks, reads, and thinks in French as easily as in Portuguese. But in the young men the influence of the United States was seen. The students had discarded their stiff collars, stiff hats, and black suits for less formal American attire. Some of the youths were bareheaded, with ungartered socks flopping about their ankles like American college boys. They admired passing feminine figures, exchanged Latin nudges and bawdry. Some got up and strayed off after a pair of gorgeous eyes or a particularly provocative curve of hip. The older men were talking politics, coffee over-production, horse racing, philosophy. North American promoters learn the art of conducting business leisurely over a coffee cup. A diamond mine or a thousand hectares of cotton land may change hands over a third cup of coffee at an *al fresco* café, whereas high-pressure procedure in stuffy offices would blow up in impotence.

At least half the world here was coloured in various senses of the word. Many with straight high-bred noses and thin lips seemed to have taken on tobacco-, coffee-, chocolate-coloured complexions from the raw products they trafficked in. Some had turned terra cotta from prolonged love affairs with the sun. Others had unmistakably inherited an ingrained pigmentation from a slave ancestor. Copper of Indian, yellow of Mongolian, brown of Hindu, every shade from the whiteness of Scandinavia to the blueberry black of the Congo, smeared the palette of the café. In a single family group, skin tones ranged from *tête de négre* to ivory.

"But the thick-lipped child," said the Rumanian, "is loved as much as the fair-haired. There is no more colour prejudice among the people than in these inlaid pavements beneath our feet." Cream-coloured pebbles were set against chocolate, white against black. "Brazil has no colour problem in the accepted sense, whether in street, shop, school or amusement place. Only in exclusive drawing rooms of the small group known as 'society' is the thing called 'a line' drawn. And even there, when fame or diplomatic expediency offer credentials, the line can be withdrawn."

On the coloured pavements under the gay striped awnings of Rio's most sophisticated street Norbourne saw with his own eyes "the most daring and voluntary acceptance of racial amalgamation in human history."

"But," the Rumanian said, "the Brazilians welcome the boatloads of immigrants. The European comes and takes a mulatto for a wife and helps to make the race more white. See how gay-humoured the people are. It's the influence of Africa."

Everybody was smiling. Where Lima reflects the sombreness of her Andean Indians, who ever thought life a serious affair, Rio responds to the good nature of her Negroes, who jest with life and aim at dodging labour. Brows are not furrowed with worry or hurry, nor mouths twisted with greed. Eyes that are hollow are not hollow from overwork, but hollow from indulgence in sensuality. Any Yankee avidity for work for work's sake sooner or later succumbs to the carefree atmosphere of laughter, song, and love-making.

"In Rio the heart is more valued than the brain," said the young Rumanian, spooning more and more sugar into his coffee cup.

"Sugar is necessary for strength in hot climates," he explained. "Here we put sugar on everything but sugar cane, and lots of it. There is nothing niggardly about Brazilians," he went on. "The people are spendthrifts, individually and nationally. That is why a European with frugal instincts rises so rapidly in business here. The upper-class Brazilian has inherited his Portuguese ancestors' distaste for work and his delight in government sinecures. Almost anyone you meet of the socially *élite* is on the government payroll. The Brazilian of the proletariat class is quick enough in intelligence, but he has little sturdiness of character. He is easy to live with and loves to be obliging. He doesn't like to work or to fight. When he protests, he uses soft language. No one kills for money here. They kill for love or for using bad words. Rio has an efficient police and detective department, but criminals get off lightly. The Brazilian is far too sentimental to tolerate capital punishment. A man charged with murder needs only to explain that he momentarily 'lost his control' and he will be exonerated on the grounds of what they call 'perturbation of the senses.' I went to a trial last year. The murderer had had his feelings hurt by his boss, who called him ugly names. He told the court with tears in his eyes how he had suffered over the insults and waited all day with a knife to kill his employer. The court wept too, and let him go free."

The Rumanian paused to drop a calcium wafer into his coffee cup. "If you want to keep your teeth you must add calcium to your diet. The vegetables lack calcium and the milk is poor. That's why you see so many snaggle-teeth among the rabble. They can't afford to buy cream."

A bus halted at the kerb behind a Rolls-Royce. It bore a placard advertising treatment for venereal disease.

"Seventy-five per cent of advertisements in street cars, newspapers, radio broadcasting, concerns medical products," he said, indicating the placard. "The French and German medical factories do more business here than in Europe. I shall never forget my shock soon after I arrived. I had been paying attention to a pretty middle-class girl. One afternoon she telephoned me to say she couldn't meet me to-morrow because she had to go to the doctor to get her injection."

"Syphilis?"

"Syphilis. Oh, yes, they have it here—plenty of it. But they treat it! They are wise not to try to hide it as they do in the United States and Europe. They begin giving injections to babies. Only yesterday afternoon a girl who spends the week-ends with me had to leave for a couple of hours to go and give her sister an injection. The sister prefers her to do it instead of a doctor."

"But your friend!"

"She hasn't it."

"But aren't you afraid, even so?"

"If I were afraid," he said, stiffening slightly, "I might begin by being afraid of this—and this—and this." He touched the coffee cup, the sugar bowl, the marble table top. "They are honest about it here. They tell you the truth, just as one does about a bad cold. By being so frank and getting treated, within another generation or two they will have it stamped out. And nature herself cures it in the malarial districts. A high malarial fever deliberately produced will kill the syphilis germ."

They left the café and strolled down a side street completely canopied with green tree branches. Like Calle Florida in Buenos Aires, where no vehicles are allowed between four and eight, no vehicles are ever permitted in the Rua Ouvidor. The shops sparkled with smartness, but among them morgues of blue butterflies and jewel-like humming birds followed one another in depressing numbers. As recently as a decade ago, fantastically lovely butterflies, "the blue silk variety," had fluttered from jungle to city gardens and into the kaleidoscope of the business district. Now neither butterflies nor humming-birds beautify the Federal District. They are all but extinct even in the mountains. They have been butchered to make a tourist's holiday more touristy. In the show windows the butterflies, luminous in death, lay ironed out under the glass of cocktail trays or spread over concave trinket boxes like Aztec captives on the sacrificial stone. The humming-birds' heads had been mounted on silver to make feathered brooches—"something original and characteristic for tourists to take back." Norbourne's gorge rose with indignation.

"It's an outrage," he said, scowling at an amazed shop proprietor, who had amiably invited him in to see other atrocities.

"The dead butterflies come now from the interior where millions are slaughtered annually," the Rumanian said, as they strolled on. "Little bundles of a hundred ordinary ones bring no more than a penny—the price of a demi-tasse. A hundred rare specimens will bring several cups of coffee. The poor set their children to catching butterflies for profit as soon as they can toddle."

"A novel kind of child labour—butterfly-catching," said

Norbourne, thinking how strange it was that the people of Rio, who value so highly their unsurpassed beauty, should allow one of the exquisite features of their scenery to be destroyed for shopkeepers' profit.

Delights and the Prince

Morning after morning Norbourne woke up feeling that Rio was too fantastic to be true. Besides being unrivalled in scenic beauty, the city combines the advantages of a modern metropolis with the facilities of a spa, and limitless opportunity for adventure in near primeval jungles. For the sportsman the racing season lasts through autumn and winter into spring. The racecourse, bearing a purple lagoon in the centre of its green and winged with bizarre spurs of rough-hewn mountains like settings for Greek tragedy, is equalled only by Santiago de Chile's course crowned by the icy Andes. The polo grounds are a greensward lying like a lake at the foot of a mountain where a virgin forest cascades and bursts into spray from thousands of great white blossoms that flower on some indigenous species of tree. At the Jockey Club and the Golf Club, where five or more languages may be heard spoken simultaneously in locker rooms, at the bar, or about terrace tea tables, big business and diplomatic bargains are negotiated with ease and friendliness.

On a tip from the doorman at the Jockey Club, Norbourne had won money on a horse named Picaflor. He had taken the aerial car at night and floated along a cable to the top of Sugar Loaf, where he sat for two hours looking down on the sparkling city. But above everything except the society of the Brazilians, he had enjoyed the beaches and the glorious sunshine. Whenever he had a spare couple of hours, he took a taxi to the Copacabana beach, alone or with friends, and baked himself in the sun and cooled himself in the green surf. On the Copacabana sands, where the local aristocrats play with the holiday-making *haute monde* of Argentina, the sight of golden bodies of women and bronze bodies of men splashing in surf, tossing feathered handballs, offering themselves in voluptuous Latin languor to the sun, was an eye-feast for epicures.

"What is responsible for this change in figure?" Norbourne said to the Hastings during a beach party. "Any book written about Brazil up to 1930 says the women grow fat at twenty-five. Look, they—you—are all superb!"

Mrs. Hastings smiled thoughtfully. "Some say *Harper's Bazaar* and *Vogue* have been responsible for the change. Others say the introduction of sports for women. But it's really the Prince of Wales who deserves the credit."

"The Prince of Wales!"

"Six or seven years ago sea-bathing and beach life here were virtually non-existent. Fashion had never considered it. We bathed at Deauville and Nice, but never here. The established hours for bathing were six to eight in the morning. Bath costumes were still hideous, like those of the nineties. Even a man whose suit was cut out too much in the back was liable to arrest. And as for a woman——" Her eyebrows elevated slightly. "But one morning in 1931 on the Copacabana beach, the Prince of Wales, wanting more sun, unloosed his shoulder straps and dropped his tops. Rio gasped. The law was thunderstruck. But the daring young men of our military school politely imitated the royal gesture, and defied arrest. Fashion capitulated. Then, if we were to show our figures, something had to be done about them. Men rushed to gymnasiums. Swedish masseurs and masseuses were cabled for. Ladies who had never sat on a horse took to riding before breakfast. Diet became our watchword. Public tennis courts were crowded. Private courts were laid out in every garden. Husbands and wives engaged trainers to come for an hour a day to put them through exercises. You saw ours. Away went superfluous flesh in chin, abdomen and hips. Bathing kits became smart and scanty. Rio took up the cult of the body beautiful with devout heart. Within four years a miraculous result was achieved. And that is the story of our regeneration."

Mountain Resort

Hastings took a day off to drive Norbourne to Petropolis, the mountain resort where the Emperor had held his summer court. The drive took them winding about the mountains among peaks and precipices of sheer beauty, where nature was at its most dynamic and bountiful. Vegetation crowded every square foot of flat surface in joyous abundance. A hundred different kinds of trees and shrubs overrun with exotic vines and unfamiliar flowers of mauve, orange, and scarlet packed the space of a single acre tight as squares of needlepoint in vari-coloured wools. From out grotesque crannies, crystal cascades gushed in jagged courses, spraying gigantic ferns and deepening the blossoms' rich pigment.

Petropolis is still neat and full of charm, like a Swiss village set down in the midst of a hundred palace gardens. Don Pedro created the town in 1845 as a model of order and cleanliness, and imported three thousand Swiss and German middle-class immigrants to inspire the lax and care-free Brazilians. Until yellow fever was conquered, all the citizens of Rio who could afford to build summer villas, came to Petropolis for the hot months, and so did the diplomats and wealthier foreign residents.

The many-bridged canal splits the long shaded shopping street down the middle. Before the humbler cottages, as well as the villas, stand the fragrant frangipannis with their salmon blossoms, and the "shower of gold" trees with gilded clusters drooping like wisteria. In the Emperor's garden between the azaleas and red japonicas, the freesias and tuberoses were in bloom. But instead of an imperial court wandering on the paths along the bamboo hedges, schoolboys take recess, for the summer palace has been turned into a state school. The one-time glamour of Petropolis is only an echo.

They passed the villa where Edwin Morgan, the United States Ambassador, had had his summer home during the twenty-two years he held his post. "When he died in the States a few years ago," Hastings said, "he requested that his body be brought back here for burial. He was perhaps the best loved man in Brazil. Between the two nations the friendly diplomatic intercourse has been unbroken for a hundred years. Brazil has always been more friendly to the United States than any other Latin American country. But Morgan strengthened the ties—and gave Brazilians a high esteem for the United States. Morgan—and the coffee-drinking custom," he added practically. "We are Brazil's best customers. If the Americans suddenly lost their taste for coffee, I fear the diplomatic relations might become strained. You can imagine the panic down here."

"What effect is this phenomenal new development in raw cotton going to have on our South?" Norbourne asked.

"I wonder. In 1933, only 147,000 tons of raw cotton were produced here. In 1934, 279,000 tons. In export value cotton has become one-fifth that of coffee and more than three times as much as cacao, which before ranked second. Jungles are being cleared for new cotton lands. Worn-out coffee trees are being rooted out and sugar cane fields are being ploughed under for cotton planting. Restricted crop in the United States is profit for Brazil. Business men and landowners from the Amazon banks to the timber lands of Paraná in the south are talking cotton, speculating with cotton, planting cotton.

"But the American business men know there is every prospect of a Brazilian economic development within the next half century equal to the expansion of the United States from '49 to to-day. And they are flocking down."

Norbourne had noticed that the hotels were full of United States business men inquiring into Brazil's vast and varied resources in mine, forest, and field. Staying at his hotel was a well-known American—he had recently sold his seat on the Stock Exchange—who was negotiating for an interest in a diamond mine. With him was his son, just graduated from Groton and ready to enter Yale in September. The youth had already begun lessons in Portuguese, to be prepared to take over his father's Brazilian interests when he finished college. Brazil's diamond fields are capable of supplying the world. Because of organized preferences given to the South African diamond trusts by the diamond-cutting industry of Europe, the Brazilian mines are scarcely scratched. But Norbourne had heard that it was most likely that soon the South African syndicate would be displaced from its monopoly of the American market, and a great American diamond-cutting industry would be established, to the mutual profit of Brazil and the United States.

The car turned up a mountain road and entered the gateway of an inn, where they lunched on a long veranda, overhanging a precipice and overlooking fifty miles of astounding beauty. All serious conversations round about Rio seemed to end in gazing on loveliness.

What an Ambassador Should Do

No fashionable dinner in Brazil begins before nine-thirty. An invitation might even read "Dinner at ten," but never "Dinner at eight." Only in provincial towns could the latter occur. The Hastings invited Norbourne to a dinner they were giving on Wednesday evening at the Copacabana Grill. Brazilians are the most considerate people imaginable. Norbourne had brought only his dinner jacket. Mrs. Hastings wrote notes to all the men requesting them to wear black ties.

On Wednesday evening Norbourne went with the Hastings to their party. Magda was demurely radiant in flame taffeta. She wore ivory-coloured dancing sandals without hose, her toenails tinted like rubies. On the way to the Copacabana they stopped to call on the old Baroness de Bomfim. Hers was the only titled family that continued entertaining after the proclamation of the Republic in 1889. Her daughter, Donna Jeronima de Mesquita, a witty and great-hearted woman who devoted herself quietly to good works, had sold one of the largest diamonds in Brazil to endow a hospital for the poor.

On the grand piano in a silver frame stood a photograph of the late American Ambassador. Beside him was one of the Emperor Pedro II. Both were reflected again and again in the long gilt mirrors that hung on the walls.

"You will see his photograph in many other Brazilian homes," said the Baroness. "He was a wonderful man—Edwin Morgan. He held our affectionate confidence as no other alien emissary ever has. For twenty-two years he was one of us. He did what all ambassadors should do. He made us love the country he served. When he died, Brazil buried him with the ceremony and honours she pays her national heroes. I understand your new Ambassador, Mr. Gibson, is a splendid man too, but I have not met him. It is good of you to send us your best."

How graciously and simply the old aristocrat expressed it, thought Norbourne.

"And when Morgan's will was read," said her daughter, "we found he had remembered us all. He left each one of his friends something—something of his he knew we had admired. He left me his reading lamp and a jade statuette."

"The samovar there on the little table was his," said the Baroness.

"He left me all his books of English poetry," said Magda.

"It is after nine—we must be going," said Hastings, whose ten years in South America had not beguiled him of his admiration of promptness.

Ladies-in-Waiting

At dinner Norbourne was to meet seventeen scions of old Portuguese nobility. Six of the men and five of the women were heirs to titles dating back two, three, and four centuries. The other seven were the President's brother-in-law and daughter, an Argentinian and his Uruguayan wife on holiday, the Danish wife of a cabinet minister, the host and Norbourne.

"I am putting you next to a woman noted even in Paris for

her elegance," Magda said, as she started into the dining room to arrange the place cards. "She is a dear friend and a political enemy of mine. Her husband is a leading coffee king of São Paulo. He inherited a truly marvellous *fazenda*. So in politics they are naturally ultra-conservative and out of sympathy with the present government." She smiled mischievously. "I am putting her husband next to the President's daughter. Opposite you will be the woman the Maharajah of Tabore pronounced the most fascinating woman in South America."

Wondering how his taste would agree with that of a Maharajah, Norbourne went off with James into the gambling rooms. The long double rooms extending the length of a city block were the quintessence of restrained elegance. They were chastely decorated in powder blue velvet and cut crystal.

The space about the roulette tables was darkened thickly with black dinner jackets and tails and black evening dresses. Here, as in Buenos Aires, quite three-fourths of the women prefer black to any colour. The concentrated odour of tea-olive and sweet shrub from the perfume of the young men's hair oil was so strong that the more delicate odours of Coty and Caron might have been wasting their sweetness on desert air. Young demi-mondaines in afternoon costume, with small hats tilted sharply to leave only one eye visible, sat about the tables and played from time to time with studied composure. They took no interest in whether they themselves won or lost, but kept their glances on the hands of whatever male was raking in the most chips. They paid the lucky one the compliment of playing his numbers exclusively and when possible they imperceptibly eased in next to him. The men who were winning tried to ignore their unspoken overtures, but sooner or later they laid a small stack of chips before the girls. By the subtleties of this gesture a *cocotte* gauges nicely whether the gentleman desires her to leave or to hang about to help him celebrate when he goes home at dawn.

By five minutes past ten all but one of the dinner guests had arrived. Cocktails were served in an ante-room. Norbourne found himself before the woman the Maharajah had admired. Tall, slender, her complexion darker than that of any lady present, she was dressed in amber velvet. She smiled. She was *simpática*. A radiance hung about her. Her voice was low, gentle, and stirring.

"Tell me, secretly," Norbourne said, after a moment, "how do you Brazilians manage—waiting so late for your dinner? Don't you slip off to the pantry and nibble a bit before coming?"

"Well," she laughed, "this evening I did have a large glass of milk about eight o'clock."

"I want to know something else. How does a Brazilian lady of fashion spend her day?"

She hesitated, as if he were making game of her. "They live much in the sun: riding, tennis, the beach."

"But it's rained all day. How, for instance, have you spent this particular day?"

"Well, because it rained," she confessed almost deprecatingly, "I spent the entire day in bed. I read French newspapers in the morning, Morgan's *The Fountain* in the afternoon—I found it very beautiful—do you like it?—and later I read Portuguese bed-time stories to my little boy. Then I had a session with a masseuse—and at eight o'clock I drank that large glass of milk—and I did eat a muffin. Then I began to dress." She laughed a self accusing little laugh as if to say, "There is a portrait of a useless, idle woman—what do you think now?"

They turned to the others as the latest guest arrived at ten-twenty by the clock. Hastings looked at it with a scowl. The girl, a last year's débutante, of the family of the Count of Estrella, was dressed in shimmering white. She made no explanation whatever to her hostess, merely a wan greeting and a dreamy acknowledgment to introductions. Extremely thin, her complexion the pallor of alabaster, her hair palest gold, the irises of her enormous eyes the blue of Chinese forget-me-nots, she too was pure Brazilian—the embodiment of one of Edgar Allan Poe's ethereal heroines. She and the full-blooded Danish lady were the only blondes among the dozen women.

At the long table in the centre of the grill-room the twenty-four place cards rested against a bank of mauve orchids a foot thick and running the entire length of the board. The lady from São Paulo at Norbourne's left, who was "noted for her elegance even in Paris," looked like a Russian and wore diamonds fit for a queen with as fresh a grace as a Devon country lass wears spring flowers. Her brown hair was piled serenely in braided coils; her complexion was smooth rich cream. She and her husband spent half of each year abroad. Oh, yes, she did find Paris a trifle more —"sustaining"—than South America, she admitted to Norbourne, as they got up to dance.

Though the twelve women differed in type from the inky-eyed, olive-complexioned to the alabaster blonde, all but one—the granddaughter of a Duke—were pretty. Their beauty was enhanced by a striking make-up of darkened eyes and no rouge except on the lips. Six followed the South American preference of dressing in black, four were in white, only two in colours—the hostess in flame, the Maharajah's choice in amber.

For all the smartness of Brazilian women there is no trace of hardness in them. They have a charm of manner to remind the world that a modern woman can be a woman and a lady at the same time. Doubtless it is some traditional overtone that distinguishes Brazilian ladies of quality from their Spanish American cousins. For despite their chic, which follows the latest gleam from Paris, a faint odour of the imperial court still hovers about them. In their gentle movement and gracious cadences there is a flavour of ladies-in-waiting to an empress.

Back at the Gloria, at the lift door, Norbourne said good-night and good-bye to these strangers who had been so extraordinarily kind. In his seven days in Rio, he had come to look upon this American and his Brazilian wife as long-time friends. In his room, his brain still danced with the champagne and the music. He went to the balcony for a breath of fresh trade-wind and a last look at the enchanted bay. But the night was black as witches' broth—the unrisen moon was in the last day of its last quarter. The cathedral clock struck two. As if it had been a signal that the dream was over, Norbourne kicked off his pumps, threw open his suit-case, and began to pack. At dawn he would begin his flight back to the secure realities of routine on the other side of the equator.

Au Revoir

Within ten minutes of the centre of the city, the incurably hospitable Rio had presented the airways companies with a terminal. Fashioned on reclaimed ground, it was surrounded by beauty in every direction. As he drove up to the temporary waiting room, Norbourne thought of the contrast with Buenos Aires' airport in a cow pasture fifteen miles beyond the city's most unattractive suburbs.

About the illuminated small building, Brazilian blue swallows, disturbed by the transport activities, made scrawls against the night's slate, like blue Neon lights loosed from their tubes. As the seaplane rose from the dark water like a lover saying farewell just before the dawn, Norbourne looked down upon Rio's voluptuous curves outlined by incandescent night lamps. The black mountains flowed gently like molten onyx down into the slumbering town and the hushed bay. Just as one often feels in a down-plunging lift that a physical part has been left behind on the upper floors, Norbourne felt that he had left a vital part of himself in Rio.

The night metamorphosing into day changed the landscape from black to royal purple. And as the thunderbird's wings bore it higher above the bay's bizarre islands, the colour turned to that of the orchids banked upon last night's dinner table.

At the edge of the east, the nearly dead moon pricked the faintest green crescent, thin like a pine shaving, in the mauve paper screen of the sky. Then as the plane flew farther towards the east before turning north, Norbourne saw that the old moon clutched in its frail arms the rotund shadow of the globe—just as Rio held between its encircling mountains samples of everything beautiful this world could offer except stalactites and snow and volcanic flame.

Curling up on the lounge, Norbourne went promptly to sleep. He had no desire to watch for the anticlimax of another sunrise.

Strayed Rebels

Norbourne did not wake up until the thunderbird dropped down into another enchanting bay by the picturesque island town of Victoria. The passengers got out to take coffee while the plane took in petrol and mail. People were riding bicycles up and down the slanting streets between rows of palm trees. Here began the older Brazil of the north half of the coast, which knew greatness when Rio de Janeiro was only a name and Santos an outpost of civilization. Victoria was founded in 1530, before Elizabeth of England was born, and nine decades before the Pilgrims arrived in Plymouth.

Back in the air, Norbourne, now wide awake, began thinking again how flying was the most rewarding way of travelling. From a god-like position above the earth, one could behold the treacheries of shoals and promontories, the capricious favour of rivers. He had seen what deserts made of men, and what men made of forests. He saw the end of Brazil's coffee lands and the beginning of square miles of cacao and the vast areas of corn and cane and cotton. He could see the influence of natural harbours, the determination and directions of climate. Scrolls of geography and history unfolded beneath him. Revelations of past, present and future were all brought within the gamut of vision like some gift of second sight.

Two hundred miles beyond Victoria the plane stopped again at Caravellas, and there at the airport Norbourne had coffee with the living ghost of a lost dream. He was a dried-up, cocoa-coloured white man, with tobacco-stained teeth, a high-bred nose and bleary yellow eyes with the spirit gone out of them. His name was Rodney Pickens. Born in Brazil forty-five years ago, he was the offspring of Southerners who refused to be reconstructed after the Civil War. His people had come from Mississippi and South Carolina. There had been a great exodus of families from the ports of New Orleans, Mobile, Charleston, and Savannah in the late '60s and early '70s. Planters, stripped of their slaves, their homes burned, their plate and horses stolen, emigrated to Brazil, which offered them land to encourage cotton cultivation. Books were written and circulated among the disrupted rebels glorifying "Lizzieland," as Brazil was called. Thousands, beguiled by a promising future, sailed south, planted cotton, held slaves for twenty more years. Some prospered, built plantation homes like those of the antebellum South, and entertained in the gracious tradition. In 1889 they again lost their slaves, this time not by bloodshed, but by proclamation, which they accepted without bitterness. With the new stimulation in coffee production, they ploughed their cotton under and planted coffee trees, just as to-day they are planting cotton where coffee trees grew. But they did not understand coffee as they did cotton. The Negroes refused to work; moved to the coast. The new fortunes dwindled. In time, most of the planters came to admit that their kind would have done better in the second generation if they had remained at home to face the rascality of carpet-baggers and the insolence of Negroes in office.

Rodney Pickens said he never expected to visit Mississippi or South Carolina, where he had many cousins. He had forgotten all the English his mother had taught him. He spoke nothing but Portuguese. Since his father died in 1922, they had had no communication whatever with the relatives in the States. His mother was well into the eighties and could not see to write. Norbourne regretted that he had not time to pay his respects to the old lady. The pilot, Captain Lanier Turner from Virginia, said she was a rare conversationalist. He had called on her twice. Even she was forgetting her English, she had such few opportunities to speak it. Marooned in this small Brazilian town of four thousand Portuguese, mulattoes, and blacks, haughty Mrs. Pickens sits nursing her hatred for the Yankees and telling tales of girlhood grandeur.

The Victoria morning paper which Pickens gave Norbourne was full of the new immigration of Texan cotton planters into Brazil. He wondered which way the fortunes of their second generation would go.

A hundred more miles and again the passengers were offered small cups of coffee at a town called Ilhéos, a name unfamiliar to the world at large, but the foremost cacao shipping port in the hemisphere. From Rio northward, as from Rio southward to Porto Alegre, the coast of Brazil was one long-drawn-out panorama of variegated beauty.

Half way to Bahia, where they would stop for the night, the steward called the passengers' attention to a sloop wrecked on a sandbar. The aeroplane passed it, turned, dropped low and circled about, got its exact position, read its name, and gave its crew the cheering signal that the radio man would call for help. The operator tapped out information to the nearest ports and to nearby ships. It was all in the day's business, yet to Norbourne there was something exciting about the event.

Wax Works

The capital of Brazil until 1763, Bahia, or "The Holy Saviour, on the Bay of All Saints," is still the fourth largest city of the nation. Once it was the centre of Brazil's African slave traffic. To-day it is the blackest city in South America. Eighty per cent of its 350,000 inhabitants are Negroes. Like Natchez, Mississippi, with its Under-the-Hill and On-the-Hill towns, Bahia is built in two stories, one two hundred feet above the other. A concrete carriage road winds around the cliffs, and four spacious lifts bear the public up and down from one level to the other. The port does a thriving business in tobacco, cacao, and hides. On the plateau are the government buildings, the shopping streets, the better residential districts, the seventeenth century corners, and most of the town's seventy churches. In the lower town are the docks, the Customs House, warehouses, the fishing smacks, the shacks of poorer blacks, the picturesque open market. At sunset the harbour was bristling with the spear-like masts of a thousand little boats, like a primitive army poised before a rush.

The thronged streets of both levels were more vivid with black faces than a town in Alabama's Black Belt on Saturday afternoons. Within a couple of streets of the leading hotel the cellar-like stalls of the alien prostitutes are set two feet below the pavement. Here and there, breaking the stalls of sin, are the butchers' shops and the shops of the Holy-Image makers, where men mould saints in coloured plaster and fashion symbols of bodily health. In black Bahia, where Voodoo mingles with ardent Catholicism, the faithful materialise their prayers against disease. A man with a broken hand buys a plaster replica of a hand and offers it sacrificially when praying to saints for alleviation. A woman with a cancered breast presents a breast in plaster. In the shop windows lay feet, fingers, noses, and hearts for sale.

Norbourne had dinner with Captain Turner and an American business man who had lived in Rio for twenty years. The American found life in the United States "dull, flat, and unprofitable" in comparison. He "would not swap a year in Rio for ten anywhere else." After dinner he and Norbourne went to take the air at a terrace café set on the edge of the cliff overlooking the town under-the-hill.

They were stopped by an altercation at a street crossing. Two black taxi drivers, swearing viciously, got out and shook their fists within an inch of each other's noses. As a crowd gathered and the rest of the traffic moved discreetly aside, they got back into their cars, put them in reverse and then charged at each other whooping like trumpeting elephants. Screaming at the impact, they reversed the cars and bumped furiously into each other again. They were preparing for a third attack when the police arrived to soothe them with soft words.

"It would have been the same," the man said, "if they had had passengers in 'em. In Bahia the chauffeurs won't fight hand to hand, but sometimes they tear their cars to pieces bumping into each other in rage. They are pardoned on the plea of 'perturbation of the spirit.' "

After the climax of Rio Norbourne did not expect to be thrilled greatly any more, but he was glad that the route still followed the roundabout coast. Perhaps he would never have another opportunity to see Pernambuco, and Natal, and São Luiz do Maranhão.

Aracajú, capital of the State of Sergipe, was the last port that sent out large quantities of coffee and cacao. From now on the exports were principally sugar and cotton, nuts and rubber. At Maceió, exclusively a cotton and sugar port, the watery space about the air station was filled as far as the eye could see with three-cornered isosceles triangle sails of dugout canoes painted maroon, terra cotta, and russet.

Pernambuco, or Recife, as the capital of Pernambuco is really named but never called, is the first western port of call of ships from Europe. It is so far east that it is only thirty-five longitudinal degrees west of London. Europeans bound for South America get their first impression of "this brave new world" from the city built in three sections on an island, peninsula, and mainland, and connected by iron bridges. Because of waterways running through the city, Pernambuco is called Brazil's Venice, but it bears little semblance to the Adriatic's gem. The population, approaching half a million, is three-quarters mulatto, as Bahia is four-fifths black. The chief sugar port of South America, the town smells crudely sweet. The most characteristic sight of the place is the file of brown sugar porters bearing brown bags of raw sugar. The heat of the sun draws juice through the mesh of the jute, the bags drip molasses and the naked torsos are streaked with rivulets of sticky sweetness as the bearers wind among cotton bales and crates of orchids labelled for European markets.

After luncheon in the air, they paused at flat, dry Natal, the town famous as the western terminus of the French and German mail planes that wing the ocean within twenty hours. It was from here that the Lindberghs hopped off to Africa.

In the late afternoon they landed in Indian-blooded Fortaleza for the night. The next morning the plane flew on to Pará, the last overnight stop on the continent.

Rubber Path to Glory

Norbourne's windows at the Grande Hotel in Pará looked across a broad avenue with a triple row of ancient mango trees to the Praça de Republica. In the golden decades from 1890 to 1910 Pará strutted and glittered with fabulous prosperity. Money grew on trees in those days, wild rubber trees that oozed black gold.

The town was established in 1615 at the junction of two rivers, both a part of the Amazon system but separated from the "river-sea" by the great island of Marajó, which is itself larger than Mother Portugal. Because the first settlement was made in the Christmas season, the founder called the place Nossa Señhora de Belém, or Our Lady of Bethlehem. Belém is still the proper name for the capital of the state of Pará, but all the world, except the local inhabitants, calls the town Pará.

In 1852 a Paraense sent the first steamboat up the Amazon. Fifteen years later the great river was to open desultory foreign navigation. In 1877 a devastating drought drove thousands inland where they began to open up the illimitable rubber fields. By 1890 millionaires had sprung up in astounding numbers. Brazil controlled the world's rubber market and was the chief source of supply. With the advent of automobiles, the rubber business skyrocketed.

Pará's luxurious expansion, however, was by no means as spectacular as that of Manáos, a village a thousand miles up the river, which unfolded like jungle magic and became known as the Orchid City. Gaudy villas, baroque hotels, an opera house more costly than Rio's, were built in a jungle clearing. Money lost its meaning. Manáos commanded performances of European opera troupes and they obeyed. Ticket speculators did business such as New Yorkers have never seen. Champagne bubbled as prodigally as the Amazonian rapids. Babies played with toys of gold. But one day into the delirious garden of monopoly came a fox dressed in the sheep's clothing of an English gentleman. Slyly he stole some rubber seedlings and smuggled them out of the country through Pará's customs inspection, vigilant against any such disastrous happening. By the fastest steamer he carried them to England. In the hot-houses of Kew Gardens expert horticulturists nurtured the seedlings, and then shipped some to British-owned Ceylon and some to the Straits Settlements in the Malay Peninsula. The climatic conditions in Malaya were more like those of the Amazon basin than any place in the world, and the cost of living was about the lowest, as that of Manáos had become the highest. The rubber trees flourished like wild mustard. Four years before the Great War, England was already dictating the world price of rubber. Brazil's mammoth monopoly was mortally punctured. The golden bubble of prosperity burst like a balloon. Manáos had refused to interpret the handwriting on the wall and had continued her fantastic orgy until the gilded denizens of the underworld began deserting the doomed city like rats. Soon the castles that rubber built reverberated with hollowness and the silent opera gave up the ghost of its glory to the spiders and the moths. The forest began trooping back into the city to reclaim its own. Weeds crept into crevices of the paved streets and rankly possessed the gardens of deserted mansions.

To-day eighty thousand people still inhabit the ghost town. The inauguration of the Pan American Airways' regular schedule stimulated the town's morale, though most citizens never expect gala days again. Some continue to pray nightly for a blight to attack the British plantations in the East. And never, they say, will they again trust the proverbial "word of an Englishman."

Although the "seaport a thousand miles up the river" is only a shell of its former grandeur, Pará, just seventy miles from the ocean retains much of its old glamour. It is still a handsome city, highly-coloured, wide-spaced, embowered in flowers such as only abundant rainfall and hot suns can produce. Norbourne had time for both a walk and a drive before dinner. The villas of carnation pink, cinnamon, and heliotrope are set among mimosa trees in gardens exuding ardent odours—jasmine, vanilla, tuberose, tea-olive. In the basin before the fish markets are acres of sailing dugouts, the pretty little *junggaddas* laden with the fruits of the lower Amazon: farina, tapioca, turtles, and tons of Brazil nuts which North Americans call "nigger-toes." European culture and the ways of the jungle meet. Boulevards flavoured with Paris emerge into weedy alleyways where naked potbellied babies tumble about and suck at bananas. At the end of the streets like the walls of a fortified town stand the pales of the jungle.

On the thousand balconies of Pará, women, ceaselessly fanning, sit behind the iron grille rails among moss baskets trailing orchids. Sometimes a broken blossom drops into the street at a man's feet as if by accident. At twilight the mulatto wenches in the poorer quarters scent their hair with an aphrodisiac of ground bark called *cheiro de mulate* and their admirers begin twanging banjos and wailing songs of love on the pavement before their murky doorways.

After dinner Norbourne sat drinking a cooling non-alcoholic *refresco* with an American business man and an old Brazilian gaolbird who had lived up in Manáos in the gala days. He had killed a man and was serving his sentence rather quaintly. He had been in gaol for nine years now. He was still in gaol. Oh, yes, he went home for his meals; it was simpler, because he didn't like the gaol fare, and by having his meals at home he saved the municipality money. True, he often stopped to chat with his friends after meals as he was doing to-night. But he would sleep in the gaol. He had not broken gaol once in all these nine years. He was very scrupulous about sleeping there. They had let him supply his own hammock. Of course he wasn't free to take a job. But in eleven more years he would be free and able to work again, if he wasn't too old. He touched his white hair. He had been very honourable to allow himself to be arrested. "If you kill a man in Pará, Señor, and get away into the woods for forty-eight hours, you won't be arrested," he explained. "But I'd rather be in gaol in Pará than free in the jungle." He must be getting on now, for the gaoler would be wanting to lock up and go home for the night himself.

Far into the evening men sat about the round tables on the pavement in front of the hotel, the pavement that is broader than many Spanish streets. Above, the leaves of the mango trees stirred with night breeze from the river. "In December the mangoes ripen and drop on the heads of café patrons," said Norbourne's companion and offered him another pink *refresco* made from *assahy*, the small fruit of a date-like palm. "Paraenses have a saying: 'Whoever stops off at Pará stops; whoever drinks *assahy* remains.' They say too that if you drink and do not remain this time you will come back." And Norbourne, sipping his *assahy*, felt he would come again to Pará—as strongly as he felt he would never see Fortaleza or Pernambuco or Bahia again.

"Soon we shall be independent of the river breeze to cool us," the man commented, when they both rose to say good night. "As a pledge to the inevitable future, the hotel and Pan American Airways are preparing to air-condition the two upper stories of the hotel. Pará looks to the new destiny of Brazil, when she shall become a queen among ports. The Amazon and its tributaries drain an area two thirds as large as the United States, a soil estimated to be four times as fertile. Pará is the gateway to this land of to-morrow—a to-morrow not like those two flashy decades of yesterday, but one to last for centuries."

At four in the morning Norbourne was up to make ready for the longest flight of his sixteen thousand mile trip. He would set foot briefly in the three Guianas and spend the night in the Island of Trinidad in the Caribbean.

From his balcony he looked down on the broad pavements lit by equatorial stars. The marble-topped tables were arranged in five long rows and the chairs leaned over them like people praying. The branches of the mango trees were still in the windless air. Across the street chauffeurs in white patent leather caps talked in low voices. The ivory marble façade of the Opera House was flecked with starlight. Some night not so far in the future the velvet stage curtains would be withdrawn to delight an audience sharing in the new destiny, which would be long lasting and not a bubble to be pricked by a gentleman with a seedling secreted beneath his Burberry.

Illusion

At the airport when his luggage had been weighed, Norbourne went outside into the faint dawn and watched the amphibian take off for Manáos. Filled to capacity with men and mail, it roared towards the murky jungle like a herald clearing the way for the coming of the sun.

The bell rang. The northbound passengers followed their pilots, took their last step on Brazilian soil, and went up the carpeted steps into the luxury of the Brazilian Clipper. The corps of brown boys manoeuvred the mammoth machine skilfully down the ramp into shoulder-deep water. The engines hummed with powerful music. The thunderbird rose from the River Pará, flew across the island that is larger than Portugal, and crossed the yellow mouth of the Amazon.

The sun rose reluctantly from behind the eastern horizon, a whitish disc in a platinum-coloured dawn, a sun with no more colour than iron that is white-hot. It was more like a transparent wafer used in the Sacrament than anything else Norbourne could think of. Below to the north and west lay an impenetrable tangle of pestilential swamp like the bottom of Panama and the top of Colombia where Norbourne had first seen land in the Green Continent. He looked at his watch. The sun cleared the horizon at precisely six minutes past six.

The steward came up and caught Norbourne's attention. He was an attractive young Puerto Rican named Lee, a direct descendant of Lighthorse Harry. His American father had settled in San Juan just after the Spanish-American War and married a Spaniard. Young Lee himself was marrying a Puerto Rican the following week.

He pointed northwest in the general direction of British Guiana and the northernmost part of Brazil's interior. "Over there is Redfern, dead or alive. It will be the biggest scoop of the times if they find him." Norbourne looked the way he directed. A flock of white cranes was flying along the line where the blue porcelain of the sky joined the jade enamel of the jungle. The Clipper passed them and the cranes looked, for all the world, as if they were flying backward. The illusion was Norbourne's last look at Brazil.

VIII

THE GUIANAS

"Aeroplanes are birds that sing the year round; they go from city to city, governed by a certain call and alighting, after a route from country to country, beneath the eye of the landing officer, as surely as the falcon on the wrist of the falconer."

Paul Morand

THE GUIANAS

FRENCH GUIANA

"It Would Bring Tears to Your Eyes"

THE thunderbird began to descend on a land unblessed by God and cursed by man. This was the hot, fever-ridden French Guiana which harboured men who lived and died in the shadow of the "dry guillotine."

It was not that the rigidities within the penitentiary walls were unendurable, but that the "double sentence" condemned the convict to spend again the length of his penal term in Guiana after his release from prison. In the prison he was provided with shelter, food, and at least another suit of red and white pyjamas and a straw hat when the old clothes wore entirely out. But outside, the *libéré* was left to shift for himself. There was virtually no employment and very small alms. He snatched his living from garbage heaps or what employment he could wangle. Out of the seven hundred convicts arriving each year from France, not more than half a dozen were destined to see Europe again. They died of malnutrition, malaria, dysentery, or leprosy. If they attempted to escape into Brazil or Dutch Guiana, they got lost in the bush and starved, or were devoured by red ants. Otherwise they were captured by Bush Negroes who returned them for the three dollar rewards. When they were returned to the authorities alive they went into the bear pits of solitary confinement. To most of the *libérés* the swift knife of the "wet guillotine" would have been a boon from heaven.

Of the 16,000 population of Cayenne, the island capital of French Guiana, 8,000 are convicts, prisoners, or *libérés*. France implies that the double sentence is for the purpose of colonization. But as a colonizer she reveals her deficiencies to her own scandal in the one piece of land she owns in South America. Less than 8,000 acres are in cultivation in a territory almost as large as England. French Guiana imports most of her foodstuffs and raises only a small amount of bananas, maize, and sweet potatoes for local consumption. With the slightest attention to scientific farming she could provide a decent living for her freed convicts and raise food enough for the entire population. She has no railways whatever and only a few miserable roads leading to the capital. She bothers with little except gold mining, the chief industry of the country, although she exports rosewood and rosewood extract. Cayenne is a miserable town, muggy of climate, unsanitary and stinking, where lepers walk the street unsegregated.

White curtains fluttered damply at the many little windows of the white landing barge where the passengers alighted. The pleasant pink-faced Dutchman in charge of the airport mopped his dripping face, as his wife offered hot chocolate. Norbourne drank his chocolate, mopped his own brow, and walked to the door to watch the white men refuelling the Clipper. Their manner was quite different from that of the others who refuelled planes. They went about their work mechanically, silently like *zombies*, with resigned shoulders and lack-lustre eyes.

"Ah, they are lucky fellows," said a passenger, noticing Norbourne's wondering stare. "*Libérés*. Pan Air has been a godsend. It provides half a dozen of them with a living. They want to go back to France. But it will be many years before they save enough. They give most of their earnings to their comrades who have no work."

On the platform, as they went to board the plane, the passengers were offered for sale little nosegays of meadow flowers. But the flower-girls were four barefooted men in ragged pyjamas and the flowers were made of the bright breast feathers of jungle birds, ingeniously wrought into bachelor buttons, daisies, primroses, buttercups, and field verbenas. The men did not urge anyone to buy. They did not even smile hopefully or pitiably. They merely stood in line, as if by accident, holding their nosegays loosely in their tough fists. They were grateful to accept any coin of any country or denomination a tourist would give them. Weeks of patient toil had gone in the making of the flowers. But *libérés* have lost all sense of time or money value. Gratefully they labour from tropical sunrise to tropical sunset for black citizens at a sum less than three dollars a month. Out of that wage they are forced to feed and clothe themselves. The Negroes exact their full toll of work, but they are not inhuman. They permit the Frenchmen to nail together old boards and palm leaves for a shelter, behind their own cabins on the other side of the ditch which they use for their privies.

"It would bring tears to your eyes to see those white boys grovelling in a nigger's garbage pail for scraps of food," a rubber tyre salesman from Akron, Ohio said to Norbourne. "I've been here a week and I've seen things with my own eyes. The wild tales people write about all this are not exaggerated, though they may have lied about themselves. It would bring tears to your eyes to see what I saw. Of course, the men are prisoners. They've committed crime and should be punished. But not in such a terrible way. Some of those boys come from good homes in France too. I talked to two who could speak English. One of them is too weak for regular work, if he could find it. He came from Nice—stole some money fourteen years ago. He makes his pennies carrying the market basket for a black wench."

Luncheon was served in the air between Cayenne and Paramaribo. Norbourne ate with the traveller from Akron who was going to Georgetown in British Guiana.

"Look at the three islands over there!" The traveller pointed out Devil's Island and the other two. "That's where Dreyfus was. Political prisoners still go there. But there are only eleven men there now. Life is better on Devil's Island than on the mainland. But one of those other islands is where they punish the incorrigibles." He screwed up his face and jerked his head. "I guess it's pretty bad, from what they say." There to the north Norbourne saw three black spots in the translucent blue of the sea. The Iles du Salut. "There are no guards on Devil's Island. The man-eating sharks do the work. Pretty thrifty of France."

If he had not been always blessed with an appetite, Norbourne's soft-hearted nature would have made him choke over the savoury hot meal from the Clipper kitchen. For like a man obsessed the Akron drummer continued to dilate on the cruel hunger of the *libérés*. Each course ended with the refrain: "It would bring tears to your eyes."

DUTCH GUIANA

The Jews Beat the Dutch

The founder of Dutch Guiana, or Surinam, was Baron Willoughby who sent Anthony Rowse as first governor in 1651 to make a settlement. Rowse wrote his wife a letter extolling the new land. He called it "the sweetest place that ever was seen: delicate rivers, brave land, fine timber." "Amongst the forty persons," he wrote, "not one of them had so much as their head-ache during the first five months. And the water so good as they never had such stomachs in their lives, eating five times a day, plenty of fish and fowl and partridges innumerable." Willoughby's first agent must have been a natural romancer or else he was deliberately trying to trick his reluctant spouse into joining him. For he did not mention the heat or the humidity.

Norbourne watched the sweat ooze from the station agent and the helpers, and felt it gush down his own breastbone as the passengers stood about the landing barge of Paramaribo, the capital and chief port. They were again offered chocolate made from local cacao, but no one felt much like drinking it so soon after luncheon. Cacao was once a principal export. But cacao production dropped from a peak of almost 2,000,000 kilos in 1917 to a measly low of 23,000 kilos in 1932. The drop was due to that same "witch's broom" which had swept entirely across the continent over the jungles and the Andes, and brought the Ecuadorian landlords sulking home from Paris.

The contrast between Cayenne and Paramaribo is marked. The latter is clean and neat and self-respecting, despite the Hindu ragamuffins. The population of the country is about 160,000, consisting of Dutch and various other European nationalities, a few North Americans, Chinese, 32,000 Javanese, and 37,000 Hindus. The most interesting element of the population and civilization is the estimated 17,000 Bush Negroes, descendants of escaped African slaves who have reverted to savagery and live in the jungle. There are also some 2,500 aboriginal Indians lurking in the hinterland.

The honest, hardworking Dutch have had a hard time making their fortunes in Guiana. It has been an expensive investment for Holland. Conditions have been bad for a long time. Gold, which was formerly one of the principal sources of revenue, has dwindled until its output is negligible. Timber is abundant, but it is difficult to get at the forest products. A profitable item of export is bauxite, or aluminium ore. The second most important product after sugar is coffee.

Since the colony's founding, however, sugar has been the principal commodity and most of it is turned into molasses and rum. The Dutchmen export only half the rum, and console themselves with the other half.

When Baron Willoughby himself came to the sweet land the year after Rowse's reports, he brought with him among the settlers many Jews. Other Jews followed, Dutch Jews, and Jews expelled from Brazil and Cayenne. On the Restoration, Charles II granted the whole territory jointly to Willoughby and the Earl of Clarendon's second son. They colonized almost exclusively with Jews, who were beguiled from their mercantile inclinations into sugar cultivation. They had just got the plantations well started when the Dutch conquered the colony. The English reconquered it. The Dutch won it back. Finally, by the peace of Breda in 1667, Holland exchanged New Amsterdam, now New

York, for Dutch Guiana. A spectacularly bad trade, though at the time the Dutch thought it very clever considering that the territory was five times larger than that of Holland. The Jews were cleverer than the Dutch. Soon they vanished from the sweet plantations of Surinam, and took up their abode in New York.

BRITISH GUIANA
Little India

Sir Walter Raleigh was the first Englishman to see and describe Guiana (an Indian name meaning "watered land"); and for his pains and because of the little brush with the Spaniards, King James cut off one of the most intelligent and noble heads in his whole kingdom. Raleigh's execution marked the beginning of the sad fate of innumerable adventurous Englishmen who wooed fortune and fame in the Guianas. Today bright young Englishmen go out as clerks and deputy overseers of vast sugar plantations, hopefully looking to gain the position of overseer or ultimately the place of manager, where they can live in the big bungalow and employ Scotch governesses for their pale children and have their wives sit sometimes at the governor's right hand at dinner and they themselves the privilege of taking in the good wife of some local officer of the Crown.

Sugar is the be-all and end-all of British Guiana. Eighty per cent of the area in cultivation is planted in sugar. But the cultivated area of the colony—it is about the size of the British Isles—to its total is much like that of a Britisher's cropped moustache to his whole body.

From the plane Norbourne could see some of the sugar mills, the labourers' villages, the managers' houses, the canals with the mule-drawn barges, and the irrigation ditches. Most of the labourers, male and female, working down there, were not Negroes or aborigine Indians, but East Indians. These Hindu coolies are brought over on five-year contracts to work on the plantations. Over half the population of British Guiana is East Indian, and a stranger who has not read his guidebook is surprised to see brown coolies in cream-coloured loin cloths and saffron turbans, and Hindu women in silk draperies and embroidered boleros, their smooth brown arms covered with bracelets and bangles of Benares silver work.

After slavery was abolished and the blacks indulged in their natural inclination to vagrancy, the British brought over Portuguese labourers from Madeira who returned home as soon as they could. They next imported Chinese; but as soon as the thrifty Chinese had saved enough pence they went into shopkeeping. The British Government at last saved the plantations by transporting indentured Hindus.

"Today," said the Akron traveller, who was getting off at Georgetown, "you can walk thirty miles between towns and never set eyes on a white man. Yet you feel Great Britain in the air. You also see in the paved roads, the sanitation, the respect for law, the Englishman's superiority as a colonizer and administrator. Only five per cent of the people are white. It's conventionally all right for an English overseer to keep a native woman —the Hindus are preferred to the niggers—but he must have his dinner jacket, his tennis racket and his tea caddy, all for the proper times of day. The one local custom that has triumphed is the use of the swizzle stick over the cocktail shaker or the soda syphon. Before dinner everybody swizzles, foams his rum and fruit juice with a twig twirled briskly between the palms. There's one other local trick they've taken up to help them get through —the arms of their chairs are three feet long."

"I know those chairs," said Norbourne. "They have a few in Bermuda. You hook your legs over one side or the other or stretch out on both, and drink your rum swizzles with your feet in the air."

Marsh birds by the thousand rose from the flooded flatlands as the thunderbird skimmed to a landing before the sea wall of Georgetown, with a mile length of warehouses. The town of sixty-one thousand coloured and one thousand whites looked very neat and clean. The English love of green lawns had gone with them to the tropics. The houses were painted white. Hundreds of people were riding bicycles down the streets shaded with mango trees and coco-nut palms.

At the airport an attendant handed Norbourne a glass of bottled orange squash, uniced, insipid; as interesting as a British dinner of cold mutton and cabbage. The orange squash attested to the British dominance as surely as did the Union Jack on the flagpole. No Latin would ever think of thrusting such a beverage down his gullet.

When the seaplane rose from the muddy water, it flew for a few minutes over a strip of irrigated land. Hindu women, knee deep in mud, were setting out rice plants in dyked paddy-fields. Out of a canebrake a pink flamingo emerged and flapped low over the ricefields like an overseer inspecting the Biblical methods of husbandry. Farther into the interior East Indian men were turning more jungle into market gardens. Between where the women and men were working a Hindu temple stood out strangely on the flat land. When Norbourne first set eyes on South America in the Bay of Turbo in Colombia, he felt he was glimpsing the heart of Africa. This last bit of the continent was like India.

Last Look

Norbourne went up towards the cockpit as the thunderbird turned its nose northwest to the island of Trinidad. Ed Schultz, the same pilot who had flown him from Havana to Mérida in Yucatan, was drinking strong hot tea poured from his own special teapot which he carried everywhere with him. It was a funny squat little teapot of glazed black earthenware embossed with blue rosebuds. Schultz, the ex-marine, who had won all his boxing matches, drank nothing stronger than tea, but he drank it every two hours he was in the air. While he sat there before the controls, gulping tea, he gave instructions in higher mathematics to an industrious co-pilot being trained for the China Clipper and the Pacific flights. Every time Schultz raised his cup to his mouth a huge star sapphire on the little finger of his hardy fist gleamed like a signal in a fog.

"Look down to the left," Schultz called back. "In a minute you'll see the end of the clipper ship days."

Norbourne glanced down at the approaching scene, then back at Schultz. More than any other pilot he seemed fashioned of the stuff of those indomitable salts who captained the old sailing vessels. Still under forty, a German-American from Warrenton County, Virginia, he belonged to that generation of strong-willed men, sailors with nose and eyes quick to detect the least change in meteorological conditions, sailors who read the sky's map in all kinds of weather with a sixth sense. Norbourne had watched Schultz with keen interest on his first flight three months ago. He had seen him swerve forty miles to dodge a squall and ride triumphantly within a few yards of it. The same gleam that lighted the eye of old sailing masters flashed in the eye of Schultz. He knew all the little secrets of the high open spaces which escape the man on the ground.

"Look!" Schultz commanded.

Below, by the Venezuelan shore, like a wavering hallucination, lay the half-submerged remains of a clipper ship, the pores of its rotting timbers tasting the salt of the breeze that its stout canvas once had swelled to. A thrilling era was dead and gone. But its spirit had been saved from oblivion by the new conquerors of the air. As the thunderbird soared on its duralumin steel-ribbed wings above the wreckage of timber and iron, Norbourne thought of the Phoenix, that rare Egyptian bird, fabled to live five hundred years and on its death to rise from its own funeral pyre in youthful freshness and faith incorruptible.

Like an instrument of destiny the aeroplane thundered on towards Trinidad.

As it passed the mighty mouth of Venezuela's Orinoco, Norbourne thought how blessed were the countries of the

Americas, in that among themselves they can supply almost everything each other needs. If the Eastern Hemisphere destroyed itself by suicidal wars, the American nations could still maintain a balanced economy. While he had no intention of urging all the bright young men of the United States to emigrate suddenly to South America, he hoped that they would familiarize themselves with the history and manners and economic potentialities of the various countries, because there was no knowing when any of them might be called upon "to act in a manner that might affect the relations between the Southern republics and the United States." And for those who were eager to seek adventure and fortune, there lay the continent with its opportunities and undeveloped resources. Now with these aeroplanes, like flashing silver shuttles, weaving a fabric of material and spiritual solidarity, the Southern continent was no longer inaccessible or remote.

Norbourne went back to his seat and kept his eyes on the disappearing land where he had found so much kindness. Gradually the green of the earth paled until there was only one tenuous thread of flickering colour, like a firefly's luminosity at daybreak. The pincers of the sky and sea squeezed the Green Continent to nothingness, and it passed out of sight. If nations travelled, he said to himself, they would not, they could not, fight each other. If they visited one another with a desire to comprehend they would find too much to like and to admire not to be friends.